PARADOXICAL UNDRESSING

Kristin Hersh is an American songwriter and guitarist. She
founded the seminal art-punk band Throwing Muses at age
fourteen and is widely recognized as an indie-rock pioneer.
She is a mother of four, and lives in New Orleans.

D1337598

PARADOXICAL UNDRESSING

KRISTIN HERSH

Atlantic Books
LONDON

First published in the United States of America in 2010 by
Penguin Books, a division of Penguin Group USA, Inc.

First published in Great Britain in hardback in 2011 by Atlantic
Books, an imprint of Atlantic Books Ltd.

This paperback edition published in Great Britain
in 2011 by Atlantic Books.

1 3 5 7 9 10 8 6 4 2

A CIP catalogue record for this book is available from
the British Library.

Paperback ISBN: 978 1 84887 239 4

Ebook ISBN: 978 0 85789 301 7

Printed in Great Britain by Clays Ltd, St Ives plc

Atlantic Books,
An imprint of Atlantic Books Ltd,
Ormond House,
26–27 Boswell Street,
London WC1N 3JZ
www.atlantic-books.co.uk

They say, "You are ill, so what appears to you is only unreal fantasy." But that's not strictly logical. I agree that ghosts only appear to the sick, but that only proves that they are unable to appear except to the sick, not that they don't exist.

—FYODOR DOSTOYEVSKY

The universe is godding.

—MICKY DOLENZ

This book is based on a diary I started when I was eighteen. Don't know why I kept the diary for so many years; the combination of nostalgia and nausea I felt when reading it was pretty rough. I sort of held it out at arm's length, the way you might keep the first fish you ever caught (*it's an accomplishment . . . it just stinks!*). I do find it astonishing that, as a teenager, I was already trying to bring music and art together; a hell of a mission to take on. If Americans thought music and art belonged together, they wouldn't have the Grammys!

I guess the diary was a bad luck charm—I really didn't want history repeating itself. 'Cause it was certainly a strange book to pick up and read. Full of holes, it dissolved along with the drowning writer and each page was oddly like crawling in a window: you had to stand up carefully, squint, get your bearings. The diary was about a year long, from one spring to the next.

I seemed awfully young that first spring and not so young the next, though this wasn't a year when a whole lot happened, in my opinion. It *was* a year when many things began, which is probably important. It was also a year I tried very hard to forget, so I know it was worth remembering. Some of it I don't actually remember; I just read about it in the diary. I'm *real* okay with not remembering this stuff, though; like a lot of people's stories, mine can be pretty embarrassing.

♋ Songs help with that. They don't commit to linear time—they whiz around *all* your memories, collecting them into a goofy pile that somehow seems less goofy because it's set to music. Songs're weird: they tell the future and they tell the past, but they can't seem to tell the difference. So I stuck lyrics from my songs into the text whenever they reflected on a moment and its reverberations.

Here's a quote of mine: "I would never paint a picture, do a dance or *write a book*." And here's another one: "I'm not in the business of *publishing pages from my diary*." I still say these things all the time. What I mean when I say them is that although I'm a musician, I'm not a particularly creative person, nor am I interested in self-expression—I don't want people to listen to my songs so that they'll care about *me*. That would be obnoxious.

I did, however, write this *book* based on *pages from my diary* because copying down a year isn't a particularly creative thing to do. And it all happened twenty-five years ago, so it can't really count as a story about *me*— that girl isn't me anymore. Now it's just a story.

And interestingly, it turns out to be a love story. One with no romance, only passion. Passion for sound, reptiles, old ladies, guitars, a car, water, weather, friends, colors, chords, children, a band, fish, light and shadow. It's dedicated to my friends Betty and Mark, who both died while I was turning the story into this book. And can I just say: everything that wacky old Betty Hutton told me was true. The craziest things she said turned out to be particularly true. She was even right about "Throwing Muses" having too many syllables.

Betty taught me that you can't tell the whole truth, as not all of it is pertinent or lovely. You have to leave things out in order to tell the *story*. Otherwise, people could miss the whaddyacallit . . . the point. Her story was full of brightly lit holes that allowed the point to show itself in sharp relief.

For what it's worth, this is my old diary's story, riddled with enormous holes and true.

Love,

Kristin

PARADOXICAL
UNDRESSING

The handmade Jesus on Napoleon's living room wall has no face, just a gasping, caved-in head with blood dripping down its chest. He appears to have been crucified on some popsicle sticks. His mottled green and gold surface reminds us of fish scales and his paddle-shaped toes fan out like a tail. It is a singularly gruesome crucifix. We call it "Fish Jesus."

The first time I saw it, I thought it was funny. It's less funny at night when you're alone. And even *less* funny tonight because next to me is a bag of horrible donuts one of the painters left for me as a joke. They look just like Fish Jesus. Oblong, greenish-gold and bloody with jelly, coconut maggots swarm over them. I really don't wanna look at them anymore, but throwing them away would mean touching them and I don't wanna do that, either.

So me and Fish Jesus and the donuts all lean against the wall, watching Christmas lights blink. It isn't Christmas, but these were the only working lights left in this empty apartment when its old man died. He was named Napoleon. All we really know about him is that he lived here in Providence and now he's dead, his body and most of his belongings carted away. And somehow he still pays his electric bill. Someone does, anyway, and it isn't me or any of the other people I've seen use his electricity.

I also know where he hid his key (under the mat—Napoleon was a brilliant tactician), and tonight I need a place to stay. So I park myself under a sad crucifix and watch tiny blue, green, red and orange bulbs blink on and off. *Insomniacs like to waste time.*

The lights are comfortingly tacky, the garish blue ones my favorites. They remind me of being a little kid, hypnotized and mystified by Christmas. I open first one eye and then the other, to see if I can watch only the blue lights and ignore the other colors, but it's hard and I'm boring myself, so I close both eyes to try and get some sleep. They pop right open again.

♋ fish

i have a fish nailed to a cross on my apartment wall

This room is not a good thing to look at, but I look anyway. The wall-to-wall carpeting is a pukey beige, bleached in the center by a stain shaped like a hermit crab. The paneling on the walls is marked by big splotches of something that once sprayed across it. It has been suggested by sleepless crashers that these splotches are a clue as to how Napoleon died. The whole apartment smells like mold and disinfectant. And now, donuts.

It's spring, but you'd never know it looking out Napoleon's window. He lived and died in a gray world.

I'm glad it's spring, though—Christmas decorations around here are the saddest things you ever saw. They hung, decomposing in the gray wind, through *March*. Just a few weeks ago, someone took down the dismal pink wreath, blackened with car exhaust, that hung around the fluorescent green sign across the street. This sign has always read, will always read: "Pumpkin Muffins 24 Hours."

All the women who work in the donut shop below the sign look the same. They wear pink smocks and lean on the counter, smoking, all night long. I'm often a sleepless crasher in this apartment myself and I've spent many hours watching them to see if they ever move. They don't. I've never even seen one light a new cigarette. It probably smells like mold, disinfectant and donuts in there, too.

The loosely associated group of people who frequent Napoleon's guest house: touring musicians, bored kids with nowhere else to go or nothing else to do, and anyone whose job isn't really a job (like "painter") have agreed that the key should remain under the mat—the first place any desperate individual would look—to honor Napoleon's memory. Not that we remember him, but he's become a kind of saint to us. He shelters the lonely and the lost, wrapping them in a soft blanket of Christmas lights and old-man smell.

So the key stays where Napoleon left it because if somebody wants to break in *here*, well then, we should make it easy for 'em. Clearly, they need Napoleon's soft blanket.

I gotta get rid of these fucking donuts; they're making me sick and they aren't gonna get any prettier. Maybe I'll leave them here on the floor for the Animal.

We don't know what the Animal is, only that it gets in sometimes and eats cornflakes out of the cabinet, which is fine 'cause I didn't like the look of those dead-guy cornflakes anyway. Once, a painter named Jeff actually took the Animal to the *face*. It leaped out of the apartment and jumped on his head when he opened the door. This is the closest encounter any of us have had with it. Unfortunately, it was the middle of the night and the stairwell was too dark for him to get a good look at it; the Animal just knocked him backwards down the stairs and took off.

Jeff was thrilled. The next time I saw him, he was still giddy, glowing with pride. "Kristin!" he said dreamily. "The most wonderful thing happened . . ."

This guy looks just like Jimmy Stewart. I tried to imagine him falling backwards in the dark, limbs flailing, fur wrapped around his head. For some reason, I saw this happening in black and white—maybe 'cause of the Jimmy Stewart thing—which made it even creepier. But Jeff was so happy telling the story, he looked dewy. Painters are so sick. I wouldn't want an animal jumping on *my* face in the dark.

I gotta admit I was enchanted, though. "Did it make a noise?" I asked him. "Was it furry? Did it smell weird?" He couldn't remember much; he was falling down stairs. Happily falling, having taken a wild animal to the face, but too distracted by gravity to pay attention to much else. In retrospect, he figured it *had* been furry and was about the size of a watermelon.

This was relevant information, as we had had a kind of meeting on the subject once, the gaggle of lost souls who use this apartment when they have nowhere else to go. The Animal hadn't yet gone for the cornflakes—it had only shuffled around the apartment in the dark, which was, I admit, a little spooky. Subsequently, there had been murmurings of "ghosts" walking around at night, and most of the musicians are such pussies they were scared to sleep here anymore. Some of them wanted to have a Narragansett medicine woman smudge the place with sage to relieve it of its restless spirits.

"Look," a drummer named Manny said gravely over the cold leftovers of two greasy pizzas. Candles flickered near the open window, the dancing shadows making it look more like a séance than the overgrown Cub Scout meeting it really was. "She's really nice, I've met her. She doesn't dress weird or anything. She charges a nominal fee and all we have to do is fast or fuck off for, like, a day and a half."

"What?!" yelled a painter, laughing. Painters think musicians are ridiculous. There seems to be a general consensus among them that painting is high art, music low. Can't say that I blame them; musicians *are* sorta ridiculous. I'm a guitar player, so technically I'm one myself, but I don't stick up for us all that often.

Manny, clearly more afraid of ghosts than painters, held his ground. "This place is definitely haunted," he said. "I hear noises, but when I check 'em out, there's nobody there!" He pushed a lock of purple hair behind his ear. For some reason, none of us musicians have normal hair—another thing that makes us seem ridiculous to the painters. Mine is blue, there is a lime green and a fuzzy-yellow-chick yellow . . . together, we look like an Easter basket. Chalk white and glossy jet-black are close to normal, but those two are goth kids—at least once a day, a painter will turn to them and yell, "Happy Halloween!"

"Fast?" The painter stared at Manny, wide-eyed.

"Don't eat," explained Manny.

"I know what it *means*. I just think you're a moron." The other painters laughed. The musicians and neutral observers sat quietly in the candle-light.

Manny shook his head. "Last night, something was walking near my face. It was weird."

"It's just the family downstairs bangin' around," said the painter. "They got like, twelve kids or something."

"No, seriously. I could feel it moving. It was right next to my face."

"Were you high?" asked the painter sarcastically.

"Yeah," answered Manny, "but . . . it was right next to my *face*!"

You can tell painters and musicians apart by their uniforms and expressions. All the musicians except the goth kids wear torn blue jeans, flannel shirts and pajama tops and look perpetually stunned. Painters dress like it's 1955, in white T-shirts, khakis and black loafers, all spattered liberally with paint. They either spatter their clothing on purpose so everyone can tell they're painters or else they have a lot of trouble getting paint from brush to canvas, 'cause they're really covered in the stuff.

Painters usually look like they're about to laugh. Not smug; they just think everything is funny. "Let's get him an exorcism," said one. "He really wants one."

Manny looked grim. "I'm not saying there's an *evil* presence. Napoleon was a good man. But he died here. A violent death," he said ominously, pointing at the splotches on the wall.

"That's Michelob," smirked the painter. "Napoleon probably had a Barcalounger and spasms. If you're worried about hauntings, worry about the guy who died in those pajamas you're wearing." Manny winced. It was a little low, I thought, going after his clothes. Everybody knows you don't buy pajamas from the Salvation Army if you're not into the dead.

Manny's girlfriend, the fuzzy-yellow-chick-haired chick, tried valiantly to come to his rescue. "Paranormal events occur in places where souls were unwilling to separate from their bodies at the time of death," she explained carefully. "What if Napoleon's soul wanted to stay home even though his body was dead?"

"This place is a shit hole. If you could fly, would you stay here?" The other painters laughed; everyone else was silent. Painters and musicians never agree on *anything*. It can be entertaining, but it can also be exhausting. They even order different pizzas.

I consider myself to be a neutral crasher; I don't wear either uniform and I don't side with anyone. The painters are almost always right, but I feel sorry for the hapless musicians who're so mercilessly ridiculed, so I abstain from arguments *and* pizza.

The painters have made it clear that they feel I'm one of them, even going so far as to try to make me paint. They claim that making noise is the heathen's way, a poor excuse for a calling. I guess they're right, but I *am* a heathen. I mean, I've met me.

But I toured their studios anyway, watched them paint, let them lecture me and attempted to absorb the process of smearing colors onto cloth in order to impress upon observers a sense of "visual feeling." I even took classes at the Rhode Island School of Design here in Providence. This is frowned upon by the "street" painters in Napoleon's gang who believe that art is something which can't be taught.

I thought some paintings were very beautiful—places to go—but ultimately, "I don't get it," was all I could think to say.

"What don't you get?" asked Jeff in his studio on a freezing afternoon, as we studied one of his paintings together.

"It's too quiet," I said.

"Even the orange?" he asked, surprised.

I stared at the orange, trying to see it as loud. "It just seems hard to make something matter if you don't yell it."

"Kristin, whispering matters."

I looked at him. "Yeah, well, you don't do that, either."

Jeff frowned thoughtfully. "Oh yeah."

It was painters who suggested that I keep this diary in the interim between making noise and artful sublimation. I don't even know what a diary is, really—a book about now? That means you can't write the ending first and work backwards, right?

"Don't worry," they said. "Painting will come. Just give it time."

So far, so bad.

Manny's girlfriend sighed, slowly pushing pizza crusts around in the cardboard pizza box like a little train, the multicolored Christmas lights creating a shifting pattern for her to drive the train through. We all watched the crusts drive around. "I'm just saying, you should keep an open mind. Maybe Napoleon's still living here. It's his house, not ours."

The painters howled. "You guys are idiots!"

Manny pouted, glaring at them. The girl shifted uncomfortably, blowing yellow hair out of her eyes, her pizza train slowing to a halt. "I said *maybe* . . ."

We decided to sit up and listen for ghosts. Staying up all night wasn't hard for the musicians, who were high, paranoid and scared shitless. Everyone else was bored until the noises began: scratching, shuffling, nothing too scary really, but when we crept into the kitchen as a group, there was nothing there.

"Told you," Manny hissed.

The mystery was partially solved when the ghost turned out to be a furry, watermelon-sized face jumper that likes cornflakes and is good at hiding. We now have tremendous affection for the Animal, which is easy because it never shows itself. It politely devours whatever it can find and then takes off.

We all act like it's a magic *bear*, but the best thing it could be, really, is a raccoon and it's probably just a cat. Though it might be Taffy, the neighbors' dog who never comes when called. Our scary neighbors stand in their yard wearing bathrobes and yell "Taffy!" over and over again, but Taffy never shows up. Maybe Taffy lives with us now.

When I give touring bands and lonely kids directions to this place, I always mention the Animal, in case it jumps on their faces. Displaced individuals can be sorta jumpy.

I wish it were here right now, 'cause nobody else is. The more promiscuous and insecure of us have a rule: *no sleeping alone at Napoleon's.* A rule I'm breaking tonight. "Taffy?" I call weakly and wait.

Napoleon took his bed with him when he left, so when you stay here, you sleep on the floor, and the floor feels extra hard tonight. Extra hard is extra lonely, for some reason. Like you're being punished for something you probably did but don't remember doing.

♋ cartoons

this war's okay
in a sweet old fashioned way
like a game we play

guilty of something we forgot

We live in the woods in a communal dwelling, a gigantic barn full of hippies, one of whom tries to write "Be Together" on a parachute that stretches across our ceiling.

He's pretty stoned, though, so what he actually writes is "Be Togeater," and no one has a replacement parachute or the money to buy one.

I'm only three years old, so I shouldn't be able to read it, but my mother, Crane, taught me to read when I was two. I'm sure she regrets having done this, as we lie on the couch together, staring at the ceiling. "I guess he just likes to spell things his own way," she says.

So we live under that magical sentiment for years, growing our own vegetables, drinking goat's milk, and feeding the rats who live there togeater with us by hand, because rats are Buddha's creatures, too.

7:00. Slept almost three hours straight—a personal best. The Christmas lights're going quietly apeshit in the sunshine, which is cooking the donuts. Reaching into the terrible bag before I can think about what I'm doing, I tear off a maggot-coated hunk and stuff it into Fish Jesus's bloody maw— whistling in the sun. Should cheer up the next lonely visitor to Napoleon's guest house, anyway.

I leave, quietly locking the apartment door so as not to wake the thousands of children who live on the first floor, then let my eyes adjust to the dark stairwell, hoping to catch a glimpse of the Animal. *Nope.* Not unless it's hiding behind a pile of old carpet at the bottom of the stairs. Then I lift the mat and place the key under it, silently thanking Napoleon for another night of creepy hospitality. On my way out the door, I peer into the pile of dusty carpet, just in case. "Taffy?" I ask it.

Across the street, Taffy's owner is standing on his front lawn in a bathrobe, smoking a cigarette and holding the morning paper. *"Mahnin!"* he shouts through his cigarette when I step outside. This means "good morning" in Rhode Island. I smile. He smiles too, takes the cigarette out of his mouth and, spitting on the ground, starts walking toward me.

Oh, crap. I can't talk to this guy; I've tried. I can't understand a word he says after *mahnin.* And he looks like a yeti, which makes it hard to listen to what he's even *trying* to say. I always just squint and nod, watching his face move until he stops making noise, then back away. Quickly, before he can cross the street, I scramble into my car and start the engine. It sputters. I try again. Taffy's dad watches. My dumb car. It doesn't really work, can hardly breathe. "The Silver Bullet," she's called, and she is in fact silver, but she's a fat-ass, logy version of a bullet. This morning, she coughs, wheezes, then suddenly heaves to life. Pulling away from Napoleon's neighbor, I wave and he waves back, looking sad, his newspaper at his side.

At the first intersection, the car stalls. I whip my head around to see if he's following me, lumbering along, puffing his cigarette—*"mahnin, mahnin"*—his bathrobe blowing in the breeze. *No wonder Taffy left.* But the street behind me is empty and the Bullet's engine kicks in again a second later, humming in her distinctive full-throated whine.

"Thank you, ma'am," I say out loud in my relief. I'm from the South. I believe in politeness, even when it comes to machines. My family left Georgia when I was a kid, a well-mannered little Gomer, and here in Rhode Island I got beaten up for both my Southern accent *and* my politeness. Damn yankee kids'd never heard the word "ma'am" before.

They tried to beat me up, anyway; I always won those fights. Didn't clobber anybody, just hit 'em real hard and they fell down. Then I *politely* helped them up. Damn yankees. I've been trying to hide my accent ever since, but I'm still polite.

Speeding is *im*polite, so I don't do that. I tear, though . . . tear down the highway, through blizzards, thunderstorms and blazing sun 'cause I love driving. It's a perfect world for a shy spaz like me. A shy person likes to be alone, and a spaz can't sit still, right? So though my car sucks big time, it lets me race around without having to make eye contact with a single human. I take the Silver Bullet very seriously for this reason. And, yes, I talk to my car. She deserves it.

```
☺ arnica montana

the desperate
tearing down the highway
like they got no place to stay
```

The Bullet and I are doing the thirty-minute drive from Providence to Aquidneck Island together so I can swim laps and shower at the Y before school. Like most of the people in Napoleon's gang of losers, I'm eighteen—the age where no one takes care of you—so most of my showers are taken at the Y. I'm not homeless, I just can't stop for very long. I'm too . . . wired. And I have this idea that you could belong everywhere rather than just one place, so I don't call anything "home." Don't know what I'd do there if I did. I'd just get antsy and wanna leave again.

People who suffer because they have nowhere in particular to go are those who can sit still, who sleep. I stopped doing these things last September, when I made a mistake and moved into the wrong place: a bad apartment christened "the Doghouse" by someone who painted that on the door. The Doghouse was the last place I played music on purpose, of my own volition.

I innocently stepped through the door of the Doghouse and put my stuff down because I thought that if I lived alone for a while, music might speak to me, tell me its secrets. Music spoke, alright—it yelled—and as it turns out, it *has* no secrets. If you ask music a question, it answers and then just keeps talking louder and louder, never shuts up. Music yelled so loud and so much in the Doghouse, I can still hear it.

I was used to sound tapping me on the shoulder and singing into my ear. I've heard music that no one else hears since I got hit by a car a couple years ago and sustained a double concussion. I didn't know what to make of this at first, but eventually I came to feel lucky, special, as if I'd tapped into an intelligence. Songs played of their own accord, making themselves up; I listened and copied them down. Last fall, though, the music I heard began to feed off the Doghouse's evil energy. Songs no longer tapped me on the shoulder; they slugged me in the jaw. Instead of singing to me, they screamed, burrowing into my brain as electricity.

I got zapped so bad in that apartment, I don't think I'll ever rest again. In the Doghouse, sleep stopped coming, days stopped ending—now sleep doesn't come and days don't end. Sleeping pills slow my thinking, but they can't shut down my red-hot brain. If I do manage to drop off, wild dreams wake me up. So I'm different now; my thinking is liquid and quick, I can function at all hours. My songs are different, too, and when I play them, I *become* them: evil, charged.

I'm actually head over heels in love with these evil songs, in spite of myself. It's hard not to be. They're . . . arresting.

Before I disappeared into the Doghouse, the songs I heard were not devils, they were floaty angels. Gentle and meandering, interesting if you took the time to pay attention, but they wouldn't necessarily stop you in your tracks. Now the songs I bring to my band are essential, bursting: harsh black-and-white sketches that my bandmates color in with their own personal noise. These songs grab your face and shout at it.

Do you want your face grabbed and shouted at? Probably not; at the very least, it's irritating. But now that it's happened to me, I know that music is as close to religion as I'll ever get. It's a spiritually and biologically sound endeavor—it's healthy.

Some music is healthy, anyway. I know a lot of bands who're candy. Or beer. Fun and bad for you in a way that makes you feel good. *For a minute.* My band is . . . spinach, I guess. We're ragged and bitter. But I swear to god, we're good for you.

When I finally left that messed-up apartment, I swore I'd never go back. I stuffed my guitar case full of frantic songs I'd scribbled down on a hundred pieces of paper, then took a minute to squint through the noise and try to figure out what exactly made the Doghouse so dark. It looked like a plain old apartment to me: wood floors, silver radiators, paint-flecked doorknobs and smudgy windows. Why this place and not, say, the house next door? *Who knows, maybe the whole block is evil.*

But by the time I raced out the door and took off in the Silver Bullet, it was too late. I was branded; tattooed all over with Doghouse songs—each one a musical picture etched into my skin.

I know that when my band plays these ugly tattoos, people can see them all over me, but I don't care too much. I mean, shy people are generally not show-offs, but the *burning* that the songs do, the fact that I'm compelled to play them, makes me think they . . . matter? Maybe that's not the right word. That they're vital. And I respect that. I can feel sorry for myself without judging the music.

Comfort isn't necessarily comfortable, after all; sometimes you gotta wander into the woods. Everybody knows that.

I never did go back there. Sometimes I park the Silver Bullet across the street from the Doghouse and stare at it, wondering what the hell is up with that place, but I don't go inside. I know if I did, the walls'd close in. I made it out with my guitar and my brain, so I can look on the bright side: I got some wild songs out of it and I have evil's big balls working for me now. Evil seems to know what it's doing, though it isn't ever very pretty.

Doghouse songs are definitely not pretty—they sound like panicking—but they *are* beautiful. The cool thing they do is, they make memories now. A syringe of déjà vu injected into my bloodstream. All the best stories work this way, but a song has the ability to tell a nice *loud* story. Louder than orange.

Which has made my band a work of obsession, a wholly satisfying closed circle. My bandmates and I are both conceited and pathetic about this: we think we're the best band in the world and that nobody'll ever like us. We play in clubs because that's what bands do, but we don't expect anybody to show up.

Really, we're just on our own planet, so it wouldn't make sense to give a fuck about anybody else, which is sorta nice. If I had to survive the Doghouse to earn this planet, I'm okay with that; it's a swell planet. I've spent a lot of time on it—almost twice as much as someone who sleeps. And this lingering Doghouse energy means that I can keep going, keep moving, keep looking around. I learn a lot, being awake all the time.

For example, I learned this: we should belong *everywhere.*

℗ calm down, come down

i don't wanna calm down
i don't wanna come down

On the lawn next to the library, I sit in the sun, my textbooks stacked beside me, and look for Betty. Peering through groups of college kids, I try to catch a glimpse of her hair. Betty's hair changes daily, so I'm not exactly sure what I'm looking for, except that she's about fifty years older than all the other students, so it's usually gray, champagne or white.

Betty and I have a study date. I know I could go inside the library and start studying without her, but we go to school on the island, right on the water, and it's just too beautiful out here. I avoid going inside buildings whenever possible, anyway; I kind of . . . disagree with them. Shouldn't we live outside?

Betty says this is never going to happen 'cause nobody else wants to live outside, just me. She says I need to learn to like buildings, that buildings aren't something you're even *allowed* to disagree with. "They're everywhere," she says. "And sometimes, you need to go inside them. Get used to it."

I get that. But I still disagree with them.

Even childhood takes place inside buildings now, which doesn't make sense—we shove kids indoors, make them sit still and be quiet when they should be going outside to run around and make noise. At least college classes allow for breaks when you can race out the door and breathe. I think I hold my breath when I'm in a classroom, "learning." Learning to hold my breath.

This university let me enroll a few years ago, before I was old enough, because my philosophy-professor father, who teaches there, told them they should. He sent them my records and then I had to have a meeting with three administrators in which I was expected to carry myself in collegiate fashion.

My dad coached me on the way to the meeting. "Sit up straight. Lie. Smile." I told him he was making me nervous. "Oh yeah, and don't be nervous," he continued. "Make eye contact. But not for too long—no piercing stares. And when they ask you a question, lie some more."

"About what?"

"You'll see."

"That's unpossible," I said. "I can't lie."

"Oh. And don't make up any words."

I squinted up at him. "I make up words?"

The three administrators I was meeting with, through glorious coincidence, all had flippy hair in the shape of yak horns. *What're the odds?* They also looked angry. Three angry yaks.

Everyone in the world calls my father "Dude" except for these three yaks. An old hippie with weird-ass white-blue eyes and big, curly hair, my dad looks like a Dude. The yaks called him "Dr. Hersh," though. I would've snickered if they hadn't already looked so angry.

"Very impressive grades," the yak man said to me with a threatening glare. His flippy horns were tiny, right at the top of his forehead, and he was neck-less.

"And test scores," added the yak woman, grimacing. When she moved, her shoulder-length curls did not.

The yak person of indiscriminate gender and chin-length horns frowned. "I think Ms. Hersh will be extremely happy here."

I sat up straight, made brief eye contact and assured them that I would be extremely happy holding my breath inside those buildings. I used only real words, as far as I know. The whole time, I was thinking *Dorks always get straight A's . . . do they not know this?*

"They weren't so schmanky," I said to Dude, walking down the hallway after the meeting, "but you don't look like a Dr. Hersh."

"What do I look like?" He stopped and posed while I stared at him.

"You look sorta like Dr. *Who* . . ."

"Hmmm." He stopped posing. "I wonder if I could get people to call me Dr. *Who*?"

"That'd be cool. It might be weird to suggest it."

"Yeah. I'll stick with Dude."

Now Dude makes me take all the groovy classes he teaches, to pay him back for getting me into college before I belonged there: *Dream Symbolism, Native American Mythology, Yoga.* "I'm trying *not* to grow up into a hippie," I told him.

"Good luck with that," he said.

One of our housemates holds a brown and white guinea pig
in his hands for me to pet. "Don't be afraid. The guinea
pig is the gentlest of all creatures," he says kindly.
"All he wants is peace."

The guinea pig looks at me suspiciously and makes
strange, underwater sounds.

"Humans enslave each other and fight wars," he continues,
pushing his long brown hair behind his ears. "Guinea pigs
want nothing to do with governments or violence. They're
our brothers in peace. Go ahead, you can pet him."

I reach out to touch the guinea pig's twitching nose with
my finger. It bites me.

Dude introduced me to Betty one afternoon outside his office, as college students who *looked* like college students chatted in the hallway, balancing books, backpacks and cans of Coke. "Kristin Hersh? Betty Hutton," he giggled. "Betty Hutton? Kristin Hersh."

Betty had white hair that day, which curved in around her jawline, framing her pink lipstick. She wore blue cowboy boots and sunglasses, which she removed to reveal enormous drag queen eyelashes. Dude cried gleefully, "It's perfect! Kristin, you're too young to make any friends here and Betty, you're too old!" Betty and I both cringed.

"I'm sorry," I said, putting out my hand. "He's not a tactful man." Betty shook her head and then roared with laughter, pulling me into a bear hug. Over her shoulder, I saw Dude beaming. Then Betty pushed me out in front of her and growled, "Nobody can fuck with *us*, right, Krissy?"

"I guess not," I said, and she hugged me again. "Wow!" I mouthed to Dude. He just stood there, smiling.

Now Betty says we need each other. That the two of us have to stick together because we're "boy-girls," independent and gender-free. I think she means "humans," but I'll take it. Betty is a shiny beast, a warm heart in a cold world, and I'm lucky to know her. She also has a great life story: she says she spent a fatherless, poverty-stricken childhood in Detroit, dancing and singing for drunks in her mother's speakeasy, and then became a rich, famous movie star in Hollywood.

I've never heard of her, but it doesn't matter. I love the story too much to question it; I don't care if it's true or not. I honor it as the pink, sparkly Hollywood tale with the dark Hollywood underbelly that we all need to hear at least once. I hear it all the time because Betty can talk and I really can't. Like most quiet people though, I'm an excellent listener.

This is a Catholic university, so there're a bunch of nuns around, though most of them disguise themselves as regular women, so it's hard to tell who's a nun and who isn't. Betty and I actually have a favorite nun, a baffling sister who takes her marital vows to Jesus very seriously—she and Jesus actually sleep together. *"And we don't just sleep,"* she revealed in a lecture, after which she was granted an immediate, possibly permanent, vacation.

I saw her in the locker room at the Y soon after this. She wore a huge, puffy shower cap and a bright rainbow-striped towel, and held a shower brush the size of a tennis racket in her hand. I was naked, about to step into the shower. I probably stared at her outfit a minute too long while I waited for the water to warm up, 'cause she caught my eye from across the room, waved her shower brush in greeting and *whistled at me!* What a nun.

Our favorite nun *name*, however, is: Assumpta Tang.

Suddenly, Betty appears from behind an enormous old tree, walking carefully over the dirt in prim heels. She waves maniacally, like people do in old home movies, and I wave back tiny. Everything about Betty is huge, bigger than life. I'm smaller than life—so unremarkable that I'm practically invisible. We make an odd couple.

"*Mahnin!*" I call to her.

"Sweetheart!" she says breathlessly, juggling textbooks and pressing her pantsuit into place. "I overslept! Did you do your workout?"

I make a face. "I don't call it a *workout*."

"Well, I do! Did you do your workout?" she asks again, piling her books up neatly on her arm.

I laugh. "Yeah."

"Oh good," she says. "So you'll be able to sit still for a little while."

We walk up the stairs together, Betty chattering loudly, ignoring glares from people who're trying to study. Because she's loud and I'm shy, Betty and I both love the library bathroom. In the bathroom, she can talk as loud as she wants and sing and guffaw without librarians giving her any shit, and I know I don't have to see anyone but Betty 'cause the door's locked.

The library at our school is a castle on a cliff overlooking the sea and its bathroom is a large, black and white tiled room with an antique claw-foot tub. When we have a study date, I lie in the tub, she sits on the toilet, and we read and talk. The doorknob gets jiggled every fifteen minutes or so by students needing to pee, but Betty just yells, "Occupied!" and they go away. This is our favorite way to kill an afternoon.

"*No, no, no, it couldn't be true . . . that anyone else could love you like I do,*" Betty sings when we get upstairs and lock ourselves in. She's hunched over her notebook, scribbling in it, a textbook perched on the radiator next to her. "Singing on the toilet! If Mr. DeMille could see me now!" She hums the same song for a minute, then sticks her pencil behind her ear and turns to look at me. "Krissy, did you declare a major?"

I keep reading. "No. Why would I do that?"

"Because you have to? Remember how they told you you have to?" She sounds exasperated. "You know why they said that?"

I look up at her. "Why?"

"Because you have to!"

"No, I don't." I go back to my reading. "I wanna learn everything, not one thing."

"Just *pick* something. It's easy. What are you studying right now?"

"Uh . . . metaphysical anthropology," I answer. "Or maybe anthropological metaphysics. I forget."

She stares at me. "You have to prepare for your future or you won't have one," she says in a singsongy voice that echoes off the walls prettily. This makes her start humming again.

"What're you, my guidance counselor?"

She stops humming. "Did you apply to McGill?" It's hard to read with Betty around; she hardly ever stops talking and singing. I don't get much studying done on these "study dates."

"They said I could go if I want to," I mumble.

Betty freezes. "That's a great opportunity, Krissy," she says quietly.

I look up from my book again. "You know where Montreal turns out to be? *Canada!* That's a hell of a commute."

She giggles, then exhales theatrically. "Oh, thank you, Jesus. I'm sorry, Krissy. You *should* prepare for the future; I just . . . don't know what I'd do if you left."

I try to read again. "The future doesn't exist."

"Well, not *yet*, bonehead!" I smile up at her, but she's looking off, humming again, so I go back to my reading. Suddenly, she stops. "Krissy, have you ever been on a trapeze?" Betty is the queen of non sequiturs.

I shake my head and continue reading. "Mm-mm."

"It'd do you good. I took trapeze lessons for *The Greatest Show on Earth* so they'd hire me instead of a trapeze artist who couldn't act," she says. "It's not that hard . . . it's like flying. Scary flying."

Wow. Circus Betty. "Scary flying sounds cool. And scary." I finish what I'm reading and look up into her huge eyes. "Why was it the greatest show on earth?"

"Well, it wasn't," she answers thoughtfully. "It was just called that."

"Oh."

Betty smiles her reminiscing smile. "It *was* great, though. It was great fun, swinging around. And Cecil B. DeMille was a great man. Who said I had great feet!"

"Great!" I laugh. Betty takes her pencil out from behind her ear and goes back to her notebook, humming.

Soon, she's singing again, *"No, no, no, it couldn't—"* then, suddenly dark, says, "I can't write this."

I look up. "The Jung paper? Why not?"

"I can't write about personality types because I don't have a personality. I was a commodity, not a person," she says bitterly.

I'm disappointed; I really wanted to read that paper. Betty can be very entertaining when it comes to psychology. She calls Freud "that motherfucker" 'cause she thinks he's the only guy who ever wanted to sleep with his own mother. I'm sure she's right about this. Her other problem with Freud is *"Talking?* Gimme a break! Talking's not a cure! Nobody ever solved a problem by whining about it!"

That's probably true, too, at least for her. Betty's had to bust her ass in order to quit drinking and taking pills and she's not a whiner. She has a strong, guileless way about her that makes a huge impression. I always assumed it was her "personality." *And she thinks she doesn't have one?* Of course, it's that same old Hollywood story again. I'm not sure exactly what happened to her there, but Hollywood haunts Betty. Both the loss of the pink, sparkly life she lived and the hatred of its dark underbelly. "What do you mean you don't have a personality?" I ask her.

Her fluttery girliness is gone. "I'm not a real person, only the shell of one. I started working on my outside when I was fifteen and showbiz never let me stop."

"But you're a psychology major . . ." I venture carefully. "Maybe you could write about *other* people's personalities?"

"How? I wouldn't know what I was talking about." Slowly, she walks to the sink, shoulders hunched, and stares at her reflection in the mirror. "There's no me in here." She looks into her own eyes. "I only sang for my mother's sake."

"Sparkle?" One of Betty's cautionary tales is about a little tap-dancing windup monkey girl, a child star with a relentlessly driven stage mother. Whenever the daughter performed, the mother would tell her to "sparkle!" which I thought was so hilarious, I started saying it all the time. Now it seems sad.

"Sort of. I just wanted to help." She looks very tired and, for the first time since I met her, old. I check her cheek for wetness. Betty cries at the drop of a hat—ladylike movie star tears, sweetly showy—but this afternoon, she actually looks too sad to cry. "And now I'm old. Who the hell am I?" she asks her mirror image angrily. "Maybe I don't give a shit."

Jesus Christ. "Betty . . ."

"You aren't supposed to have feelings in Hollywood," she spits. "The product must go on and Betty Hutton was the product." Her skin seems to vibrate with feeling, but the dullness in her eyes is more terrifying.

I put my book down and kneel in the bathtub, watching her curved back and the half of her face I can see in the mirror. She looks so sad. "A minute ago, you were enjoying your memories," I say. "Why'd they turn on you?"

"I have very mixed feelings about my memories."

"But Betty, you can't be empty; humans don't have that option. Maybe your outside is sparkly, but you aren't hollow on the inside. And the outside isn't as fake as you think." Her eyes glitter and she twists her mouth up in the mirror, trying not to cry. I can't bear this; I start babbling. "And it's so cool! You're a Catholic boy-girl with lipstick and big muscles. I love your singing and your hair—"

"This isn't *my* hair, sweetheart! It's a wig! I wear wigs because I can't let anyone see the real me!" She sounds desperate.

"But it *is* the real you! More than keratin pushing out of your follicles is. You chose it, so it's you. I'm not a natural blue, you know." She just keeps staring into the mirror. "I can honestly say you're the most 'you' of any human I've ever met. In fact, you're so *much*, you make other people seem like zombie . . . dolls."

"Zombie dolls?" She turns to look at me kneeling in the tub and smiles sadly.

"Personality-free."

Betty shakes her head. "*Zombie dolls.* Just don't be easy to control, Krissy. They're going to want to wake you up and put you to sleep, and they'll do it with drugs."

We have this conversation frequently. Betty's afraid some cigar-chomping studio mogul's gonna stuff me full of pills just because I'm in a band. Whether or not she was actually a movie star, it often seems like she just stepped out of an old movie; she's a walking anachronism. "Who's 'they'?"

"Listen, this is important. Judy Garland and I had a long talk about this once, in Vegas—"

Geez, sometimes she just seems nuts. "Really Judy Garland? From *The Wizard of Oz*?"

"*Listen*. You'll end up dead, like her. Nobody'll care about you once they can't make any more money off you; they'll just go get another girl—"

"But I'm *not* a girl. I don't think they do that anymore, anyway."

Betty stares at me for a few seconds, then turns back to the mirror. "Look at my ugly mug," she presses her hands to her cheeks, pushing them up into her temples. I feel so bad for her. Betty sees herself as a young, beautiful starlet. Then she looks in the mirror and an old lady looks back.

I thought getting old meant getting wise. Or at least secure. I don't know why I thought that; I don't know any wise, secure old people. Maybe I inferred it from after-school specials. And I'd like to think that by the time you die, you've figured *something* out. That you aren't lying there wondering what the hell just happened.

Betty's old and she isn't at all together. In fact, she often seems to be falling apart. Time is like a hurricane to her—a big, fast mess, sweeping her away. What a scary vision of the future. I'd have liked to see time as my friend; Betty makes it look like a black hole.

The doorknob jiggles and someone knocks. Betty shrieks, "Occupied!" at her own reflection and the knocking stops. Wearily, she sits back down on her toilet. "Promise me you'll stay you, Krissy. No one should have to sparkle."

"Don't worry. I *can't* sparkle and I'm not scared of them," I say. "I'm not scared of anything."

She turns slowly and gazes out the window at the ocean. "Maybe you should be." The silence that follows this grim prediction is so long and uncomfortable that I interrupt her gazing.

"So you were in Vegas with Dorothy, huh?"

She narrows her eyes at me. "Don't make fun."

"Sorry . . . it's *interesting*."

"I was lucky she talked to me at all. I stole the role of a lifetime out from under her." Sometimes Betty says things that are so foreign to me, I don't know how to respond. I can't even pretend to know what she's talking about. If it's craziness, it's certainly fascinating craziness. If it's real, well . . . it's still weird. "Don't try to meet your heroes," she says sadly. "You'll only be disappointed."

"You just say that 'cause other people say it. People who have assholes for heroes."

She looks at me pointedly. "This is important, Krissy. The entertainment industry got Judy hooked on drugs that killed her, my addictions almost killed me and I don't want the same thing to happen to you. Christ's love saved me, but you're never going to let that happen."

Betty says she converted to Catholicism "as an alternative to freaking out." I think it's her new drug, but in a good way. She gets all hopped up on Jesus and good works and heaven within and starts telling people that His love is out there for the taking and she means it. She can see them looking at her funny, but she knows too much about how a light heart can replace an old, used-up, heavy one to care. I don't necessarily love Catholicism, but I love *her* Catholicism.

"Oh, I don't know," I answer. "I might go get religion someday." She says nothing, just looks at me. I grope for a change of subject. "Do you . . . do you miss it?" I ask. "Drinking, I mean?"

She thinks about this. "No. Alcohol was heavy. I miss pills. Pills made me great."

"Really?"

She nods emphatically, eyes big.

"You aren't supposed to say that, you know, Betty. In the movie of your life, you'll find out they were placebos."

She smirks at me. "I really do worry about you."

"I know you do, but I'm invisible, I'm nobody. I'm not *in* the entertainment industry, so no one cares enough to drug me up." It occurs to me, not for the first time, that Betty talks to me as if I were her younger self. Poor thing can't find a better younger self to talk to than me—I have no ambition, no sparkle.

"But you *will* be in the entertainment industry, Krissy. I'm trying to prepare you for what's to come."

She doesn't get it. "Why will I be in the entertainment industry?" I ask her. "I'm not entertaining."

"I'm talking about your dreams," she says gently.

"My 'dream' is to live in a van."

Her eyes widen. They're enormous. "Your dream is to live in a *van*?" she asks, appalled.

"Yeah, that's the plan. See the country, play every night. We just can't afford a van yet." Betty looks sick. I think she just realized I'm not Little Betty. "Does that not sound good to you?" She shakes her head. It's confusing that she's in so much pain. I much prefer the superhero Betty, kicking ass and making noise.

"You told me music was your religion," she says quietly.

"Music. Not the music *business*. Nobody's ever gonna let us into the music *business*."

She sighs, "Maybe you *should* declare a major," then turns back to the window.

"Hey, quit looking at the ocean," I say. "It's making you sad."

"Is it?" she looks genuinely surprised, then sits bolt upright. "I do this, don't I? I fall into holes." She looks around the room as if it's different now, like the light shifted. "Holes I dig myself, trying to be deep—yuck!"

Phew, she's back.

"You're a nice girl, Krissy," she says enigmatically. "I hope you stay nice."

I check my watch. *So much for studying.* "I have sound check in Providence at four, gotta load gear by two, but I could squeeze in a student lounge lunch . . . ?"

"Oh good," she chirps, stacking her books on the radiator. "We can talk showbiz!"

I laugh and climb out of the tub. "Get right back on that horse! You wanna be on the guest list?"

"It's Friday night! Of course I do." Betty comes to every show. Probably because she doesn't have anything else to do, but I always ask. I don't want to be caught *assuming* she's got nothing else to do.

"Okay. What should we have for lunch?" I ask her, taking my books out of the bathtub one by one. "Candy? Or candy?"

She stands up and flutters her fingers around her necklaces in an idiosyncratic gesture I always find charming. It makes her look like a queen. She does it to shift modes, it seems, or when conversations get too serious. Then, scrunched up in excitement, fists clenched, she squeals, "*Candy!*"

♋ call me

i'm in a deep hole
i dug myself

Dude races upstairs to the roof and begins throwing pot
plants into the woods while Crane talks to the policemen
at the door.

She keeps me with her so the cops can see she's a
wholesome young mother. Eventually, they leave—false
alarm.

"See, Kristin?" she says, shaking. "Another reason why
being nice is important. It can keep you out of jail."

After sound check, while I write set lists in the dressing room, our bass player tells a story about her former life in Santa Cruz that involves living in a tree house, falling out of the tree house, breaking her leg and being attacked by banana slugs. Leslie's stories are very soothing, and I only half listen until the banana slug part. Then I stop writing and look up. "What's a banana slug?"

"They're big," answers Leslie.

I hold up the magic marker I'm using, sideways. "What, like, this big?" She swings her waist-length dreads over her shoulder and puts her hands in front of my face about a foot away from each other. "No!" *Cool.* "And they attack you?"

"They attacked *me,*" she says.

"Wait a minute—" I begin.

My sister, Tea, interrupts. "But how fast are they? And what could a slug do to you even if it *could* catch you?" She talks to the ceiling because she's lying on a Universal Couch, the disgusting old sofa covered in stains, gum and cigarette burns that's common to all dressing rooms. We think this is how aliens'll colonize earth: in the form of unassuming, filthy sofas. They're everywhere. Everywhere *we* go, anyway.

"Yeah, Les," I say, "are they poisonous or something?"

Leslie shrugs. "They're really gross."

"Do the one about your hair in the pool drain," says Tea.

"Yeah." *I love that one.* "When you almost drowned. And make it suspenseful."

"How can I make it suspenseful?" asks Leslie. "You already know the ending."

"We figured out the ending to the banana slug story, too," says Tea.

"Yeah. You live." I start another set list. "Do the pool one, it's my favorite."

"*Well,*" Leslie begins dramatically, when an elderly woman carrying a chafing dish bangs open the dressing room door and slams the dish down on a table next to a pitcher of warm orange soda. We thank her brightly. She ignores us and leaves.

"Bye!" we call after her, watching the door swing back and forth.

"Who was that?" asks Tea, lifting her head.

"I don't know. Club lady, I guess." The three of us continue to watch the door swing back and forth as if it might explain who the old lady was.

"She was like, a hundred and ten years old," says Leslie.

"Maybe she was thirty," I answer, still watching the door. "And just in bad shape."

"I guess that's what we'd look like if we lived here," says Leslie thoughtfully.

Tea sits up. "We do live here."

It *is* unfortunate that we spend so much time in rock clubs. Sticky, beer-soaked floors, stale cigarette smoke and scuz dripping off walls covered in Sharpie drawings of naked ladies . . . it can hurt your feelings after a while. Leslie walks over to the table, lifts the cover of the chafing dish and squints into it. "What is it?" I ask her.

"Looks like horse," she says carelessly.

"Horse in gravy?" asks Tea.

"Yep. Could be goat." Leslie's a vegetarian, so she thinks all meat is funny. "There is no love in this food," she murmurs. Carrying the chafing dish over to me, she shoves it under my nose and lifts the lid. "Here," she says. "I got this for you."

I pull my face away. "Stop that."

Tea gets up slowly. "Beer for dinner," she says, and walks out of the room. Tea and I are stepsisters—we introduced my mother to her father and they got married, of all things—but even though there's no blood between us, we look very much alike: puny little dishwater blonds. When people ask us if we're twins, she tells them we're "*step*-twins" and they always nod, like they know what she's talking about. Tea also says this about us: "It's good that we're ugly—it makes us funny." Of course, we think ugly is beautiful.

Leslie yawns and stretches. "Where's Dave?"

I look around the empty dressing room. "Lost?"

"You *lost* him?"

"*I* didn't lose him, he just *got* lost. I'm not my drummer's keeper."

She studies the chafing dish. "I wanna show him the horse-goat."

When I finish the set lists, I stack them on the table, then notice that the bottom one's stuck to a wad of bright green gum. Peeling it away from the gum, I look at Leslie. "She shouldn't eat beer for dinner, it's too sad. Let's grab her and go out." Leslie nods, puts on her jacket, then leaves, calling Tea.

Dropping the set lists back down on the gum, I grab my hat and follow her out to the bar where Tea's talking to the soundman. The soundman's laughing, but Tea looks annoyed. "That doesn't make sense," she's saying as we walk up. He turns his back on us and walks away before she can finish. "What a dick," she says, shaking her head.

"What's the matter?" Leslie asks.

"He said our equipment sucks."

I look back at him, then at Tea. "Our equipment does suck."

"Yeah, but he called us 'rich kids from Newport.'"

"But if we were rich, we'd have *good* equipment."

"That's what I told him. He just laughed. He thinks we're too *dumb* to have good equipment."

"Dick," mutters Leslie.

"He wouldn't put kick and snare in my monitors, either," I bitch. "He just kept *saying* he was doing it. Too lazy to push a fader."

"He thinks you can't tell the difference," says Leslie. "C'mon, let's go find food." The three of us walk slowly toward the open doors of the club. "What the hell makes people think bad shit doesn't happen in Newport?" she grumbles. "Bad shit happens in every city."

"Well, to be fair," I say, "the only bad shit we have in Newport is tourists."

"Yeah, but I'll take a mugger over a tourist any day."

I nod. "Muggers are at work, tourists are insane."

Tea sighs. "We can't win. It's 'cause we look like little kids. Nobody listens when we talk."

"Did he say you can't play guitar 'cause you don't have a penis?" asks Leslie.

"No."

I look at her. "That's something, anyway."

"Some-*thing*," corrects Tea. "Not some-*thang*."

"Some-*theeng*," I repeat. Tea's been helping me kill the vestiges of my Southern accent for years.

When we reach the entrance, Leslie looks at me. "Think we can get back in?" We've been playing shows since we were fourteen, but won't legally be allowed in clubs for three more years. And we all look much younger than we are, so if we leave after sound check, door guys don't let us back in. Even though we always leave very carefully. "I'll do the talking," says Leslie, as we approach the door man. "I look the most like a grown-up." She looks at me. "And you make up words."

"I don't make up any more words than y'all do." Leslie rolls her eyes at Tea, who looks at me like I should know better. I look from one to the other. "But you can still do the talking," I add. "You're the tallest. Just don't get flitchy. Be cool."

The door guy is an oily, tattooed man in leather with many piercings—door guys always dress the part. He's sitting on a stool by the entrance with his back to us, writing on a clipboard, so we stand a respectful distance and stare at him, waiting for him to notice us. "If you don't want people to know you're Southern," Leslie says to me, "maybe you should stop saying *y'all*."

"Well, I didn't make up *that* word. You yankees don't have a second person plural."

"You could try *vous* instead," suggests Tea. "It sounds more cultured, less Gomer."

"Okay. *Vous* don't have a second person plural. Hey, that *is* better!"

Leslie chuckles. The door guy hears her, turns around and looks at us, bored, then goes back to his clipboard. "*He's so grody*," she whispers.

"If you don't want people to know you're from California," I say to her, "maybe you should stop saying *grody*."

"I *do* want people to know I'm from California! It's better than here."

The guy keeps writing, showing no sign of paying any attention to us, ever. I look at Leslie. "I think both our accents drop our IQ's a bunch of points, though."

"Try 'gross' instead," suggests Tea.

"*He's so gross*," Leslie whispers, then clears her throat and steps up to him. We stand behind her. The door guy looks at Leslie like he hates her. "Hi! We're Throwing Muses, the band that's headlining tonight," she says sweetly in bouncy Californian. "That was us onstage, sound checking. There's our poster on the wall next to you with a picture of us on it." Silence. They *never* talk. "So anyway, nice to meet you," she continues. "Apparently, we sort of don't look like a band, but . . . that's who we are." Laughing weakly, she pauses to let this sink in. "And we're underage, but we're still: *Throwing Muses*. The band that's headlining tonight." He stares over our heads. We look at each other.

It's painfully obvious that the three of us are sandy, salty little islanders—beach kids who don't belong here in Providence, the Big City. We're clean and healthy, which is very uncool. And we don't hide it by trying to look like junkies, which is what you're supposed to do. Our clothes might be dirty, but our bodies are clean, inside and out. We practically smell like sunshine.

We know this is dumb, but it's dumber to lie about it. Also, for some reason, we dress like old people, or refugees, which makes us look . . . I don't know, easy to beat up? Club guys love to hate us, anyway; they bully us with silence. As if they could *scare* us, for christ sake.

"So, listen," I tell him, "we're going out for a while, but we'll come back in time to play the show, okay?" I study his face for evidence of comprehension. "Tonight. In your club." He looks away. "Hello?"

Jumping into his line of vision, Tea tries to annoy him into paying attention. "We just wanted to make sure we wouldn't have any trouble getting back in, 'cause we don't have ID's, but we're still, you know, that band." She points at our poster. "That band that wouldn't shut up, right? *Heh heh* . . . so you'll remember us?" she asks. The guy finally nods reluctantly.

Later, though, he displays marked symptoms of short-term memory loss. He squints as we pose in front of our poster, trying to look like ourselves, pointing out our equipment sitting on the stage and the fact that we're supposed to be on in ten minutes.

"Please remember us," we beg. "We're the people that asked you to remember us, remember?"

Tea vibes him under her breath. "*Let . . . us . . . in!*"

"It was just a little while ago, remember a little while ago?" I say. "It was right before now!" Throwing up my hands in frustration, I try once more. "Is there someone else back there we could talk to? Somebody who actually talks?" He stares blankly and gestures toward the "Must Be 21 Years of Age or Over" sign. "Yeah, we've seen that," I tell him.

"Why's live music associated with alcohol at *all*?" mutters Leslie, who doesn't drink. "It's insane that we can't get in to our own show because of drinking laws. We should *refuse* to play."

"Like anybody'd care," I grumble.

"Why don't we have fake ID's?" asks Tea.

Leslie stares at the door guy, looking thoughtful. "Maybe he doesn't speak English."

Eventually, we have to pool our money and buy tickets to our own show. For four years, we've been buying tickets to our own shows. Apparently, it's okay to be underage if you spend money, which is also how it works with drinking. The other bands get pitchers of beer in the dressing room and we get pitchers of orange soda, but nobody's ever tried to stop us from buying beers at the bar, which is where I'm headed.

While I wait for my drink, I realize I can't move—I'm stuck between two drunk frat guys who are squeezing me so hard I can barely breathe.

They're the rich kind of frat guys: brand-new baseball caps and expensive clothes, trying unsuccessfully to focus their eyes, shattered by the alcohol in their bloodstreams.

I ask them politely to shift, but instead, they move in closer and one of them pulls off my hat. "Blue hair! Is *all* your hair blue?" He laughs, surrounding the three of us in a beery cloud, then shoves me into his dumb-ass buddy, who's concentrating hard on trying to wind an arm around my waist. The guy's arm slips and he falls off his stool, pushing me back into the first guy, who takes off his baseball cap and carefully balances my hat on his head.

I always want guys like this to fall in love with each other—they have so much in common! And it would solve *so* many problems.

⤳ portia

```
like frat boys who sleep together
we party better
we know what it means to be a brother
```

I grab my hat, duck under the other guy's arm as he tries to steady himself on the bar stool and leave without my drink. I don't need it. If I go onstage without a beer, somebody in the audience'll buy me one. They're mystifyingly kind. But I still stare at the stage like I always do before we play, terrified, thinking *What the hell am I doing here? I'm not the type.*

I get really bad stage fright, 'cause I'm so shy and 'cause I really don't understand what happens up there—I can't prepare for it, it's too freaky. So I picture the audience as an amorphous horde, waving clubs and torches and yelling at me. But look at 'em: they're happy as clams and sweet as pie and they buy us beer. I'm just a sissy.

And this is interesting: they aren't the unruly mob they appear to be at first glance. They've neatly organized themselves into little factions. The front row is the most overtly enthusiastic. They're often drunk, but they're never drunks—they can think thoughts and string sentences together, and then jump around like psychos. I wonder if they do this in real life, too: in the middle of conversations suddenly jump up into the air screaming, pounding on the guy next to them and running around in circles.

The goth chicks who knit in the back of the room are lovely, soft-spoken and graceful, and they appear to be music appreciators, chatting during shows and then thanking the band politely afterward. They're nice to look at, with their knitting needles flashing, their black lips and white lips.

Directly in front of the knitters are the hippies. Well, neohippies. The kids of either real hippies or CPAs, they're friendly, harmless, a little soft around the edges. It's hard to tell hippie chicks from hippie guys; they all have the same hair, the same voice and the same clothes, none of them wear makeup, and they all dance like goofballs. When they aren't dancing, they're sitting on the floor like they're at a sing-along.

Musicians gather in front of the hippies. There are two different kinds of musicians here in Providence: one kind's lost in a scene, the other kind's lost in space. The ones lost in scenes are easy to pick out 'cause they look like they sound—their outfits match their musical styles. I find this bizarre. I like the confused, spacey musicians better. Non-competitive and sweetly scared, their carriage implies a question: what happens next? Both male and female musicians wear eyeliner.

Then come the junkies, precious to me. A ghostly group but livelier than you'd think, they don't really have a "look." They don't look anything like the people who *try* to look like junkies—they're just sort of unwashed. I put them on the guest list because they're dear to my heart and 'cause they really don't have shit.

The junkies are shy, but they're shy as a group. They hang together, whispering to each other, like a tiny cult. The little girl who dyed my hair blue waves when I walk by. She's probably my age, but, god, she looks eleven. Don't know how that little body handles heroin.

She and her half-dozen or so friends move around the city in a herd. You see them sitting on the sidewalk or at parties in ragged apartments. In warm weather, they sleep in Dead Girl Park near Wayland Square or on the hill, piled up like puppies near a statue of Roger Williams we call "Jiving Man" 'cause he looks like he's truckin' off the edge of a cliff. Which is, coincidentally, what this little girl and her friends appear to be doing.

One day, she noticed that the blue in my hair was disappearing and told me to bring some Manic Panic and a scarf to the park. "Blue is where it's at," she said. "Don't let it fade." I did this 'cause I thought that was good advice. While she mixed the dye, her friends talked about heroin, their favorite subject. I was interested, because I had imagined all sorts of cold childhoods for them: desperate, dark life tunnels and at the end, a numb light. These kids didn't seem to be "user-posers" with the disenfranchised affect; they looked fragile and real to me.

That day, the funny one—the only junkie with heft ("I'm a husky boy!"), the one who actually refers to the group as "the junkies" rather than just "my friends"—told me that the escape they're looking for is from: boredom. They *numb* themselves out of *boredom*.

Geez.

While we talked, the little girl rubbed the blue goo into my hair, then expertly wrapped my blue, gooey head in the scarf and told me I could rinse it out whenever I felt like it. Because she wouldn't accept the ten dollar bill I held out for her, I put them on the guest list for the show that night and now they come every time we play. Tonight, they look really happy; their whispering is making them laugh. They don't *seem* bored.

Painters stand between the junkies and the psychos. They don't move, they don't jump or whisper or dance; they listen ferociously. I admire this.

I'm sitting on a folding chair backstage, dressed as a cardboard cowgirl. I wear a cardboard cowboy hat and a cardboard vest and swing my tiny tap shoes back and forth over the linoleum floor. I am riddled with terror.

My parents kneel on the floor in front of me.

"After the recital, we'll go get ice cream," says Crane, a tense smile on her face.

Dude fishes around in his pocket and pulls out a five dollar bill. "I'll give you five bucks to go out there," he says.

I shake my head. "I'm just not the type."

Far from everyone, huddled in a corner of the club, are Betty and her priest. I've never asked her why she brings her priest to shows, but he's always there. I know they're very close. They're sort of dating . . . spiritually. And they never miss a show. It's funny, like every day is Bring Your Grandma and Her Priest to Work Day. Betty can't even pronounce the name of the band; she says that "Throw-ing Mu-ses" is too many syllables. I told her "Bet-ty Hut-ton" has just as many, but she ignored me.

"We never call ourselves *Throwing Muses*, anyway," I said. "We say *Blowing Fuses* or *Spewing Mouses*."

She didn't think that was funny. "Krissy! That's *just* as many syllables!"

Tonight, Betty's hair is gold and she's wearing her blue cowboy boots and a cowboy hat. Her priest is dressed as a priest. The two of them lean against the back wall of the club, talking. Betty has gigantic sunglasses on because she doesn't like being "recognized."

Now that I know her deep, weird need for stardom, I act like a tiny bodyguard when I'm with her, shielding her from invisible autograph hounds wherever we go, as I'm sure her priest is doing now. I think this has backfired a little. She now believes fans are everywhere: at school, at the beach, at Dunkin' Donuts. I have to buy our coffees in the morning, she's so scared to be seen. It's strange; she's no fading flower—she's really fucking loud—but unusually fragile. She seems to love the *idea* of fans and hate the fans themselves. Or else she's just afraid of them. Of course, there *are* no fans. This minor detail hasn't dented her persona a bit. Betty is a movie star, through and through.

When we play gay bars, she and her priest look like a coupla nifty drag queens, but in this dismal rock club, they look small and lonely—out of place. It's sad that this is their big Friday night out on the town. There are probably better things for an old lady and her priest to do on a Friday night.

But Betty thinks she *has* to come to all of our shows because I need help (sorta true). She says I'm a reluctant performer (also true) and that she can learn me up to sparkle (this will never happen). According to her, one more thing she and I have in common is *music*. This is wholly psychotic.

Betty grew up in the golden age of Hollywood, back when movies were Broadway on film, so her idea of music is "singing as entertainment," and you can't call what I do singing *or* entertainment. I hiss and yell and wail. Sometimes I make seagull noises, unfortunately. Music is something I have almost no control over. Like well-rehearsed Tourette's.

When Betty sings, she sits at a piano and says lovely things about hope and broken hearts. I often sing phonetically, as if I don't speak English. The words climb out of my throat and into my mouth. Then I have to spit them out.

Betty sings about starlight and champagne. I sing about dead rabbits and blow jobs. When I say playing music is owning violence, she says it's owning love; when I say it's math, she says it's tap dancing; when I say it's my gun, she says it's her dance card.

I've also noticed that she sings notes that go with the chords in her songs. I have yet to do that. It sounds pretty when Betty does it; it sounds boring and goofy when I do it. So I make up new notes, ones that don't belong anywhere near the chords I'm playing, and I sing those. People must think, *It's so nice of them to let that deaf girl sing.*

I can't imagine what I sound like to Betty. Not boring, I bet. Maybe goofy. I actually drew a Goofus and Gallant–style cartoon once called "Kristin and Betty" and passed it to her in class. I drew her as a sparkling Amazon sashaying across the stage and me as a little rat girl with spirals for eyes. I thought it was hilarious; she thought it was Art and hung it up in her house.

Later, it occurred to me that she has no idea who Goofus and Gallant are; she's too old to have read *Highlights* magazine in her grammar school library when she was a kid. She was probably raised on Dick and Jane books. Maybe I'll do a Dick and Jane cartoon for her: "See Betty tap dance. See Kristin spaz."

Maybe not—she'd hang it on the wall. Betty's crazy enthusiastic.

Which is part of why I love having her here. My stage fright melts away when I see Betty 'cause she's the opposite of a rock club: she's the anti-scuzz. And getting felt up by frat guys doesn't seem so bad when you have a secret superhero standing in the back of the room who could kick their asses. She totally could, too; she's got big muscles and those guys were already wasted. I'd love to see Betty take on some drunk frat boys. She'd make them *die*.

Her priest is a really nice guy, too. A little tense maybe, but pretty normal for a priest, from what I hear. He smiles encouragingly and gives me the thumbs up whenever I so much as glance at him. Right now, he's watching the opening band studiously.

Betty catches my eye from across the room and does her joyful home movies wave. I wave back and join them in the corner to watch the end of the opening band's set. This band is in the throes of an outro balanced on top of another outro on top of something that was probably an outro. Other bands fascinate me. They're so *fun*. Nobody would ever call us "fun."

Unfortunately, these guys're playing music they've heard before, which is comfy but easy. And musicians get smarmy when they aren't busting their asses. They don't have to concentrate on what they're playing, so they concentrate on how they look while they're playing it: they grimace and jump around. Trying to get laid tonight, I imagine. *I wonder if it works. I should ask them.*

The song ends with a big finish. Then another big finish. Another one. And . . . done. The musicians jump off the stage, cheering along with the audience. *Gosh, they're having a good time.* As the lights come up in the room and the clapping peters out, the band members high-five each other and their friends in the front row.

I look at Betty, concerned. She's still hiding from fans who aren't there. "Do you wanna hang out in the dressing room?" I point over her shoulder.

"I'll think about it." She looks around nervously and pulls the brim of her cowboy hat down lower. "But Father McGuire likes the people-watching out here."

Father McGuire smiles engagingly, his mouth widening to the point where his face must hurt. "There's so much *energy* in the room," he says. "Everyone's excited!"

Betty is businesslike. "Oh, yes. Including us." Father McGuire sticks his thumbs up, nodding happily. "We can't wait for the show to start," Betty murmurs, glancing around the room distractedly. I find this hard to believe. They see *every* show. At this point, we could only be making them tired and confused.

Then, giving me a sly wink, she snaps into "showbiz tips" mode. Betty's showbiz tips are heartbreakingly bizarre. "What're you gonna do tonight, Krissy?" she asks gaily.

I think for a second. "I don't know, what?" *I hate being quizzed on this stuff.* Father McGuire's eyebrows shoot up past his glasses and settle high on his forehead.

"String 'em along!" she squeals, spreading her long, frosty nails like cat's claws. "Play with 'em! Cats and mice! It's spring, sweetie, and you're a super kid! Fall in love!" Father McGuire nods and smiles.

"Okay, Betty."

"And remember: don't just stare into space! Ask 'em with your eyes: *Do you want some more?*" She says Al Jolson told her to do that.

"But I already know the answer, Betty: *No*." And she giggles.

Guys from the opening band file past us on their way to the dressing room, which means it's time for us to set up. My stomach lurches with stage fright. "Good show!" I call out to them, wringing my hands nervously. Father McGuire sticks his thumbs up at them.

The guitar player stops and looks at me. "What's wrong with your hands?" he asks. "Are they sore? Lemme get you some Tiger Balm; I got some in my backpack." He disappears into the dressing room, then returns with a tube of this ubiquitous ointment, which is sorta like vegan Ben-Gay. I've never really needed it, but everyone seems to use it.

He squeezes a generous amount of Tiger Balm onto my palm. I rub it all over both hands and up my arms—can't hurt, right? *Holy crap!* It feels crazy. Searing ice. *Jesus.* "Thanks!" My voice sounds really high-pitched. He grins and takes the Tiger Balm back to the dressing room, returning a minute later with a beer that he presses into my greasy hands. "Shit . . ." I say when he leaves.

"Yeah, Tiger Bomb burns like a motherfucker," says Betty. Her priest smiles brightly.

"And I haven't taken out my contacts yet." Not seeing is a very important part of playing music for me. I stare into space and get lost in a warm, fuzzy sensory deprivation tank of sound. No audience, no club, just my best friend: noise.

Betty claims it's nearsightedness that keeps me from "falling in love," which is what she calls singing *well*. She's never actually come out and told me she thinks I sing badly, but I sing so weird, I don't see how she could think anything else. According to her, I have to make eye contact with audience members . . . and something about mice playing with cats and cats flirting with mice. Or vice versa. I don't know. I don't try very hard to do this 'cause I can't imagine anything worse than trying to play while looking at people who are looking at me.

"So leave your contacts in," says Betty. "And ask 'em with your eyes, *Do you want some—*"

"I can't," I whine.

Betty throws her hands up. "So take 'em out." Father McGuire watches with an animated frown.

I take out my contacts and hold them in my hand. Tears roll down my cheeks. Squinting at Betty and her priest through a thick fog, I announce, "I just set my eyeballs on fire."

It's worth Tiger Balm tears to fuzzify all the faces in this room, but they're looking *really* fuzzy right now. I wonder if I'll be able to see my effects pedals or the set list. I look down at my hands—they're a soft blur. Betty takes a handkerchief out of her purse and, grabbing me by the chin, wipes away my tears with it. "Wow," I say through her hand. "I thought only my grandfather carried a handkerchief. How old *are* you, anyway?" This makes her angry and she spits on the handkerchief, rubbing it into my eyes and ranting about how bad blindness is for musicians. "Stevie Wonder's blind," I mutter.

"Steve who?" she asks loudly. People at the crowded bar next to us turn slowly around on their bar stools to watch. "Where're your glasses?" she demands, taking my beer and wiping *it* down.

"I can't wear 'em onstage; they fall off." More tears stream down my face, so she switches from the beer bottle back to my face.

"Father McGuire wears glasses, don't you, Father?" Father McGuire nods and points at his glasses. Then Betty steps back and sighs, folding up her spit-kerchief. "You have to sing *to* people, Krissy. How can you do that if you can't look at them?" Father McGuire nods sadly.

I hate this conversation. I hate it every time we have it. "I can't *sing*, either."

She puts her hands on her hips. "That's no excuse! I can't sing, never could," she says proudly. Father McGuire shakes his head.

I squint at her through burning eyes. "What're you talking about? Singing's your . . . thing."

"Nope. I just yelled with a big smile on my face!" She stuffs the folded handkerchief into her sleeve.

"Hey, like me!" I say. "Except for the smiling part."

"Yeah," she continues. "I gave it my all. I *sold* it and nobody noticed that I couldn't sing."

She's gotta be lying. "You could *too* sing, Betty. Can I have that back?" I ask, reaching for the beer. Glancing at the bar, I notice that the line of faces is still staring.

"No, really, I couldn't." She studies my face. "So I *sold* it," she says pointedly, gripping my beer tightly.

"Oh." *I get it.* "I don't sell it, do I?"

Betty and her priest both shake their heads. "Listen," she says. "Show the audience how the song makes you *feel*. Your face is a blank when you play, dear—it's disconcerting. You gotta show off more." She glares at the staring drinkers who, one by one, turn back to face the bar.

Show off? That's what that dumb opening band was doing. "I don't show off at *all*," I say quietly.

"What?" she yells, startling a nearby goth couple.

"I said, I don't show off!" I yell back. The goth couple shuffles away. Father McGuire looks alarmed. Wiping more Tiger Balm tears off my face, I apologize. "Sorry. I didn't mean to *holler* at you. I'm just nervous. I think I have to set up now. What I meant to say is"—I stand on tiptoe and whisper into her ear—"*I don't show off.*"

Betty's feeling sassy. She leans in, pressing her gleaming curls against my cheek, and whispers, too. "*You said it, not me.*"

"Well, it's not *about* the show, it's about the *work*," I say into her cheek. "I'm working too hard to think about anything else. Can I have my beer back? You don't drink anymore."

"And you don't drink *yet*," she says quietly, then straightens up and chirps, "Have fun!"

"Fun's stupid."

"Fun's not stupid, it's *fun*," she says, then sing-songs, "Work plus salesmanship equals success!"

"Hmmm . . . I've never heard that saying before," I grumble. *Why does she always do this to me before I play? Why can't she wait until after the show to give me shit?*

Confused members of the opening band walk by on their way to the bar with *Shouldn't you be on by now?* expressions. They stare, wide-eyed, at the old cowgirl and the priest before turning to order their drinks.

I look at the dressing room door. *Where the hell is my band and why aren't they rescuing me?* "Playing this kind of music isn't an exercise in showing off," I whine quietly to Betty.

"What is it an exercise *in*, then?" she asks gently.

"I don't know," I answer, trying to sound pitiful, ". . . shame?"

"In *what*?" she shrieks, jumping back. Father McGuire looks sad.

I am instantly defensive. "Shame's nothing to be ashamed of!"

She drops her jaw and stares at me for a second, then says briskly, "Oh, for the love of . . . quit that staring-into-space thing." She pushes the beer bottle back into my hand. "You look without seeing. It hurts people's feelings."

"But I don't *want* to see them."

"Krissy, look at people!" To illustrate, she grabs my face and looks into my eyes fiercely. This seems to make them hurt more. "I'm telling you this for your own good. You don't even blink when you play! It's disturbing. Just look at the people you play for—they love you! Show them you're in love with *all* of them!"

I look at her, confused. "I'm not in love with *any* of them."

Her mouth tightens. "All you have to do is look at people," she says slowly. "What the hell are you afraid of?"

"People!" *Duh-uh*. The weird thing is, I don't know anyone who's more afraid of people than Betty.

She sighs. "I knew you had to be afraid of *something*." Then she pulls a tube of fire-engine-red lipstick out of her purse, grabs my chin and rubs it all over my mouth. *I wish she'd stop grabbing me and rubbing me with things.* Father McGuire studies the results and puts his thumbs up, nodding. "At least they'll look at *you* now, Krissy," says Betty. She stands back to admire her work and her face softens.

"It's okay to be scared, sweetheart," she says. "How're you gonna give 'em your heart if you don't have one?"

She says Al Jolson told her that, too.

⊚ elizabeth june

and you were right
it was okay to be scared

My grandfather carefully parts the sheer curtains of his
bedroom window on Lookout Mountain, then rests a rifle on
the ledge. He stands quietly for a long time, gazing out
the window at the peach trees in his backyard.

Suddenly, he fires the gun. A deafening crack and then
silence.

"What did you shoot?" I ask, wide-eyed.

"A squirrel," he says calmly. "He was after my peaches."

Then he takes a handkerchief out of his pocket and begins
wiping the gun down with it. "I shoot that squirrel every
day and every day he comes back for more peaches."

People mill around the dressing room, talking, laughing and drinking. The chafing dish of horse-goat in gravy sits on the table, untouched. So does our warm orange soda. The other bands' pitchers of beer have all been emptied, however. In the center of the commotion, my three bandmates are hunched over the set lists I wrote this afternoon. Leslie's telling Dave the banana slug story while Tea pokes at song titles that Dave then crosses out with my magic marker. Dave is a puny little dishwater-blond like me and Tea, just a boy one; he *also* looks like a child.

"Who gave the drummer a pen?" I ask, carefully putting my Tiger Balmed contacts in their case, then leaning over his shoulder to look. My carefully written set lists are blackened with lines and arrows; songs are crossed out, moved around, exchanged for other songs. "You fusted it all up," I tell him. "Nobody can read it now; everything's crossed out."

"Ev-ree-theeng," coaches Tea kindly. "Not *ev-ruh-thang*."

"Ev-ree-theeng," I repeat. "Eh-vree-theeng's fusted."

Dave looks up at me and smiles. "Hi, Kris. Your set sucked, so I made up a new one."

"Oh," I squint at it. "Okay. I can't see very well right now. Is it good?"

"No, this one sucks, too," says Dave, "but less than yours." He stares at me. "Are you *crying?*"

Leslie stands and stretches. "We should probably play it whether it sucks or not. We're supposed to be on now."

"There's gum on those set lists," I offer helpfully.

"There's gum on *ev-ree-theeng*," says Tea.

Our band was started on these two bullshit principles—well, they're more like bullshit *wishes*, but here they are:

1. That people should be able to touch one another and feel each other's pain. Physically, like you could place your hand on someone's cheek and feel their toothache; and emotionally, if you move someone, touch them deeply, you have to take responsibility for that depth of feeling and care about them.

So it isn't just pain that we should feel in each other—happiness should seep out of pores, and clouds of jealousy and all the different kinds of love and disappointment should float around us. We could walk in and out of people's clouds to know what they're feeling. That'd be the kindest way to live on planet earth.

2. That maybe our essential selves are drunk—not wasted, just kinda buzzed, enough to let go. If we were always a little tipsy, we'd be light, nonjudgmental, truthful. Our hang-ups'd be shaken off, there'd be no second-skin barriers to honesty. Oh, and also no hangovers.

We figure that if these two things were true, then it'd be okay for a band to sound like we do: sorta painful and a little out of control. We'd play what the audience felt and feel it at the same time and they'd feel it reflected back to them in sound and we'd all care about each other's stories and clouds of feeling and . . . *good luck with that*, I think miserably through my stage fright, trudging past the knitters, hippies, junkies, drunks, painters and psychos.

I follow Leslie through the crowd, keeping a close eye on the fountain of dreadlocks making its way through the fuzzy room. Clearly, it *isn't* okay for a band to sound like we do. If it was, nobody'd think we came from outer space, which is what everybody seems to think. *Whatever.* Don't have time to care about that right now.

We don't just have equipment to set up, we have a whole stage set: TVs tuned to static, a busted old Moog synthesizer (also tuned to static—it basically just sits onstage, drooling, like a demented robot friend), an ironing board we use as a percussion stand, lamps (because we prefer mood lighting to rock-show lighting), various car parts and kitchen utensils (for hitting), a movie screen we project slides onto and a pair of mannequin legs in a gold lamé miniskirt with a TV for a torso. All this may sound arty, but really, it's just overenthusiastic.

All four of us believe our stage set is beautiful, but it probably isn't, which is why we call it "the crap." Once in place, the crap becomes a dimly lit obstacle course. Tonight, it is a smeary dimly lit obstacle course with a halo around it.

A blond cloud next to me comes into focus as Tea untangles her guitar cord from the mannequin legs. I stare too long, trying to figure out which blur is Tea and which is the legs. She stops. "Are you okay?" she asks.

I squint at her. "Is that you?" I ask, pointing. "Or is that?"

"Holy shit," she says, walking away.

The lights go down, but it doesn't matter 'cause I'm working in a fog anyway. I find center stage and drop the mic stand about a foot 'cause the singer in the first band was tall. Feeling my pedals to make sure they're in the right order, I carefully place the greasy beer bottle down on top of my set list, then run through my settings as fast as I can with the guitar volume low. When I hear Dave's sticks count us in, I turn the volume back up and hit the two pedals I need for the first song, ready to focus. Well, ready to *lose* focus. *Trying not to see won't be too hard tonight*, I think to myself as the song starts. Now: no more thinking.

Wait. Is that smoke? *A smoke machine?* We're only halfway through the intro and there's already choking smoke everywhere, billowing onto the stage; it looks like we're on fire. I didn't know this club *had* a smoke machine. They must've just gotten it 'cause whoever's working it is really enthusiastic. We repeat the intro.

Then the clouds start flashing; it looks like lightning. *Aw, crap. Strobe lights.* Strobes're supposed to make you look cool, but they make you play retarded. 'Cause the last time you saw your hand, it was on a different fret, and brains aren't smart enough to fill in the missing milliseconds. Mine isn't, anyway. Maybe I didn't play enough video games as a child, so my reaction time is slow.

We play the intro a third time. *Aaaah! This sucks.* We're all playing our parts, but just barely. It looks like a war zone and it feels like total chaos.

Tea walks over to me through the smoke and flashing lights, rolling her eyes in frustration, then presses her face up against her guitar neck and laughs, shaking her head. As she walks away, Leslie comes from the other side and peers at me through a flashing cloud, mock coughing. We wrote our parts with the intent to make every measure fascinating, which is great when you're sitting in a circle facing each other in your practice space, less so when the complexity of the material is lost on a visually overwhelmed audience, and just annoying when we can't even see our instruments. I have to sing in a second—we can't play the intro *again*—and the microphone's lost in smoke. So's the guy working the smoke machine, wherever he is. I'd like to find him and hurt him. I can't even stare into space; space is gone.

This is so dumb. Closing my eyes, I try to lose myself in the pounding noise. I let my hands feel their way along the neck of the guitar and let my lips find the microphone by themselves. When they do, I bump into the mic with my whole face, which makes a loud *thunk*. The band sounds like a confused thunderstorm, though, and a sweaty, shirtless guy in the front row keeps jumping up through the smoke, yelling "You're so *RA-A-A-A-W!*" over and over again, so I figure I'm the only one who hears the face-thunk.

Then, suddenly, after the first verse, my guitar sound gets very loud and bright. I whip around and see the shape of a body on the floor near my amp. *What the hell? Somebody's messing with my amp?* I shoot a get-the-fuck-out-of-here look in the shape's direction, but it just slithers under the smoke like it's escaping the fire and reaches for my pedals, so I step on its hand. It turns over and lies back on the floor, smiling up at me—a leering drunk. Nobody I know. The second verse is gone; no idea what I'm supposed to be singing. I can't think up here. I mean, I can't *stop* thinking. *I wonder what Tea's playing. I can't tell. I can't even hear Dave. Wish that dick soundman had actually put kick and snare in my monitors instead of just saying he did it.* The drunk guy just lies at my feet.

Leslie looks at the figure on the floor, disgusted, and moves toward it ominously, the silver buckles on her motorcycle boots glinting in the lights. I recognize in her movement the intent to *kick the jerk* and shake my head at her, alarmed.

She shrugs and walks away, keeps her bass line going the whole time. Distracted, I've stopped singing; I'm letting chords ring out and losing track (*god, poor Betty wanted me to flirt up here*) but Leslie never misses a beat. *Never.* Dave never misses a beat, either; he smashes delicately, the deep sound of his kit punctuated by the metallic knocking of cowbells, mixing bowls, hubcaps and busted tambourines. It's beautiful. But Dave never messes up because he *can't* be distracted. He's just as nearsighted as I am and lost in his own world back there behind the drum kit. If he looks up, it's like a mole digging his way up from underground, squinting in the sunlight.

Dave and I both love the gentleness of blurry vision. "We're lucky to have the option of a visual softening agent," he said once. "I can talk to someone for an hour thinking they're someone else. It's so *Shakespearean.*"

Right now, he's liquifying the song, somehow murdering perfectly, with finesse. Thank god, 'cause I'm not. I'm *sucking* perfectly. I've sung one verse and one chorus, but the rest of the song has been a pretty goddamn free-form instrumental. I cue the band to end it. *Ugh . . . make it stop.* As the last chord fades, the drunk stands up triumphantly, with my beer in his hand—*hope he gets Tiger Balm lips*—sways dangerously for a few seconds, then stage-dives into the crowd. They separate and he plummets to the floor. Instantly, the first couple of rows close in again around his still form; they aren't missing a beat, either. I love it when a crowd effortlessly swallows a whole human.

Making my way through the smoke to fix the settings on my amp, I bump into Tea. She grabs my arm. "Sorry!" she says. "What'd he do?"

"He fusted my amp."

"Fusted it permanently?"

I mess with knobs until it sounds good. "Nah."

"What'd he do that for?"

I shake my head, shrugging, and then go back to the front of the stage, bend over my set list and try to follow Dave's magic marker arrows up and down the paper. They go in all directions, blending with scribbled song titles. There's also a dark green smear across the middle of the paper that looks like . . . guacamole? *We had guacamole? I thought they only gave us horse and orange soda.*

I'm still trying to figure out what song is next when I realize that the beer the drunk took has been replaced with a new one. I look up to thank the person who gave it to me, but all I see is jostling crowd bodies talking, laughing and hooting. Then the smoke clears and a gentle blue light washes the stage. As a cue, Leslie leans over me and smiles, then starts the next song.

"Stand Up." Good. That's as easy as Throwing Muses gets: no time changes, fairly predictable chord progression and almost normal chords; it just has to be really tight. And Leslie's always tight. As long as I can remember the words. *Don't think.*

"See no evil, think no evil, speak *only* evil" is how the band describes my MO and it's a pretty accurate description. *I* don't know what I'm doing up here, but evil knows. Evil tells stories from my life that I can't follow, makes Throwing Muses sound like the Doghouse. Like finding home in a foreign country, I'm here, but I take nothing for granted.

And I take no responsibility for these wicked déjà vu syringes.

♋ ellen west

my mouth is full of demons
i swear to god

The creepy, goofy mess that is our sound is finally playing itself—song tattoos glow all over me, I'm looking and seeing nothing, and I'm nowhere. Nowhere at all.

Every few minutes, I *am* again. Just to check in, keep the counts going and untangle the fingers as they slam away at the guitar, lost in *their* own world. I listen to Tea's guitar, make sure we're meshing, try to sing in tune with her, then yell in tune by myself. Squeezing the sweaty guitar pick tighter, I'm aware of a sensation, familiar but too strange to be okay. Something crawling into my chest and swelling up inside my throat.

I can start a song just sorta, you know, singing along, and then, before I know it, inflatable words fill my rib cage, move into my mouth. I gag on them and they fly out, say whatever they want, yell and scream themselves.

And *blecch*, that voice—it's wretched. My speaking voice is low, husky and quiet. The *song's* voice is loud, strangled and wailing: thin and screechy. A squashed bug might sing like this.

Going away is my only real talent. Betty's right: I'm a reluctant performer . . . not a performer at all. I need to go away so the song can play it*self*. When it ends, I take a deep breath and turn to look at Leslie. She's still smiling.

We pull up at a cliff by the ocean. The grass is so green
and the water so blue, I can't move; I just sit in the
backseat and stare out the window.

Dude and our dog Zoë hop out of the car, and together
they run toward the ocean. Eventually, I get out and
follow, but I'm too little to catch up with a full-grown
man and a dog, so I stop and watch them run through the
grass. For some reason, when they get to the edge of the
cliff, they both unhesitatingly jump off.

I scream. Racing to the edge, I look down, ready to see
my suicidal dad and dog dashed to pieces on the rocks.

They're both looking up at me, perched on a ledge roughly
four feet below.

"What're you screaming about?" asks Dude.

So many people tonight. Three or four hundred, someone says, a real Friday night crowd. Of course, we still make only fifty bucks, and they don't want to give me *that*. In the back office at settlement, one of the club guys puts a gun on the desk between us and asks if I really expect him to give me fifty dollars. His cronies are silent, counting piles of money with dismal expressions.

I don't think a question like that deserves a response, especially with that ridiculous prop between us. *Even this idiot isn't dumb enough to shoot a teenage girl over fifty bucks.* I realize now that these guys thought they were paying us in orange soda and horse-goat for the privilege of playing their club. So, while the audience files out of the club and the other Muses pack up gear and crap, I stand in the office and wait for this asshole to count out our goddamn gas money. Which he eventually does. *Jerk.*

Snatching the money off the desk, I shove it into my pocket without counting it. If you think, then you care. He doesn't think, so he doesn't care. Shitty attitude in a shitty back room. Why does music gotta be here?

♋ flipside

there's always drooling zombies
or at least one dick

The first time we played this club, they *paid* the audience to come in. We have pictures of the sign: "Throwing Muses—We Pay You $1." We took the pictures because it was both sad and funny. Sad because nobody was gonna show up, funny because we didn't care. They really should have offered people more than a dollar.

Ever since the Doghouse happened, though, we've been on fire and so have our crowds. I don't like what that apartment did to *me*, but I love what it did to our sound and so do a lot of other people. We were sorta counting on nobody *ever* listening, but outer-space music or no, they seem to relate. That fucking guy with the gun must think I'm an idiot. It isn't complicated math: a few hundred people at ten dollars a head, everybody drinking five-dollar beers, and they don't wanna give us fifty bucks for gas?

I'm pretty pissed off, walking to the alley for load-out, thinking that tonight I'll be in the backseat of the Bullet or on Napoleon's floor, while that loser goes home to his house, that I've got nothing to give my bandmates except a ride home (*orange soda and horse, those assholes . . . and possibly guacamole, but I never actually saw that*) when I see an enormous and hairy man crossing the room, grinning like a crazy person.

Instantly, I forget to be mad. He is . . . a Mexican biker? I've still got Tiger Balm vision and can't quite pinpoint the look, but he's walking toward me, both fists in the air, growing taller and wider with every step. "That song!" he shouts.

Oh, good, he's happy. "Which one?" I yell back.

"It has two chords and a million words!" Now he's in my face. Yep, Mexican biker, wicked-cool accent, genuinely huge, smells like smoke and cologne. He towers over me, his smile as big as my whole head.

I look up at him. "Oh god, 'The Letter'? That's a terrible song."

"No, it's beautiful," he says. "And you play it crazy—like *The Exorcist*! I thought your head was gonna start spinning around."

I wince. "That's a *bad* thing."

He shakes his head as we step outside together. "No, it was muscular, man!" he laughs. "And you look like such a *nice* girl."

"I'm nice!"

He laughs louder. "No-o-o-o, you're not! You play that song for me next time, okay? Promise? I'll come to every show if you promise to play that song." He holds out his hand for me to shake. "Deal?"

"Geez, can't you just play it yourself? I'll teach you the chords; there're only two of 'em." But I shake his hand anyway.

He laughs again and walks away, yelling "Promise!" one more time. I laugh, too, and grab the other side of an amp Dave is loading into the back of the Bullet.

"Promise what?" he asks, grimacing over the top of the amp. Together, we shove it in, crushing the kick drumhead and narrowly missing an unprotected guitar neck. The mannequin legs jut out of the trunk at odd angles, their high-heeled feet pigeon-toed.

"He *likes* 'The Letter,'" I answer.

"Really?" Dave asks, confused, studying a thigh injury he sustained during the set.

"Yeah." I stare after the biker guy. "That's what he said, anyway."

Dave talks into his leg. "Maybe he feels sorry for us."

I take the money the club guy shoved across the desk out of my pocket and count it. Forty bucks. Our tickets to get in cost thirty. "That could be."

"Where did you go?" he asks, squinting at me and rubbing his leg.

"I was settling, picking up our no-money. It took 'em a long time to cough it up. Did y'all get everything?" He nods. I look at the sky. It's a muted haze of slate and deep royal blue. Must be late. And it's starting to drizzle. "We should go. Did you bring your glasses?" I ask him.

"Nope."

"I'll drive."

ॐ the letter

i'm turning up in circles
and i'm spinning on my knuckles

By 2 A.M., we've crammed ourselves into the Silver Bullet. I'm on an interesting planet of pain, having just reinserted my contacts—sitting in the driver's seat, my hands on the wheel, staring ahead. My ears ring loudly, a discordant hum—the perfect sound track to how my eyeballs feel right now. A club guy appears outside the club with an industrial-sized garbage can, sees us sitting there and yells, "G'bye, Throwing Up Mucus!"

We wave and smile. Pathetic. "It's okay," says Dave pleasantly. "Being nonviolent people makes us a more violent band." We are, all four of us, sitting in the front seat; the equipment fills the back. It's cramped, we all smell like cigarettes and sweat, but we're finally alone. The girls sit between me and Dave, leaning on each other sleepily as I start up the Bullet and its familiar wheeze builds to a deafening scream.

"Where to, kids?" I ask over the noise of the engine.

"Santa Cruz, California!" yells Tea.

Leslie perks up. "Alright!"

"Look out for banana slugs," warns Dave.

The poor Bullet shakes badly when she goes over fifty, and in addition to the scream, there's a constant rattling noise I can only assume is made by something necessary which will soon fall off. Fumes fill the car at stoplights and the brakes screech when they feel like working, though they often do nothing at all. I've perfected the art of slowing to a stop rather than relying on them to actually *stop* (not hard to do when a car doesn't actually *go*). In the winter, the Bullet is basically a sled.

This past winter was really rough—long and so cold. Inexplicably warm and awake at all times, I found the cold air invigorating, but the other Muses wanted to hibernate and, of course, club hours don't change. Musicians are still expected to stay up all night, no matter how early the sun sets, no matter how late it rises, no matter how cold it is during a predawn load-out.

It was surreal: the fluorescent light of the New England winter days became the fluorescent light of convenience stores at night, an endless cycle of icy greenish-gray that matched our skin. We didn't think winter would *ever* end. After shows, we'd get coffee at Dunkin' Donuts with the downtown drag queens and then slide home on the Bullet sled.

A few months ago, during a particularly wicked cold spell, one of the drag queens gave me a box of wigs she was no longer using, whispering conspiratorially that our shows could use a little "spiffing up." I agreed, thanked her enthusiastically and carried the box out to the car. "Check out the schmankiness!" I yelled to a chorus of *ooh's* and *ahh's*.

We loved the wigs so much that we took to wearing them home after shows—the Bullet's heater is busted and the wigs were surprisingly warm. Plus, they made our conversations much more interesting. You can't be boring when your head looks like a burnt bomb. And if our mascara was running, so much the better.

♋ carnival wig

that looks like a carnival wig and two shiners

One night while wearing our new wigs, we discovered that listening to bad radio was so angrifying, it raised our body temperatures and *really* warmed up the car. Once we started slamming Top Forty, we couldn't stop. We creamed everything anybody likes, adjusting our wigs whenever they slid down over our eyes.

Leslie, sporting a red bouffant, yelled angrily over the music, "Those smug bastards!"

"Smug jerks," growled Tea under a white cascade of disco hair.

"Smug fuckers," I added. My wig was pointy and black. "Listen to that crap! Goddamn Church of the Rock Star televangelists and their fashion noise."

Dave pushed his glittery brunette afro to one side in order to see us. "They're our royalty. In a bad way: inbred anemics. They all sleep together and think God gave 'em their money as some kinda . . . spiritual *reward*."

"Ugly Barbies."

"Dumbasses."

"Pop music is potentially an effective tool for communication on a mass yet *personal* level," I insisted, tilting my head back to see through the windshield past my pointy black bangs, "cutting across classes, races, religions and genders, and it grows on trees! But this corporate crap is chemical candy. It's bad for you."

"Pop music could be, at the very least, intellectually stimulating," Dave said, pushing his 'fro too far to the other side, making his head look lopsided. "But they've replaced thinking with simplistic politics—"

"And passion with melodrama," I added.

"God, yes," he agreed, as his 'fro slid down the side of his face. He grabbed it and placed it back on top of his head. "That is *so* true: 'war is mean and so is my girlfriend.'"

I laughed, blowing a sticky tendril out of my eyes. "Well, corporate product will *always* be removed from human experience because it's denatured, whether you're talking music or food or sex. It's a profitable endeavor, not a visceral one."

"It is *now*," said Leslie, her bouffant smashed against the roof of the Bullet.

"Yeah," agreed Tea. "There's too much money to be made."

"They think they can charge us for telling us what to like," I grumbled, "so they dumb everything down and pretty soon we're all eating paste."

"Smug Barbies," said Tea, idly winding a white tendril around her finger.

"Smug idiots," added Leslie.

"Godless scumbags," said Dave.

Self-righteousness'll keep you warm for hours.

⌒ baseball field

talking at the radio
just one of the places to shoot off your mouth

It isn't nearly cold enough to rant tonight, plus it's hard to hate anything in this lovely pink and green springtime weather. We try for a while, but we're half-assed in our hatred of a pop song that's not quite stupid enough to be entertainingly bad—it's just *bad*, which is boring. "That's not really angrifying," I say, reaching over and turning the radio off, "but I don't wanna listen to it, either." We drive in silence.

"Spanish?" suggests Leslie, fishing around in her bag for her Spanish language tape and coming up with a squished, old, linty protein bar instead. She holds it out to Dave. "Here, I got this for you." He leans away from it, so she drops the bar back in her bag and finds the tape she makes us listen to in order to "improve ourselves," then inserts it into the crappy old boom box we keep on the floor of the Bullet.

A soft female voice filtered through crunchy little speakers then asks us to repeat everything she says, which we all dutifully try to do. We name numbers and colors, are introduced to imaginary doctors, waiters and policemen, ask where post offices and bathrooms are, then list unrelated nouns. "*La casa*," the voice says.

"*La casa*," we murmur in unison.

"*Zapatos*."

"*Zapatos*," we mumble.

The girls' responses grow quieter and quieter as they fall asleep, until it's just me and Dave whispering in Spanish. "Can we turn it off yet?" he asks, poking the mound of girl between us. It doesn't move, so he stops the cassette and drops off to sleep, too.

♋ spring

```
nothing like chrome when it shines
no better weather to drive
```


Spring air even *sounds* nice. At this time of year, air doesn't just feel thick, it *sounds* thick; you can hear the humidity in it. I like driving in this weather, breezes blowing in over the sleeping pile of band next to me. Spring weather is one more thing that keeps them asleep and keeps me awake.

When I stop at a gas station, Dave opens his eyes. "I'll pump, you pay," he says, yawning.

"Okay. You want anything?" He shakes his head and I get out, shutting the door as quietly as I can. Tea and Leslie wake up anyway, so I stick my head in the window. "Ladies?"

"Clamato and Sno Balls," says Leslie sleepily.

Tea lifts up her head. "Mr. Pibb and a Sky Bar."

"Nothing?" I ask.

"Slim Jims and a Moxie," replies Leslie. I walk away, rolling my eyes, as they call after me, "Pork rinds and a Yoo-Hoo!" "Bugles and a Sanka!"

"I'll drive, you ride," says Dave when I return with a drink and a magazine. "What'd you get?" he asks, swatting bugs in the greenish light of the gas pump. I hold the drink and the magazine up higher for him to see. He squints. "What'd you get?" he asks again.

"*These*," I answer.

"What are they?"

"It's a drink and a magazine," I say, crawling into the passenger seat. "What're you, blind?" He's still swatting bugs. At least he can see *those*. "Maybe you shouldn't drive."

Dave gets in and starts the engine. "You don't need to *see* in order to drive, grandma," he says cheerfully, as we pull out of the gas station.

I look out the window. "Yeah, but now you're a jumpy driver. That she-cop scared you so bad, you're all flitchy." A few weeks ago, Dave was pulled over by a big, scary police woman 'cause the Bullet had a broken taillight. This was a lady of impressive voice, size and attitude—an Amazon with a gun. We will never forget her.

"The cop-ette?" he asks. "Nah, she didn't scare me."

"She scared me," I say, turning pages in the magazine.

"What drink? What magazine?" he demands, peering over Tea and Leslie, who've fallen asleep again.

"Well, it's all the different kinds of soda put together in one cup," I explain. "Figured I'd get my money's worth."

"But it's just a little bit of each soda, right?" he asks. "So you didn't get any more than you would have if you stuck to the one soda."

"I got my money's worth in *entertainment value*." I taste it. It's awful.

Dave glances over the girls. Lights from passing cars run across their still backs. "Is it entertaining?" he asks.

I hand it to him. "Here, I got this for you."

He takes it and tries some. "It's not that bad. Like a Long Island iced tea."

"Yeah, I guess . . . a pointless one."

"Right. Like a pointless Long Island iced tea," he says. "Where's my Funyuns and Fresca?"

"Nobody said Funyuns to me. Want me to read to you from—" I check the name of the magazine in the light from the glove compartment, "*Woman's Day?*"

He sputters into the straw. "Yes, please."

"Okay, I'll read, you drink. First I'll describe the cover since you're blind. It's a picture of a huge pink cake with flowers and rabbits on it."

"Edible flowers and rabbits?" he asks.

"It doesn't say . . . maybe you have to read the article. All it says on the cover is that you can lose ten pounds."

"You can?" he asks through his straw.

"Sure."

"By eating the cake?"

"Maybe. Hey, there's a quiz! Wanna take it?"

"I don't know," he answers. "I'm busy drinking and driving. And I don't want to find out anything about myself that I'm trying to repress."

"Like what?" I ask.

"Don't say that. I could blurt it out and then I'd know it forever."

"And I'd know it, too, 'cause you said it out loud." I look at him. "And I'd bring it up all the time."

Dave gestures with his straw. "*That's* what I'm afraid of."

"Okay. I'll honor your feelings," I say, closing the magazine and looking out the window again. The Bullet's headlights illuminate gnats and dandelion fluff in the air and make the grass on the side of the highway glow an eerie purple, for some reason. I stare at the purple grass for a few minutes, then turn to watch Dave drive and the girls sleep. The three of them are so still, they look like photographs of themselves.

I don't remember meeting my bandmates; I just know them. And when you really know someone, you don't know their face, just a thousand moments you can't freeze-frame and wouldn't want to. I guess you could create your own static impression of someone, but it'd be inaccurate, limiting. A static being would offer no hope of bursting into a room, different. People are movement, structure built on fluidity. Which is why I never know what my loved ones look like, I guess. I stare at their faces, trying to commit them to memory, but their features are always overwhelmed by more fascinating flashbacks.

Like songs—a fake song is a static being. A real one is buzzing with potential: structure built on fluidity, body as movement. *Jesus, shut up. I can't believe I can bore my own brain just by using it to think.*

"Honoring your feelings is boring, Dave. Maybe the psychological tension'll keep you awake." I flip through pages and find the quiz. "Okay. I'll ask, you answer. But I won't tell you what this quiz is delving into your psyche *for*, okay? You just have to answer honestly." Dave is silent. "Question number one: your husband has a—"

"My what?"

"Hmmm . . . okay, question number two: a work associate (I guess that could be me) is—"

"It could be one of *them*," interrupts Dave, pointing his straw at the girls. Tea turns over in her sleep.

"Okay, it's one of them. Leslie, okay?" I whisper. "You with me?"

"Leslie," he repeats.

"Right. *Leslie* is having an affair—"

"A saucy quiz."

"—with another coworker."

"Who, Tea?" he asks.

"Well, it isn't me."

"Leslie and Tea are having an affair." He thinks. "True or false?"

"No, it's not a true-or-false question. It's a *psychological* one."

"Okay."

"This affair makes you uncomfortable," I continue.

"I'll say."

"Do you: (A) avoid both parties—"

"Parties?" he asks.

"Not literally parties, they mean *people*. (B) have a heart-to-heart with your coworkers, or (C) . . ." I squint at the magazine.

"What's C?" he asks.

"C is . . ." It's hard to see the page. I move it around the car, trying to catch some light. "C is 'attempt to end the affair by telling your boss.'"

Dave laughs. "Really? Break up Tea and Leslie? What *is* this quiz? Find out if you're an asshole?"

"You win!" I yell. "You're an asshole!" The girls jump.

"I knew it!" says Dave quietly, whapping the steering wheel with both hands.

We've been driving for days through summer heat, going
back home to the South to visit relatives. Zoë's head is
on my lap; my little brother plays with her tail. It's so
          hot we can barely keep our eyes open.

Crane and Dude have run out of activities for us except
for the occasional Slurpee at a gas station. The Slurpees
melt into gross syrup instantly. There is nothing to do
      but watch fields out the window and hope for a
                      thunderstorm.

To entertain ourselves, my brother and I decide to make
 up stories about a sister and brother riding in a car.

      We can't think of anything for them to do.

A few minutes later, we're on the island, we can smell the ocean and every-thing slows down. It's so quiet and sleepy that Dave and I stop talking and just watch the dark houses go by. The Bullet creeps along. I guess 'cause Dave doesn't wanna wake anybody up.

We practice in the attic of the giant, haunted-looking Victorian where Dave grew up. During rehearsals, his parents open the attic door and place comfy chairs at the bottom of the stairs so they can hear us play. We know this because we've peered down the stairs at them. His mom knits and his dad reads the paper; they nod their heads, tap their feet and discuss each song, even if we play it six times in a row. Either they're very, very nice or they have brain damage.

Pulling up outside the house, Dave sings gently, "Ki-i-ids . . . we're at Grandma's." Poor Tea and Leslie are so tired. They stumble out of the Bullet, hair all messed up. I don't remember tired, so I try to do more than my share of carrying gear and crap up three flights of stairs, but they won't let me; they grab shit outta my hands. Then, tiptoeing past bedroom doors, we bump guitars into walls and amps into doorways. The girls're punchy. "*We're so bad at this*," Leslie giggles.

On the way up the stairs, one of the mannequin's high heels gets stuck on a picture frame, threatening to send either the frame or the mannequin's TV head crashing to the floor. It takes three of us to extricate it in the dark. "Geez, we *are* bad at this," I whisper.

When the equipment is safely home, we hug, then scatter. My band-mates are so tired their hugs are like dance marathon rests. They get heavy on my shoulders for a second, then shake themselves awake. When they leave, I look at my watch. Technically, it's tomorrow and I need to swim.

♋ crabtown

underwater
i swim sound

Swimming's the only thing that makes me really, truly tired. It's not a nervous energy I carry around; it would never allow itself to dissipate in movements like fidgeting or smoking a cigarette. It's weighted, focused. People describe me as "calm." I am often very still, trying to keep the en-ergy in check, but that's *outer* peace.

So, yeah, I have a swimming problem. I have to swim every day or—I

don't know what—conflagrations, I imagine, chaos. Big, bad. I've never
tried to make it through a whole day without swimming. Water temporar-
ily washes off song tattoos, so I made it my drug.

I like the idea of drugs; humans seem to need them. They're personal,
private, sort of *precious*. We value so few private experiences on this planet
and we celebrate so many conspicuous, attention-seeking ones—like it only
counts if someone's watching. I love that the junkies seek an internal pur-
suit, but I didn't adopt their drug 'cause they looked sad to me. I couldn't
relate to their high.

Really, from the outside, what they call a "high" looks a lot like a low.
Heroin doesn't seem to add the color to their lives that water adds to mine.
Swimming sweetly reflects the human condition: we're never on solid
ground. And there's a whole story down there, like a love life. Underwater,
it's quiet and otherworldly; even a stormy ocean is quiet underneath. And
there *is* color—there's no bluer blue than swimming-pool blue and the
ocean is slate green and alive. I've never found anything better than water
for putting out fires.

♋ cold water coming

cold water coming
for the warm water junkies

I shut the car door slowly, as quietly as I can, just pressing it into place, and
walk down the dark street. It's silent at this time of night. Everything is.

I know that the pool gate is covered in vines and about three feet from
the end of the stockade fencing, so I feel my way down, pushing my hands
through ivy, and find it with the tips of my fingers. When I lift the latch, it
creaks loudly and I freeze. The sound brings a dog over, but it always does
that. He doesn't bark; he's happy to see me.

All dogs on this island are named "Bailey," so I call him that, ask him
how he's doing and slip into the yard, rubbing his ears until he calms down.
Then I take off my dress. I always wear a bathing suit under my clothes.

I try not to swim in other people's pools too often 'cause it's tacky and
illegal, but at 3 A.M., the Y and hotel pools're all closed, and, well, I have to
swim.

Sitting at the edge of the pool while the dog ambles back to his bed, I
watch the blossoms of a dogwood tree flutter. I love those trees. Elegant in

the spring, dogwood flowers are even more beautiful in autumn when they become sepia-toned; then they look like old photographs of trees. The yard is dimly lit and the swaying branches create an interesting lighting effect: movement, I guess.

Sudden loud jingling from the dog's collar as he scratches his ear sounds like cymbals crashing. I whisper "No!" at him. He stops, then walks over sweetly and sits next to me. I put my finger to my lips and he lies down. While I pet him, I try to imagine that the people inside the house who feed and care for this dog are kind, lovely people who might have invited me over to swim in their pool, had we ever met. *Probably not in the middle of the night, though.*

I slip into the water as quietly as I can. This pool's heated, but just barely; the water feels icy. Good. Unless I'm chilled to the bone and exhausted, I can't sleep. I have to be almost dead before I can rest. Shivering, I roll onto my back so I can see the stars glow again. I like the moving light; it looks like the yard is breathing. But I have laps to swim before someone wakes up and calls the police, so I kick off and kill an hour underwater with only the sound of bubbles as a distraction.

Drying off on the sidewalk with a towel I swiped from the Y, I whisper goodbye to the dog. "See you later, Bailey." He barks at me through the fence. "*Now* you bark?" I ask him.

Then the Bullet and I drive to the beach. Maybe I'll get a couple hours of sleep, but the sun'll be up soon and then I'll be off the hook as far as sleep goes. At the beach, I can blend in with the dog owners who get up early on Saturdays to watch the sun rise. I just don't have running shoes or a thermos full of coffee. Or a dog. Wish I could borrow Bailey.

Can't wait for summer and real beach days. I *love* swimming in the ocean. There's nothing like being knocked around by waves, turned upside down, getting the shit beaten out of you by something so big it couldn't care less, all in vivid silence. I can't think underwater—I'm too busy making bruises. Add numbing cold and I'm giddy.

A nice storm'll beat the living daylights out of you, too. Hurricanes're good, blizzards. A natural disaster'd be *perfect*: untamed energy and destruction—vandalism on a biblical scale—and none of it my fault. Short of that, I run outside whenever I hear thunder, hoping to get my head bashed in by pounding rain.

The band thinks this is very funny, so I have to sneak away when I hear a storm brewing if I don't wanna be ridiculed. They don't know what they're missing. Neither Tea nor Leslie nor Dave can relate to my desire to have my skull caved in and my body pummeled. They claim that a healthy organism moves toward pleasure and *away* from pain.

I say endorphins mean I'm having it all.

I watch my little brother eat a caterpillar as a storm
   approaches. The sky is a deep cornflower blue with
patches of lavender. He kneels on the ground, delicately
  lifting the writhing caterpillar to his lips. Bright
    green goo oozes out of his mouth as he chews.

          "What are you doing?" I ask him.

He looks at me, then at the piece of caterpillar between
his chubby fingers, then back at me, still chewing. Light
    rain begins to fall, a faraway crash of thunder.

I spend Saturday afternoon studying at the beach, books spread out on the hood of the Bullet, watching the water in between paragraphs. I read only science books, so that's what I see in the water, in the air, flying around, eating out of garbage cans—science doesn't lie. I make sure my eyes and ears are filled to the brim with its clean information, that nothing else can creep in and wreck up the place with false impressions. Science is clarity goggles.

I know this means I'm lacking, somehow; that's what I've been told, anyway. That more evolved people have an emotional attachment to what's around them, so they *enjoy* putting fictions in their head to help their feelings along. That's probably true—that imagination works like dreams and comes with a message. It just doesn't sound very reliable. And when I see a diagram of a cell, or DNA, it looks so perfect—*the essence of something: essential*—that I'm moved. Isn't that emotion?

I guess when I've got the science down, I'll make room for the rest.

As the light begins to fade, my friend Mark pulls up on his moped, smiling. He's always smiling. Mark is a monochromatic boy. Everything about him is beige: his skin, hair, clothes, eyes and backpack, which probably doesn't sound as attractive as it is. Mark *matches*.

Leaning his moped against the car, he takes off his backpack and joins me on the hood without saying anything, just smiling. I smile back and then laugh at him. He turns to look at the water. "Why do the buoys have antennas?" he asks, like it matters.

"*Antennae*."

He looks at me. "Why do the buoys have antennae?"

I watch them, poking out over the water, bouncing around. "I don't know. It looks like the ocean's full of narwhals."

"Mmmm. Unicorns of the sea," says Mark dreamily.

I shake my head. "Don't say 'unicorns of the sea.'"

"Too late." Mark lies back against the windshield, folds his arms behind his head and switches from water to sky. I join him.

The first time I met Mark, he asked me if my parents were divorced. When I said they were, he nodded. "I can tell. You wear 'broken home' on your face."

"I do?"

"Yes," he answered, looking sad. "Was it ugly?"

"I guess. I had a beautiful family that broke into ugly pieces."

"Stepparents?" he asked.

I nodded. "They don't like me." Mark looked even sadder. I chuckled. *Who is this kid?* "Do you know anybody whose parents *aren't* divorced?" I asked him.

He shook his head. "Not really. But not everyone wears it on their face."

Mark is very, *very* kind.

Our shoes match: four motorcycle boots in a row on the hood of the Bullet. Beyond our black leather toes is an orange sky, reflecting orange into the ocean. "How was the show?" he asks after a few minutes.

"Frenetic."

Mark laughs. "No shit!"

"Yeah, but this time it wasn't all our fault. There was a smoke machine and strobes and a drunk."

He smiles at the sky. "Was it poetry?"

"Was it *poetry*?" I laugh. *"What?"*

Mark thinks. "Was it beautiful and necessary?"

"Hmmm. Mostly, I guess."

"I'm sorry I missed it, then." He sits up. "There's a party at the Bells tonight. People are staying over and camping afterwards. You wanna go?" The Bells is on the other side of the island. It's a spooky shell of a building in a field by the water. It looks like a movie set or a place where burnouts would go to party; it's not much of a campsite.

"Camping?"

"That's what they're calling it. Don't you like camping?"

"I don't know. The Bells smells like cat pee."

"It does," he agrees. "You could leave the Bullet here. I'll take you over."

"You mean on that moped?"

"Yeah," he nods. "But I won't blow the horn."

"Why, what's the horn sound like?"

Mark stretches an arm out to his moped and pushes down. It sounds like someone squeezing a very loud hamster. I jump up. "Holy shit. Never do that again."

Mark frowns. "I already told you I wouldn't." We stare at the water for a few minutes. I don't feel like going anywhere. A good show last night, swam laps early this morning and the beach is both calming and invigorating. For once, staying still is okay.

"I don't know if I *want* to sleep at the Bells, Mark. It isn't even nice in the daytime."

"Yeah," he said. "It's pretty creepy. If you don't like it, we can leave." He's smiling again. Mark's smile uses his whole head—all gums and goofiness. I can't say no to it.

"Okay." I jump off the hood and open the driver's side door. "But this doesn't make me your girlfriend." He smiles even bigger. Mark is, as he puts it, *queer as a gay dollar bill*. "Get in."

"Uh . . . no." He looks suddenly serious. "I know you love the Bullet, Kris, but she just isn't safe."

"Shhh . . ." I whisper. "Not in *front* of her."

Mark looks stern. "It's not funny; you should get a bike or something."

"Carrying an amp on a bike doesn't seem very safe, either." I shut the car door and look at the moped. "You *really* want me to ride on that?"

"*I* ride on it."

"Well, not on the bitch seat."

"The moped *works*," he says, annoyed.

"The Bullet *works*, she just works badly. I can't believe you're scared of her." I climb onto the back of the moped and wait. "What a chicken butt."

Mark sits in front, then turns around to look at me. "You're so stupid."

"You're so gay."

"Noted." He grabs his helmet off of the handlebar, presses it onto his head and fastens the chinstrap.

I watch. "Can *I* have a hat?"

"I only have one helmet."

"Well, how safe is *that*?"

Then he turns the key and the little moped springs to life. Mark turns to me. "I think this'll be fun!" he shouts over the noise.

We're already going much faster than I had anticipated and the moped's sorta . . . *bouncy*, making it difficult to stay on my fakey bitch seat. I cling to him as we pull away from the beach. "Geez, Mark!" I yell into his ear.

"Geez what?" he yells back, as we zoom up the hill.

When we get to the Bells, the sun is down and the deteriorating stone walls look very beautiful, like ancient ruins. Inside, orange light from fires and an enormous grill lights skateboarders who glide past its graffiti-covered walls, music is playing and it doesn't smell like cat pee for once, it smells like hot dogs and smoke.

Mark takes a package of hot dogs out of his backpack and balances it on top of a huge pile of similar packages next to the grill, the pile with an index card that says "PIG." The other enormous hot dog pile's index card says "SOY." The kid who's cooking them nods a solemn thanks and graciously salutes Mark with his spatula.

We wander over to a window we can't see out of; the darkness outside is enhanced by the glow inside the building to the point of . . . thickness? "Yep," said Mark. "I guess that's what they mean when they say darkness is thick."

"Is that what night looked like before light pollution? I don't know if I like it."

"Well," he cranes his neck out the window, looking up at the sky. "There used to be a *moon*. Didn't there?"

"Oh yeah! I remember the moon . . ." I stick my head into the darkness, too, trying to find the moon. "Nope. It's not there."

"No," answers Mark.

Pulling our heads back in, we slide to the floor, watching skaters whiz by. After a few minutes, I get the distinct impression that couples around us are making out. Mark and I sit in silence. Every few minutes, someone skates by. The griller kid piles hot dogs onto a tray, opens packages of more hot dogs, grills them, sticks them in buns, then adds the cooked ones to the others on the tray. No one seems to be eating them. I worry that the pile of hot dogs will tumble if this kid keeps cooking. It's starting to smell like cat pee again.

"Are we bored?" Mark asks quietly.

We both stare at our boots. Like many people from this island, we wear motorcycle boots in slightly different sizes. My left boot is a half size smaller than my right; Mark's are actually two sizes apart. It makes him walk funny.

A few years ago, a ship dropped its cargo near the shore and a bunch of crates washed up on the beach. There was no official cleanup because it wasn't an oil tanker or anything, so beachcombers opened the crates and found motorcycle boots inside. Salty, wet, mismatched motorcycle boots. But free shoes are free shoes. People wandered up and down the beach for days, pulling seaweed off of boots and trying them on, trading with each other, looking for matching ones. I was there on the first day and did pretty well, but Mark didn't get there until most of the boots were gone, so his feet usually hurt.

"Yeah, we're bored," I answer. "That was fast."

"Camping's boring," he whispers. "Wanna go?"

"Sure," I whisper back.

The silent griller stops us on our way out. "Soy or pig?" he asks.

"Soy," I answer.

"Pig," says Mark. We carry our hot dogs outside and eat them standing in the grass, looking up into the orange windows. Yellow jackets buzz around our faces. "Look at that," I say. "Night bees."

"Bees aren't nocturnal," says Mark, swatting one away.

"These are."

"What's wrong with them?" he asks.

We listen to their buzzing. "Maybe they can't sleep."

"Do killer bees sleep?" he asks suspiciously.

"Now there's a thought."

"You were right," says Mark, finishing his hot dog. "This was a bad idea."

"Just too *much* fun, I think."

"Can't handle it?" Brushing light brown crumbs off his light brown shorts with a light brown hand, he straddles the moped and turns to me. "Where to?"

"I don't know, but I don't care, either." I throw the rest of my hot dog into the bushes and then sit behind him, my arms around his waist. The moped lurches into the darkness.

There are no streetlights on this part of the island. We ride by the sea-wall, where the only light is far, far out in the ocean. It feels nicely scary.

I notice that Mark's a good moped driver; not only does he wear a helmet, he follows traffic rules, even in the dark when no one's around, sticking his arm out to signal turns, stopping at lights and waiting patiently for them to turn green. He lives his life that way, too. He has to be good because he *is* good. I squeeze his middle tighter because I love him so much.

We drive across the island to a very nice neighborhood, winding through quiet streets, then pulling into the driveway of a big Victorian house. There are no lights on in the house and no car in the driveway. If Mark's into breaking and entering, I don't want to know. There I was, thinking he was so *good*. "What are we doing here?" I ask him quietly.

"I used to babysit for these people," he whispers, taking off his helmet and walking the moped up the driveway.

"That's a good story. What are we *doing* here?"

"Don't worry, nobody's home."

I follow him up the driveway, hissing, "I can see that. What are we *doing* here?"

"Be quiet," he hisses back. "It's the middle of the night." Leaning his moped up against the garage, he walks up the hill behind it in the pitch dark. I follow.

"Mark. What. Are. We. Doing—"

"We're camping," he says, annoyed.

"We're *still* camping?"

He reaches the top of the hill and begins feeling around in the dark. "What the hell happened to the moon?" he mutters in the blackness.

I notice a bulky, pyramid-shaped piece of darkness slightly to our left. "Is that a tent?" I whisper.

"Where?" he asks excitedly.

"Uh . . ." I feel around too, then bump into something. "Here."

"Good work!" he whispers happily.

"Thanks. This is so not legal."

Mark is shuffling around at the base of the tent; I can't see what he's doing. As my eyes adjust, though, I begin to make out the shape of the thing. It's dish-mouthed, like a bulldog. In fact, it has little eyes and doggie ears sticking up on the roof—it *is* a bulldog. The kids he babysat for probably use it as a playhouse. Mark's struggling, trying to get the bulldog's mouth open. "It's a dog," I say, forgetting to whisper.

"No," he pants. "It's a tent."

"It's a dog tent."

He corrects me. "*Pup tent*." After that, he can do no wrong. *Pup tent.* We all had dismal summer jobs and he was hanging with toddlers in Pup Tent. I don't care if Mark gets me arrested anymore; I'm ready to do whatever he tells me to.

Suddenly, there is a ripping sound as he gets the zipper loose and then a splash as the bulldog vomits copious amounts of fluid. We jump out of the way. Pup Tent is puking a truly impressive amount of water out of its half-open mouth. Plastic toys ride the rapids down the hill: little action figures and Lego pieces. It goes on and on.

Eventually, the torrent slows to a trickle. Neither of us moves. I think we both expect it to start up again, like Pup Tent is actually sick.

A light rain has begun to fall. I look at Mark. He seems deflated, though it's hard to make out much more than his posture in the dark. "Um . . ."

"I know," Mark sighs.

"No, I was just wondering if there was somewhere *else* we could camp."

"Where, in a tree?"

"Well . . . is there a porch? I can't see." When I was a kid, I'd crawl under the porch when it rained and spend hours there. Mark is silent. "It'd probably be drier than inside Pup Tent."

He walks slowly to the moped and grabs his backpack. "Yeah, there's a porch," he says, sounding a little less deflated. "By the back door. And I have a candle and some matches we could start a campfire with."

"A campfire?"

"To roast marshmallows." *Poor Mark. Forget breaking and entering— he's gonna get us arrested for arson.* "The Bells didn't seem like a marshmallow party, so I held on to them."

"This *is* a marshmallow party?"

"It *will* be."

I pick up every snake I see. Every single one, and I see a lot of snakes because I look for them. Now that spring's here, they're everywhere. Snakes're perfect. What a handle they've got on locomotion . . . they swim, climb trees, glide across rocks and sand, through grass and leaf litter. I can only do a couple of these terrains comfortably and I'm fairly sporty. Snakes can eat things that weigh more than they do, they come in all sizes and colors and they can adjust their temperature just by hanging out in the right places—they soak up weather and wear it. Snakes win; the rest of us should quit.

♋ snake oil

```
soak up the weather
suck up the sun
into your bones
then move on
```

When I was little, I carried snake books with me everywhere I went. I had the books memorized, but I carried them around anyway, on a pathetic hunt for rosy boas and green tree snakes, cottonmouths, sidewinders and any number of other snakes I wouldn't see. I found only garter snakes.

But I didn't care. A snake is a snake. They don't bite if you hold them. Jerky movements freak them out and they strike, but if you move slowly and become their climbing surface, they fold into your warmth and calm right down. It's an honor to spend even a few minutes with a snake.

Right now I can see one a few feet away, right over Mark's head. It's looking right at me. I don't want to scare it, so I'm not moving, but Mark's squirming around, waking up, and I'm scared he's gonna startle it. A frightened snake'll disappear in a flash.

"What are you doing?" Mark asks sleepily.

"Writing in my diary."

"About me?"

I think about that. "What's the right answer?" He smiles, then turns over and goes back to sleep. I consider waking him again to tell him about the snake, but decide against it. Some people don't like snakes, and he's had a rough night. He changed into sneakers under the porch, Mister Rogers style, and then set a sneaker on fire trying to balance dryish leaves on top of a candle. Eventually, he coaxed some paper and what looked like old birdseed into burning brightly enough to singe a marshmallow or two, and in fact, the birdseed is still glowing. But I don't know that he's calling this "camping" anymore.

My childhood camping memories consist mostly of mosquitoes and Sterno, so I wouldn't call it camping, either; this was way better. It was *fun*. Not stupid fun, either. Mark made a little orange light, like the big orange light at the Bells, but just for us. *That's* poetry.

☞ rock candy brains

your orange fingers are glowing hot
i think your sneaker's on fire
up in flames

I spit on the glowing birdseed till it goes out. I have to leave. A song is starting; its jangly, rattling tones barely discernible over the industrial whine that precedes every song. Soon I won't be able to hear anything else, so I gotta be alone.

I draw a heart on a page from this diary and stuff it into Mark's backpack, then wave goodbye to the snake.

Allen Ginsburg writes a poem for me that goes like this:

> "I have two eyes because I have two eyes
>
> I have a nose because I have a nose
>
> I have two ears because I have two ears
>
> I have a mouth because I have a mouth"

That's true, I think. But it's not a very good poem.

Sunday morning.

I left Mark sleeping last night and walked back to the Bullet in the rain, this new song playing louder and louder. Poor, old shitty Bullet looked so forlorn, sitting at the beach alone, like a sad dog left behind. She leaks, of course, so I had to jam my YMCA towel into the crack in the door where the seal should be.

Mark's gonna wake up wet and alone this morning . . . with a snake next to his head.

Gotta face this music. I lean on the damp Y towel and watch water pour down the windshield, the song rattling along with the pounding raindrops. Man, our sky. What are the odds it would turn these sick colors and spill pretty liquid all over us? What I see through this windshield is incredible. And when it isn't, I drive away. That's what I like best about the Bullet: she makes me a moving target.

Of course, she can't help me escape a song.

◎ styrofoam rattlebox

i'm shatterproof
but cranial impact
taps something true

It was a witch that gave me the double concussion that made me start hearing songs in the first place. A couple years ago, this old witch drove her car into me as I raced to a summer job on my bike. She wasn't a bad witch necessarily, but she wasn't a good witch either. I remember her blank face over the steering wheel, about to plow into me, like she was on a mission. I pedaled as fast as I could, trying to escape her speeding Chevy, but I never made it to work that day.

Instead, I flew up into the air: one minute, everything was like it usually is and the next, I was flying. Flying through the air in vivid slow motion, thinking, *so this is what this feels like.*

As the pavement came toward me, time stopped abruptly. I hovered over the street; tree branches blew in the breeze; I could smell cut grass. Somehow, I hung between flying up and falling down. A thought occurred: *"You're about to hit your head harder than you've ever hit it before, so maybe you should . . . you know . . . go limp."* I did.

As soon as I relaxed my muscles, time sped up and the ground jumped up in the air, crashing into my head. I slid down the street on my face for a while, then flipped over; my neck snapped back and my legs twisted up underneath me. The witch and her Chevy were long gone—she hit and ran.

I lay there on the street, feeling the brand-new sensation of a lot of blood leaving my body, then tried to unfold myself. Lifting my left leg, I noticed that there was no longer a foot at the end of it.

Suddenly, I was very, very thirsty. Blood spread across the ground in a deep red puddle, pouring into the sewer. I'd never seen blood pour into a sewer before (it looks *really* cool). Then a woman appeared from nowhere and leaned over me. She was wearing mirrored sunglasses. What I saw in her glasses was bizarre: I had no face. The front of my head was hamburger and blood with two blue eyes staring out. Even my hair was red with blood. It snaked out from under me, unrecognizable as hair—*Medusa*, I thought. Behind the woman's head and my monstrous reflection was a clear blue sky.

When I turned away to look for my missing foot, the woman grabbed what used to be my face and turned it toward her. "You were hit by a car!" She spoke loudly and slowly, carefully articulating each word. "You're going to be fine!"

Why is she talking to me like I'm foreign? I flashed on seventh-grade health class, where they taught us what to do in case we ever came upon an accident. We learned to tie tourniquets and perform CPR, how to recognize the symptoms of shock and what happens to the person in the backseat if you keep a crowbar on the dash (hint: *don't*).

They also taught us how to talk to the victim. You speak loudly and slowly, carefully articulating each word. You tell them what's wrong and then you tell them they're going to be fine: "You have a crowbar through the middle of your skull! You're going to be *fine*!"

A few more people joined the mirrored sunglasses lady, kneeling on the ground, looking concerned. I thought about asking them to help me look for my foot but figured, if I were them, I wouldn't want hamburger talking to *me*, so I felt underneath my leg and found the foot myself. I was sticking it back on when I saw my mother's face floating in the clear blue sky.

Aw, geez, I'm dead! You're definitely dead if you get hit by a car and then see your mother's face floating in a clear blue sky. *Wait . . . my mother isn't dead.* I noticed her car parked by the side of the road. "Hi, Mom!" I said. She looked upset. "What's wrong?"

I heard sirens as she started to cry.

♋ pretty ugly

look up
a clear blue sky

In X-ray, I lay on a metal table wiggling my front teeth with my fingers. The X-ray technician noticed and asked what I was doing. She was a typical Rhode Islander: Irish, rough-hewn, thick New England accent, heart of gold. I remember her type from when I was growing up: *everyone else's mother.* "My teeth are loose," I said.

"Really?" She peered into my mouth, interested. "They might turn black and fall out, honey."

I put down my hand.

A few days later, lying in my hospital bed, I heard my first song: a metallic whining, like industrial noise, and a wash of ocean waves, layered with humming tones and wind chimes. Intermittent voices talked and sang. I thought it was the TV in the next room. The TV never shut up, though; nobody ever turned it off or even changed the channel. I started to worry that the patient next door had died or slipped into a coma.

When the noise increased in volume, I asked a nurse what it was. "I dunno what you're hearin', dear," she said kindly. "Dear" is pronounced *deeya* in Rhode Island. They take the *r*'s off words here and put them on other words. For example, *boa constrictor* is pronounced *boer constricta.*

"This room over heeya's empty and little Josh on the other side is takin' a nap. He's got a compound fracksha, too. He isn't watchin' TV." She frowned. "I have no idear. Maybe ya hearin' . . . machines?"

"Machines?" I asked.

"Machines?" she asked again, perplexed. We stared at each other, but neither of us could answer the question. I was sure she was wrong. *Josh is a little kid, right? He's gotta be watching TV.*

Over the next day and a half, the tones began to distinguish themselves from the industrial noise; different frequencies were clarified as notes, though it still didn't sound like music, just disparate melody. Percussive sounds, like someone banging on metal, kept time for a few moments, then gave way to slow cymbal crashes that blended with the ocean waves. I lay in bed and listened until the noise became intrusive. *I gotta turn off that kid's TV.* "Can I meet Josh?" I asked the next nurse who entered the room with a tray of hospital food I didn't want. Her response was buried in a ringing wash of sound. I didn't know it had gotten so loud. "Excuse me?"

She leaned in. "I'll get you a wheelchair, deeya. But first, eat your lasanyer." I was scared of the lasagna; thought it'd make me throw up. It already looked like vomit.

"I'm not hungry!" I said loudly over the noise. The nurse looked startled, but she left and returned with a wheelchair a minute later. Then she pushed me into Josh's room and left the two of us alone. *Hope Josh likes people with monster faces.* I wasn't allowed to see my face, but I had a feeling it wasn't pretty.

Josh was about ten years old and his leg was in traction. His TV *was* on, but it wasn't playing what I was hearing. He was watching a cartoon that both mimicked and clashed horribly with the song noise—lots of banging and crashing, unrelated melodies and grating voices. I had really, really hoped Josh's TV was making the sounds I heard. Seeing him watching Looney Tunes was like having a weight dropped on me: an Acme Products anvil. *The noise is mine.* I was deeply ashamed that I'd asked the nurse what it was.

"Hi, Josh," I said through the waves of sound. He smiled and his lips moved. He was talking really quietly and his TV was screaming. *Now what do I say?* "Does your leg hurt?" I asked him. Josh stopped smiling and nodded. *Poor kid.* I pointed at the TV. "What're you watching?" and his lips moved some more. *Gosh, this is hard. Everything's noisy but this sad little boy.*

My song moaned and rattled, talked, crashed, hummed and whined; Looney Tunes did the same. But Josh was lonely, bored and hurting and wanted someone to talk to. I listened as best I could, picking out words here and there, trying to get him to smile and wondering what the hell was going on, until the nurse came and brought me back to my room. I waved to Josh and he waved back sadly, then turned his attention back to the TV.

Soon, the song began organizing itself into discernible parts that sounded less like "machines." Instruments played melodies rather than disembodied tones in the bed of ocean waves: bass, guitar, piano, cello. Punctuated clanging became drums and percussion. I guessed that my brain was making sense of something, turning this sonic haunting into vocabulary with which I was familiar.

It was all so irresistably *colorful.* Every chord I heard carried with it the impression of a color; these colors blended along with the chords in gentle swathes of sound-light. Each beat had a shape that appeared and then disappeared instantly, creating its own visual pattern that coincided with the rhythm. I watched and listened, bewildered and enthralled, as sound and color filled my empty hospital room.

One of the humming voices eventually . . . *refined itself*? enough for me to discern syllables in its talking and moaning. Unintelligible at first, the syllables eventually arranged themselves into words that told stories from my life, clarified by dreamlike images—animated home movies, a mythology of reality. The lyrics were at once impassioned and removed, as if someone else, someone who cared, was telling me what happened in black and white and then coloring it in with dream crayons.

I had a few weeks in the hospital to figure out that a song was writing itself, but I have yet to figure out *why*. Or what made the old witch drive her car like that in the first place and cast this music spell on me, making me a lightning rod for songs. She's dead now, so I can't ask her. She ran me over and then went and died, like, immediately. My impression of the event is that she was born in that Chevy seconds before she hit me. Then, her work done here, she just pulled over and expired.

I really didn't mind getting hit by a car, though—it was interesting, and probably my last chance to fly through the air in nonjudgmental fashion. I think if I got hit by a car *now*, it'd bug me, but before we learn to be whiny about our existence and how comfortable it isn't, we're still open to being thrown around, even if we bust our faces when we land. So what if sudden contact with the street makes your teeth fall out, maybe snaps off a foot or two? At least you know what that feels like.

But the musical bump on the head the witch cursed me with means that every few weeks, song noise will begin again, and when its parts have arranged themselves, I'll copy them down and teach them to the band, making them hear what I hear. As soon as I give the song a body in the real world, it stops playing and I breathe a sigh of relief, in precious silence.

I revisit this experience when the band plays, but the re-creation of a musical event, as charged as it is, doesn't take the journey from chaos to song; the song just walks into the room, a fully formed being.

It's *not* me. I don't talk that way because I'm not always "right now." A song lives across time as an overarching impression of sensory input, seeing it all happening at once, racing through stories like a fearless kid on a bicycle, narrating his own skin.

Dude sets our projector on the windowsill and we sit in
the dark yard while he shows home movies on the side of
the neighbors' white house. In the movies, my parents hug
each other and make goofy faces, take turns riding my
tricycle, paint a third eye on my forehead.

It's amazing to see the skin spaceship you inhabit,
running around on the side of your neighbors' house.
Right now, I think, *I'm a little kid.* I'm amazed by this.

Crane and Dude and I smile at each other in the starlight
and then grow solemn, watching another now move across
the wall.

The birth of a song, the wackiness that's going on as I watch rain fall on the Bullet's windshield, is always disconcerting. It interferes; it's lonelifying. I wanted to spend this rainy morning with Mark and a snake, under the porch. Instead, the ocean waves outside, the wind, the sound of cars racing by blend with the knocking, talking music I hear.

When I was younger, music was sound: moving, but not *alive*. My guitar was a pretty hobby, not a passion. I wrote songs before the witch ran me over, but they were ideas, making stuff up. Now, "writing a song" means listening, buzzing an energy, my skin dancing with sparks. It really does feel like religion. Or a disease. Like a religious disease.

The effect a song's birth has on my body is sickening. Literally. The buzzing can actually make me vomit. Songs get stuck inside me and when I finally let them out . . . they're too big, they make me sick.

If I fall asleep, the song wakes me up, whispering, chanting and shouting, suggesting bass lines and backing vocals, piano parts and guitar solos. It's that—the clattering noise of the thing, louder and louder, first whispering, then gasping with its own impact—that's so upsetting, so overwhelming. A sickening frenzy. *Ugh, lemme out of here.*

This is a goddamn song. I have a genuine love/hate relationship with these things.

☺ fear

this is much better than me, okay?

I grab a guitar from the backseat of the Bullet and try to find the notes I'm hearing, pick 'em out of the *other* notes and the pounding raindrops—a riotous mess of color.

Each major chord is a primary color, its associated minor altered with a tinge of another color that makes it sadder; sevenths are altered by a secondary color that makes them twangy, and minor sevenths combine the original primary color with the sad shade and the twangy one, etc. Chord structure follows a logical pattern, in other words, until I start making them up. When I invent a chord, I invent a color. I mean, I don't *really* invent a color, but it sure sounds like something I've never seen before, if that makes any sense.

Sometimes a song will play a frenetic melody that achieves a rolling impression of a chord. The notes still vibrate against each other, but in a hypnotic rhythm that achieves its impression over the course of a phrase rather than a word, a color building itself out of its constituent colors in a pattern. The confusion is dazzling.

Years of classical guitar lessons kept my fingers nimble enough to keep up but couldn't prepare my brain for this . . . slow-mo implosion. It's hard to concentrate.

This part isn't art, though; it's science. Not *rocket* science—anybody could do it—but there's no way it's art. Art's a mess, too emotional for its own good. Cool science counters hot art, takes sober measurements. It makes magic clean, refines the intangible.

Dude unwittingly taught me this when I was six years old. He carefully placed a nylon-strung Yamaha guitar behind the living room couch and told me never to touch it because it wasn't a toy. To a little kid, this means, "It's not *just* a toy, it's a *great* toy." For months, first thing every morning, I'd run downstairs to stare at it.

The guitar was so golden it looked fluorescent orange, with lovely, intricate patterns around the sound hole. I knew it was capable of great things, lying there in its case: mysterious, untapped potential, like an ancient farming implement or a magic wand. I particularly liked how the ends of the strings were frayed and textured, almost falling apart, yet stretched tight enough to do their work. Work I couldn't hear because this was a forbidden instrument.

It didn't stay forbidden, though. Dude eventually felt bad enough to let me hold the guitar. He sat on the living room rug with me and placed my hands in the correct positions, right hand over the sound hole, left on the neck. The neck was huge. The instrument was huge; my tiny hands didn't come close to having an effect on the guitar.

"It's just like that stupid horse," I said, and Dude nodded sympathetically. I had recently ridden a horse for the first time and this experience had taught me that the space a six-year-old takes up on planet Earth is dreadfully, painfully small. Both the horse and the guitar had seemed attractive from a distance, useful. Up close, though, they were unmanageable. Beautiful behemoths.

I was driven to play the guitar, but I hadn't really wanted to ride the horse. I did it only because my mother came home from the grocery store one day and told me she'd seen our neighbor there. This was a boring story until she mentioned that the lady had invited me over to ride her outsized,

bad-tempered ex-racehorse. I waited for Crane to tell me she'd politely de-
clined for reasons of safety. Instead, while unpacking the groceries, she said
lightly that accepting the woman's invitation was the nice thing to do.

Alarmed, I suggested that *she* be the one to ride the giant horse, as she
was a giant lady and I was only six, but she shook her head at me, saying,
"You like horses."

"I *like* them," I replied. "I don't need to get *on* one. Especially not *that*
one." I saw this horse bite his mistress on the shoulder once. She hit him
really hard when he did this. Then the horse pranced around, angry, and
the lady grabbed her hurt shoulder and kicked dirt. I just didn't wanna get
mixed up in anything like that. They seemed troubled.

"It'll be fine, Kristin," my mother sighed. "Run along."

"What, right *now*?" She gave me an impatient look I knew well, and
which I took as my cue to give up. Slowly, I walked next door and crouched
near the corral, staying low so the neighbor lady wouldn't see me out her
back window. I figured if I waited long enough without her catching sight
of me, I could just go home and say that I'd done the polite thing by showing up, but it hadn't worked out.

I watched the horse through the wooden fence as it stood at the far end
of the corral, staring into the distance. He looked like a toy horse, very
pretty and delicate. I decided I should probably get used to the idea of
making friends with him. *Wish I'd brought sugar, or a carrot.* Maybe I'd be
the only person he didn't bite or something. Maybe he'd just been waiting
for a child to come along and understand him. And not hit him. And we
could jump the fence and go off into the fields beyond and—*well, she didn't
see me, guess I can go home.*

I spun on my heels and headed for my house when the neighbor lady
came out of hers. *Dang!* She herself was very horsy: she looked and smelled
like a horse, and when she talked, it sounded like whinnying. I was intrigued
by this world of horse-ness that was powerful enough to turn a human into
an equine version of a human. It reminded me of the Greek myths Dude
read to me in which people were condemned to live as trees and cows. I
wasn't intrigued enough to want to be a part of it, though. "Hey!" the horse
lady called, walking over. "You want a Coke or you just wanna start
riding?"

I wanna go home. Did she ask me if I wanna go home? "No, thank you,
ma'am."

She towered over me. "No what?"

"Thank you."

She squinted down at me. "D'you wanna Coke or not?"

"Um, no," I answered. "Thank you."

She smiled sideways. "I remember being your age," she said, hopping the fence. "I couldn't wait to start riding either." Whistling for her horse, she added, "All little girls love horses."

"Yes, ma'am," I answered sadly. I watched as the horse came sauntering over, growing exponentially larger with every step. He was a toy, then a dog, then briefly, a pony, then a normal horse, an elephant and finally, a building.

The neighbor lady grabbed him by the reins and laughed at me. "C'mon!" she shouted happily, like she was telling me to jump into a pile of candy.

Gingerly, I climbed over the fence and positioned myself under the horse's chin. He was a twitching skyscraper and I was an ant. My neighbor whacked him with the palm of her hand and told him to stand still. I thought whacking him was a bad idea, but I said nothing. "You climb up over *here*," she said, pointing to his side. "Whaddya, gonna ride his head?" she laughed. I laughed, too, as if I'd made a joke. "Go ahead, climb up." She struggled to hold the reins as the horse waved its head around in an agitated manner.

Walking to the side of the horse, I squinted up at the saddle. *Climb a skyscraper.* The massive ribcage in front of me heaved and trembled. I put my foot up in the air, past my own trembling, heaving ribcage, and shoved it into the stirrup. Hand over hand, I climbed the swaying leather straps and swung myself onto the horse's back. *Not too shabby*, I thought, gazing out into the pasture, feeling like a cowboy, my heart pounding.

But instead of the horse's mane and ears in front of me, I saw its butt and tail. *I got up backwards*, I thought. "You got up backwards," whinnied the neighbor lady.

♋ soap and water

in her doghouse
she does it backwards

"I won't play guitar backwards, though," I promised Dude and he smiled. But the guitar was uncomfortable to hold. It didn't fit on my lap; I was simply too small. And its shiny finish was blinding, flashing light into my eyes whenever I shifted underneath it. Zoë lay next to me on the living room rug, her chin on her paws, looking worried.

Zoë was way smarter than any human. Small enough to sneak around and watch whatever was going on and learn from it, with brilliant brown eyes that seemed to know . . . everything. Zoë was never wrong. She could catch a Frisbee ten feet in the air and catch a problem ten minutes before it happened. She'd refuse to get in a car headed for the vet's office, but she'd leap joyfully into one that was going to the beach. She loved children and cats and hated snotty rich people. She was psychic. So when Zoë worried, I worried. I looked down at the guitar, then at her. Her eyebrows knitted. "What?" I asked her.

Dude leaned over and carefully placed my fingers over the smooth strings, helping me thumb through my first "song." *E/ G/ A.*

It was disappointing. I had expected more impact. Nylon strings sound soft and muted, different from the shimmering clang of steel strings I thought I would hear, but I could get used to that. Something else was wrong.

I frowned. "What is it?" asked Dude.

I didn't like how the chords sounded and I told him that. He looked hurt. "Why don't you like them?"

"They're boring."

"But Bob Dylan plays these chords. And Neil Young."

"Mm-hm." I looked down at my hands, willing them to play better. "They're probably nice guys." Handing the guitar back to Dude, I stared at it, perplexed. *Why doesn't it sound as cool as it looks?* I glanced at Zoe and she looked back sadly.

Dude took the guitar, then sat, staring at me. "'Nice guys'?"

I complained that the chords we'd played didn't sound magenta enough. ". . . you know?"

"No," answered Dude, bewildered.

"Well, *red*, I mean. I've heard red before. A million times. The first chord was red. And boring."

"E major's red?" he asked. "E never sounded particularly *red* to me. You mean you think it's a primary color?"

"Yeah. We didn't even play green."

"What chord is green?"

I shook my head at Zoë, then glared impatiently at Dude. "Mix a blue chord with a yellow one. *Duh-uh.* It's stronger and prettier that way. Like those fish." The fish I meant were African cichlids, who change color when they lose too many fights. They get their asses kicked enough times and grow pale, while the winning fish develop bright, colorful scales and beautiful patterns. Dude and I always loved that these fish wear their hearts on their sleeves. I looked up at him. "If you play too many wimpy chords, you're just asking for wimpy scales."

"Because the guitar kicks your ass?" He squinted in thought. "Are you calling Bob Dylan a loser?"

"No, just a pale fish."

"Are you calling *me* a loser?"

"*No . . .*"

Dude looked at me sideways. "Are you calling my scales wimpy?" I shrugged and he handed me the guitar. "It's yours," he said. "Play colors."

♋ spring

all i want is green

Play colors, I think to myself, as the swishing voices conspire against me. This song doesn't sound like colors, it sounds like . . . machines. That nurse was right; I do hear machines.

There are notes in there, though. I find them and play them, reduce the industrial orchestra I hear to a pathetic *plunking*. That melody needs a bed and chords come only through trial and error. So when a sound the guitar makes matches the sound that's filling the Bullet, I keep that chord and move on to the next one. It gets easier each time, as one chord will set up the next, words in a sentence, then sentences in a paragraph.

Voices playing counter to the guitar parts then form themselves into a kind of phonetic melody. These syllables pile themselves up into words and say things that are hard to grasp, hard to control, and I plug my ears to their meaning. I know I've lived the stories they tell, but I never wanted to tell them; the songs do. I'm just playing along.

These are words that don't talk to brains. Instead, they thump into chests, bashing and shrieking like poltergeists. If I try to jump into the song and write it myself, sorta hurry it along, my lyrics'll stick out like ugly relatives. You can tell it's me talking because suddenly the song isn't beautiful anymore—it just makes sense. Or worse, it's *clever*.

The real song waits patiently for me to shut up and then picks up where it left off: time-tripping, speaking in math, bodies and dreams, landscapes, passed notes, pages from this diary, conversations, memories, newspapers and unmailed letters that crawled back out of the garbage—sometimes sweet, sometimes angry, sometimes funny, but always twisted up and painted in extravagantly ugly Technicolor: well-rehearsed Tourette's.

It's not like I've embraced the songwriting process. I haven't even accepted it; it's too creepy. There's an electrical component, for example— the lightning rod thing. I get all flitchy and my hair stands on end, like a seizure. With a heightened awareness of . . . *meaning*, for lack of a better word, that feels like possession. Whatever is important at that moment will jump up into the air and grab my electrified brain.

ⅾ the fuchsia wall

then suddenly everything i see's a love letter

Playing a real song is like keeping a wild animal for a pet: gorgeous and terrifying, it lives in your house, but it's never really yours. It's an honor to stand next to this beast, and yet at the same time, you know it can kill you. It's bigger, better, more important than you and scarier than any person could *ever* be.

A real song doesn't count listeners; it doesn't even give a shit about the musician who plays it—it exists only for itself. So spiritual that it's physical, so basic that it doesn't say "look at me," it says "look at *us*."

Listening to it is like watching nature: gross and great.

So I respect music; it's powerful—gods and devils. But I would never do this on purpose. Dave says that's part of it: unless you *have* to do it, you could be lying.

I watch Dude carry our TV up a winding staircase. He struggles, jammed into a narrow corner. He can go neither up nor down the stairs without dropping the television. He swears loudly about this.

Then I hear a soft fluttering sound as a big moth flies in the open window next to Dude's head. *No, it's a bat! I love bats!* The swearing escalates as the bat flops around on Dude's head, tangled in his hair.

The bat squeaks, Dude yells. It's gross and great.

Mark pulls up on his moped in the gray dawn and beeps the wretched thing outside my window. *Wow, he's up early.* Smiling at him through the rain-spattered glass, I push the passenger side door of the Bullet open and he climbs in, soaking wet. "You okay?" he asks through the song he can't hear, taking off his backpack.

"Sure. Are *you*?" I pull my Y towel out of the crack in the door and hand it to him.

Mark puts the towel over his head and rubs his hair vigorously. "Thank you."

"Guess what? There was a snake next to your head last night."

He stops rubbing. "There was?" Peering from under the towel, he wipes his wet face with his hand. "Jesus, Kris. Why didn't you wake me up?"

"'Cause you were sleeping." He gives me a blank look. The song dances around, begging for attention. I've gotten really good at hearing two worlds at once. I can carry on conversations now, albeit feebly, when a song is playing.

I watch Mark fold the towel carefully. When he hands it back, I jam it into the door again. "You didn't have to fold it, sweetie. I was just gonna do this with it."

"So you aren't mad at me?" he asks.

I turn to him, astonished. "Mad? At you?" He just stares, waiting for an answer. "Mark. I don't get mad at you. I *can't* get mad at you."

He stares for another second to make sure I'm telling the truth. "Okay."

"Has anyone *ever* been mad at you?" He nods. *Sometimes I really hate songs.* "Never think that again."

He isn't smiling. "Okay."

I made smiling Mark stop smiling. What a terrible person. All that beige beauty; I don't deserve him. Suddenly, it occurs to me that "camping" was probably his way of trying to find a place for me to sleep. *Oh, god.* He still cares where I sleep, still thinks I have a broken-home face. He's so very kind. Mark is *made* of kindness. Kindness and fragility and beige. You have to be gentle with people like that. "Look in your backpack," I tell him.

Reaching in, he pulls out the heart I drew for him. The song jangles, whooshes and clatters. Mark looks at the drawing for a few seconds, then folds it up and sticks it back in his bag. "Thank you."

I can hardly hear him. Mark puts his backpack on and hugs me, then smiles a dim version of his gummy smile and leaves me with my lonelifying noise.

♋ him dancing

i'll be the runner
you can love me anyway

New song is done. It's burgundy and ochre with a sort of Day-Glo turquoise bridge—another tattoo on this pathetic, little body. *I'm running out of room.* I almost called off the Muses' weekly Sunday afternoon practice, thinking I'd be in the throes of musical whooshing, but the song finished writing its parts and organizing its thoughts by the time the rain stopped.

I'll teach it to the band this afternoon; they'll like this one. It's a Doghouse song, of course. All songs are Doghouse songs now. I can't even remember what it was like to hear a song that didn't grab my face and shout at it. Must've been soothing. But this is *electrifying.*

And now, everything is okay: the world is silent except for real things. I hear birds again, cars. When the rain stopped, dog walkers just *appeared* on the beach, like spontaneous generation—they seemed to rise up out of the sand with their Dunkin' Donuts coffees and Labs named Bailey. I could hear them talking to their dogs, to each other; it was beautiful. I'm so relieved the song is over and so happy with it that I *love* the dog walkers. All of them. And the birds and the cars and the damp sunshine.

I hear the song, too, but the sound it makes is *inside* my head, not outside. It's only there because it got stuck there, the way any song will if you hear it too many times. Inside means everything is fine.

♋ carnival wig

i won't be afraid
when my ears ring
and my head spins

Dave is late for practice, so while we wait for him, Tea and Leslie and I pick up cans of spray paint and draw and write with them on the walls of his parents' attic. This goes on for hours. Dave's parents are parked at the bottom of the stairs, newspaper and knitting in hand, but no sign of Dave. So the girls and I play spray-paint tic-tac-toe, draw spray-paint portraits of each other and leave spray-paint messages for Dave about how late he is and how we have better things to do than spray paint messages on the wall to him about how late he is.

Eventually, the air is full of paint droplets and noxious fumes, so we have to open a window and lie on the floor for a while. "I bet he's picking up garbage," says Tea slowly and deliberately through her dizziness.

I'm also having trouble thinking clearly. "I *know* he's picking up garbage."

"There's an actual cloud of paint in here," adds Leslie dreamily.

The Muses' sound is something of a free-for-all: we can play whatever we want, as long as it doesn't remind the others of a beer commercial. Dave has embraced this anything-but-suck aesthetic with charming exuberance. He is a classically trained snare prodigy who refuses to play cymbals but is willing to hit just about anything else—hubcaps and mixing bowls, for instance, or whatever he finds in the street on the way to practice. We've all watched him get lost in the world of *pings* and *knocks*; he definitely loses track of time. Lying on the floor is really all we can do about this. "Are his parents down there?" whispers Leslie. Tea nods.

I lift my head, whispering too. "*They* weren't late."

Leslie looks concerned. "What's wrong with them?"

"Brain damage." I let my head drop again. "From paint fumes."

"They're proud of Dave," says Tea. "They like everything he does."

"So, what, we're, like, a finger painting taped to the fridge?" asks Leslie.

"Sure."

I think about this. "That's amazing."

"It *is* amazing," says Leslie.

"It is." Tea thinks. "They might still have brain damage, though."

When he finally appears, Dave has an armload of garbage that will be his instrument for the day. Shaking up a can of spray paint, he begins decorating the garbage. We all groan. "Put that away!" yells Leslie.

"Aren't you a *snare* prodigy?" I ask him from the floor, through my headache and nausea. "Why don't you just play the goddamn snare?"

"Look at this!" he exclaims, holding up a piece of twisted metal and spraying it red.

Sitting up to admire his garbage, I notice that he's wearing a coat. I'm stunned. "Dave . . . what the hell?"

Dave and I always believed that coats were for wimps who couldn't handle seasons: "coat slaves." *Geez, people, get a grip! Seasons happen!* And that vision was for wusses: people who couldn't hack the rough-hewn, fuzzy life we lived—slaves to their glasses—when we could play entire shows without seeing anything. It was the only thing we were smug about, really, our ability to live blind and cold.

Then, a few months ago, he showed up at our attic practice space *wearing* glasses. I felt betrayed, but he was transformed. "Trees have individual leaves, even when they're far away!" he insisted, his eyes and new lenses shining.

I tried it 'cause I do everything Dave says. I bought black square men's glasses like Dude wore when I was a kid and I loved them but I wasn't prepared for vision. Such sharp edges . . . vision hurts. There was a lot of stuff my glasses showed me that I really didn't want to know about. Plus, in the mirror, without the forgiving Vaselined lens of nearsightedness, my face was disappointing. It had *individual* pores. "I'd rather navigate in a cloud," I told him, taking off my glasses. "I like sound. Hearing is an honest sense. I can do without the others."

"Mmmm . . ." Dave frowned thoughtfully. "It *could* make us look clumsy, though, to be, you know, bumping into stuff all the time."

"Yeah," I admitted. "Sometimes we seem illiterate, too."

He nodded. "I've noticed that."

I put my glasses back on and looked around, wincing. "God, there's just too much stuff out there. I don't like being forced to see everything I'm facing."

"I get that," he said. "There *is* too much stuff out there. But maybe some of it's . . . good?"

૭ flood
my aching eyesight

Dave was right. Dave's always right. I even bought contacts so I can look at stuff all the time, because he said some of it was good. I pick and choose among visual elements as best I can—have joined the ranks of the glasses slaves. But a coat? A *coat*? *Et tu, Dave?*

Dave unzips his coat to show me how it works. "See? We can still wear T-shirts, but if we wear our T-shirts *underneath coats*, winter won't hurt!"

"But it's spring!"

"Winter happens annually, Kris."

"So?" I whine. "Wear a wig!"

"Seeing turned out to be okay sometimes, right?" he asks gently.

"What?" I whip my head from side to side. "Who said that?"

He sighs. "It's dumb to live blind and cold when we have *tools* at our disposal to prevent it. It just weakens us, gives everybody else a head start."

"*Coat slave*," I mutter under my breath.

Dave sits behind his kit, zips his coat back up and reaches for his sticks. "I heard that." Taking a deep breath, I stand at the mic, focus on the far wall of the attic and start the new song. I forgot what it sounded like; quietly, it had tiptoed out of my head.

So here's what it sounds like: ugly. Butt ugly. The strange kind of butt ugly—clay molded into some weird shape you've never seen before. Organic, yeah, but . . . organic what? And why would you wanna look at it? It's an owl pellet, a deformed stalactite. But it's great. This tattoo is wicked cool.

Tea and Leslie sit on their amps, holding their guitars and watching me, the floor in front of them littered with Leslie's sheet music. *Can't they close their eyes or look somewhere else? Singing is such a dumb thing to do. I guess that's why normal people only do it in the shower.*

Soon, though, the girls're blotted out by burgundy and ochre, shot through with neon blue-green. When I finish the song, there's a little freak standing in the middle of the room: a song body, and I'm burning hot. A song may be born of electricity, but it lives as heat. Now I don't just resent Dave's coat; it's actually making me sick to look at it. How can he be cold? *He's just being stubborn.*

I look at my friends. They all look back at me, but no one smiles or acknowledges that they've heard anything. They just look thoughtful. *God, it's hot.* I can't swim or race out into rain right now, so I suck down a glass of ice water Dave's mother gave me and it helps. Water is the perfect antidote to the musical desert, the hot, dry, killer-beautiful landscape of songs.

Focusing on the far wall again, I start the song over from the beginning. Two bars in, there is a shattering *bang*! Sudden gorgeous noise all around me, the sound of three musicians jumping in with six feet. Enormous, crazy big. They play so *loud*. And somehow, their entrance is timed perfectly. They seem to have worked out their musical responses in their hands, knowing intuitively to bypass their brains: a gut reaction poured through muscles. What kind of love is that? What kind of trust? I watch them as they play, touched and baffled. They work hard, temples throbbing with the effort, locked in to shifting time signatures they've never heard before. It's like I've been playing with matches, my bandmates turning my sad little arson into a celebratory bonfire.

Their musical replies are elegant: Dave's manic snare patterns that mirror my guitar parts plus a hypnotic rolling over the whole kit; Leslie's complex, melodic bass lines, more like bass *leads*, first pounding, then airy; Tea's distinctive guitar parts, neither rhythm nor lead, bouncing off mine, high melodies jumping up above the mix, low ones pushing up from underneath; and then fractured vocals, all mixed up, dancing in and out of rhythm, banging into each other. My bandmates are a freakin' *superteam*; look at 'em go.

That Mexican biker was right—it's muscular. Sun-dappling splashed across the fog I brought to practice. Still not pretty, but at least I'm not alone in it anymore.

♋ honeysuckle

your temples throb with effort
and your notes hit every target hard

There is a phenomenon known as "paradoxical undressing" that affects those dying of hypothermia. Freezing to death, people tear off their clothing as they're overcome by imaginary heat. Lost in blizzards, on snowy mountains, in frozen forests, their bodies become convinced that they're burning, not freezing.

Honestly, I'm so shy that I find most contact with people deeply unsettling, but songs—the alive kind in the air, injected with evil from the Doghouse—mean that I'm burning with sound, not frozen with fear. 'Cause they're my way down to where we all are.

I didn't *ask* to go down to where we all are, but as it turns out, I'm a member of a deeply social species in which the only truths worth speaking are the most naked. In other words, I had planned on wearing *all* my clothes into these freezing woods—songs ask me to wear none.

♋ serene
lose control

But way beyond stripping off clothes, the musical kind of paradoxical undressing strips you down to your bones. And as it turns out, we all have pretty fucking similar bones.

Who knew?

Dude plays guitar for me before school, to cheer me up.
I have a school-morning stomachache and can't finish
my oatmeal.

He sits at the table with me and plays "Wabash
Cannonball," "The Cuckoo" and "Go Tell Aunt Rhody," which
is not a very cheerful song. It's about a dead goose and
the gander who's crying because his wife is dead and all
the little goslings who're crying because their mother's
dead. My oatmeal gets colder and colder.

Eventually, I drag myself out the door to catch the
school bus, the sad melody of weeping baby geese
in my head.

A few hours later, Crane is called to the school because
I'm crying behind a bookshelf and won't come out.
"She says she's crying about a song," the teacher tells
her on the phone, "but I think she might actually be
sad about something."

I have no idea how many times we play it, but when the new song begins to sound realized, we're completely spent. This one's so intense, it's making me overheated and sick. So is Dave's dumb coat. And the lingering paint fumes. We're catching our breath before starting again when Dave suddenly stands up and drops his sticks onto the snare drum with a clatter. "Shopping!" he announces. The girls unhesitatingly stand up to leave.

"What?" I ask into the mic.

"You're getting a coat today," says Dave.

I freeze. "Unpossible."

"No," he answers matter-of-factly, "it's not. You'll see." Checking his watch, he says, "St. Paul's is still open. C'mon."

"Only if they come, too," I say, pointing at the girls.

"*I'm* not shopping," says Leslie.

Tea, placing her guitar on a stand, shakes her head. "I *have* a coat."

"Aw, come on," I plead. "Get *another* coat."

Leslie holds her bass in its case and waves. "Have fun!"

"Bye!" calls Tea, already halfway down the stairs.

I look at Dave. "I hate shopping."

"I know you do," he answers. "Which is why you don't have a coat, which is why you need to go shopping."

So Dave and I walk to the thrift store to buy me a goddamn coat. The rain stopped early this morning—it is a warm, glistening, sunny day. Not the sort of day that'd make *anybody* buy a coat. Days like this make people throw coats *away*. "I'll try it," I tell him. "But only 'cause you said to."

"Mm-hm."

"Sometimes you're right about things."

Dave nods emphatically. "Yes, I am."

"But only sometimes."

His mouth tightens. "Right."

"I'm not *promising* anything."

"No."

"It's spring."

"Yep."

I look at him. "Even coat slaves stop wearing coats in the *spring*."

He rolls his eyes. "Yeah."

"And I'm *always* hot."

"I know."

"And it smells weird in there."

Sighing, he holds the door open.

While I plow through hundreds of gigantic old-lady coats that smell like mothballs and dust and are too big to fit my *car*, never mind my body, Dave holds up different combinations of feather boas and golf shirts, asking if they "work." I say that they all do. He drops his arms to his sides, framing himself in pink and yellow feathers. "You can't like all of them."

"I don't like *any* of them. I just think they work." Dave stares at the neon-pink feathers, then the neon-yellow ones. "If that's the look you're going for, you succeeded."

Then he sticks both boas on a hat rack and pulls a big old-man suit off a hanger. I stop plowing through coats and watch as he drapes the heavy brown jacket over his shoulders, pulls on the fat-old-man pants that go with it and walks up and down the aisle.

"Those pants are way too big," I say, staring. "So's the jacket. The whole suit is too big. Maybe you should look for a Sunday-school suit in the kids' section. You look like you raided grandpa's closet."

"I did. Just not *my* grandpa." He stares at the floor where his feet used to be, then looks over at me. "You should take fashion risks."

"You shouldn't wear *that*, though."

"Too risky?"

"Too hot."

"It is hot in here." He lets go of the suit and it falls to the floor. Stepping out of it, he pulls a small blue wool coat with a fur collar off of a hanger and hands it to me. "Here," he says, "I got this for you."

I'm sure that when this coat was made in the forties, it was a fancy item for a fancy lady, but I got it at a thrift store in the eighties and it looks it. It's ragged and most of the buttons have fallen off. I already looked a little bag lady to begin with—my skirt looks like it was made from curtains, my T-shirt's torn and grimy. This coat isn't helping.

♋ marriage tree

like an old man in a dress
treat me like a twelve year old man

I'm practicing wearing my new coat. Driving the Bullet around, all wearing a coat and whatnot. I'm sweltering, but, as I understand it, that's what a coat is for, so it's going pretty well, I guess. Only thing is, nobody *else* is wearing a coat. The sidewalk people look happy and sunshiny in their T-shirts.

Driving to the Doghouse, I park across the street from it and stare at it through my fur collar, just to think for a minute. That place was a cartoon nightmare. It wrapped me in my own skin, crammed it full of explosives and locked it shut. *I couldn't move when I lived there. Now I can't be still.*

I start the engine. The Bullet shudders and coughs. *Stillness is dangerous, anyway; it's best to keep moving.* The engine heaves, then settles into a comfortable rumble and I pull away from the Doghouse.

Gonna head back to Providence, back to Napoleon's. Gotta find somebody to crash with me under those sad Christmas lights, though; I don't wanna sleep alone tonight. And I really hope those godforsaken donuts're gone. At least let godforsaken Fish Jesus be funny again.

I pull my collar up around my face and swelter some more.

♋ fish

lonely is an eyesore

I drag my mother's wedding dress down the attic stairs
and put it on over my jeans and T-shirt so I can watch TV
in a wedding dress. The dress is very long; I have to
stand on a footstool to keep it from dragging on the
ground.

It's still too long, though, so I get a chair and put the
chair on top of the footstool.

Balancing on top of the stool and chair, I spread my
white pearled skirts around me and watch game shows.
Women scream and cry, but they're happy.

Happy about dinette sets.

SUMMER 1985

Betty stands in front of the main doors to the O'Hare building, holding a jar of brown liquid up to my face. "We're gonna drink this under the fairy tree," she says. Students stream in and out of the building around her as she grins at me through the glass jar.

I stare into it. The liquid inside looks like pond scum. "We're gonna drink it? What is it?"

"Bieler's Broth. Dr. Bieler invented it." Betty's wearing a white pantsuit with a turquoise scarf around her neck; a shiny white vinyl purse swings from her shoulder. Licking her shell-pink lips, she coos, "It's amazing stuff."

So we walk to the fairy tree in the sunshine to drink a jar of pond scum. It's one of those super windy summer days before the air slows down; clouds are tearing by overhead. Cool breezes and warm sun make dogs goofy and they seem to do the same thing to Betty. When we get to the fairy tree, she lifts a branch up for me as if she's holding a door. "Madam . . ." she says in a snooty voice.

I crawl under the branch. "When you were rich, did you have a butler?" I ask over my shoulder, peering at her through the leaves.

"Probably," she answers noncommittally, following me in and dropping the branch door behind her.

The fairy tree is an enormous, ancient, crawling thing, old as Jesus or something. It's like a fort. You climb in on your hands and knees and then let the branches snap shut behind you. Lots of students hang out under here, so it's not a private fort—more like a gazebo. A way to be outside without the elements shining or falling on you. Plus, it's cool and middle-earthy.

Betty pushes her jar, purse and textbooks in and then crawls in herself, absentmindedly brushing the dirt off her knees. She leans against the gnarled trunk next to me with a sweet half-smile on her face. Carefully lifting her jar of pond scum, I turn it from side to side and stare into it; little orange and green specks float by. "Betty?" I say. "This looks like sea monkeys."

"You know, it *does*." She grabs the jar, opens it and takes a swig. When the sea monkeys drip down her chin, she wipes her mouth on her clean white sleeve. "Want some?" she asks, holding it out.

"I don't think so."

"Trust me."

Squinting into the jar, I watch the specks circle. "I trust you. I just never ate sea monkeys before."

Betty takes another sip. "It's vegetables."

"Is this a new diet?" I ask her. Betty doesn't diet to lose weight; she just reads a lot of books about not getting old. She did a goat milk diet and a seaweed one. Sometimes she makes me do them with her. "You're gonna live forever," I tell her. "I hope you're ready for that."

She drinks some more monkeys. "I'm fasting a day and then drinking this magical broth, and then fasting the next day and then I drink the broth again. And it tastes good."

I look at her. "That's 'cause you're starving. You fasted yesterday? All day? *Dirt'd* taste good today."

"That's true. And Bieler's Broth tastes better than dirt." She takes another sip and closes her eyes blissfully. She does make it look good, but cows make grass look good, too.

I don't think I'll do this diet with her. "I miss the goat milk one."

She nods, her eyes still shut. "That was fun. And our skin looked pretty."

I pick up the jar but can't bring myself to try any, now that I know she's starving. Also, it still looks like sea monkeys, so I just stare into it, swirling the specks around. "I think we just imagined that."

"Maybe," Betty says. "And goat milk's . . . goat-y."

"It is. Why isn't cow's milk cow-y?"

She thinks. "It probably is, but we're used to it."

We sit against the lumpy bark, thinking about milk. "Milk's weird," I say.

"Milk *is* weird." She nods, wide-eyed. "We shouldn't drink another animal's milk. It's like something ants would do."

"I think ants *do* do something like that. And ants are weird, too."

"Mm-hm." She takes another sip. "They have war."

"And slavery." I study her. She's like a thoroughbred, but an uncomfortable one. You get the feeling that she shouldn't have been domesticated. "How long're you gonna do this diet?"

"Just for the summer."

My jaw drops. "The whole summer? You aren't gonna eat for the whole summer?"

"I'll eat Bieler's Broth."

"How about just, you know . . . food?" I ask her. "Why don't you eat that?"

"Eat food?" She thinks. "But I want to be lovely."

Oh, no, not again. "Betty, you're the fairest of them all."

She picks up her purse and fishes around in it, then pulls out her wallet. "I never stopped wanting to be pretty," she says. "Is that silly?"

"No, I don't think so. You want people to like you." I pick up a stick and draw some lines in the dirt with it, tracing a circle of light that's shining through the branches. "But pretty's a weird club; the rules are always changing." I try to draw Betty's face in the light circle and make it pretty. "And then if you get in, they say you're stupid."

Betty slumps against the tree, flipping through the pictures in her wallet. "You're right about that. But you can't get a foot in the door without being pretty in *our* business. It'd be stupid *not* to look pretty." She holds the wallet out and shows me a picture of herself a million years ago: the young Betty, with a big American smile, standing by a desk with a clock and some books on it. Same lady, but the face is unlined, with a different expression. Less worried, more nervous, if that makes any sense . . . a desire to please?

I put my stick down and take the wallet from her in order to see the young Betty up close. "I never thought about it that way." Something about the smiling face is not happy. I can't put my finger on it for a minute, then I realize it's desperation. A desperate desire to please. And she thinks *these* are desperate times. Handing the wallet back, I point to her dirt portrait. "Look," I say, "same face."

She smiles. "That's *me?*" Studying my drawing, she reaches for the stick. "I'll draw you. I'll make you look as good as you made me look."

I watch as she draws. "I don't get wanting to look good; it seems rude. Just makes other people feel bad, doesn't it? Trying to look better than them?" Betty's ignoring me. "How can you say one person is nicer to look at than another, anyway? I mean, if you gotta try and look like something, how about *kind?*"

She smiles and keeps drawing. "Oooh . . . I like where this is going, sweetheart. But I think it's sex appeal we're after. We all wanna go to bed with somebody. Or just know that we could."

Oh, geez. "Ew. You think so?" She's drawing a very nice picture of me in the dirt. "But no one wants to sleep with looks," I insist. "They want to sleep with a person."

She looks up from her drawing, stunned. "That is such a lovely thought! But entirely untrue." She giggles and glances at her old picture before stuffing the wallet back into her shiny purse. "They want to sleep with a person . . . who's *hot*."

"But people who think they're hot have that 'I think I'm hot' expression and that's *ugly*."

"Yeah. But we all want to be loved. It makes us feel lovable."

"Betty, sleeping with hot people isn't *love*. It's just sleeping with hot people." *Maybe it's a generational thing.*

"True . . ." She brushes some powdery dirt away from her sketch. "We want to be *valued*. And that makes us feel *valuable*." Pointing at my dirt face, she says, "That's you."

"Wow, I'm pretty dirt."

"Yep," she agrees, admiring her work. "You're pretty dirt." Leaning back against the fairy tree, she sighs. "You know what runs the world, Krissy? Fucking. It's about time you learned that. Fucking runs the whole fucking world."

I stare at her. "It does?"

"Pretty much, yeah." She wraps her sea monkey–stained arms around her mud-stained knees. "You'll miss fucking when it's gone, you know."

Jesus. "Can you call it something else, please?"

She rolls her eyes. "You'll miss 'making love' when nobody wants to sleep with you anymore because you stopped being pretty."

Poor Betty. It bugs me that she wants to be pretty. She's better than that. And I'm sure she was better than that a million years ago when she was unlined and desperate. "In that picture, you looked like *yourself*, right? Like a real person?"

"No makeup," she says proudly, "just crushed walnut shells."

"Yeah, see? You weren't trying to look better than anyone else. You were a feminist." I catch her eye. "Wait, what? Walnut shells? On your *face*?"

"That's right," she answers proudly. "I was pretty dirt. But they didn't say 'feminist' back then, Krissy."

"What'd they say?"

She looks thoughtful. "I don't know; they didn't really talk about it."

"Suffragette?"

She winces. "I'm not *that* old."

Change the subject. "So you had a butler? Probably? What was that like?"

The branches around us brush the ground. It's such a windy day that we're even getting breezes under the fairy tree. This makes me miss the speedy clouds and I start to feel claustrophobic, so I crawl to the edge of the fairy tree and lift a branch to look out. The grass is a humming, clashing chartreuse, the underside of each wildly dancing blade a rich, pine green. "Wowee, Betty, look at this." I turn around, grinning at her, and point at the crazy grass.

"I had a hundred people on the payroll," she says absently, ducking her head to see under the branch. "I'm not sure what they all did, but whatever it was, it cost me ten million dollars."

My grin fades. "Ten *million* dollars?"

"Yeah." She smiles at me. "It's just money—numbers and paper. It was time to leave Hollywood anyway." Our dirt faces blow around in the breeze, disappearing. Betty pulls her books to her and presses them against her chest. I always assumed she'd been a chorus girl or an extra or something; a bit-part actress with Hollywood dreams that never quite came true. I thought blending these dreams with reality to create her pink sparkly / dark underbelly mythology was a good idea. *But ten million dollars? How did she work that in?* "Whadda you mean it was time to leave? Didn't you like Hollywood?"

She leans her head back against the fairy tree. "I liked how it *smelled*," she says dreamily to the branches above her. She liked how L.A. smelled. Nobody ever says the stuff Betty says.

"What about show business?"

"I liked the *show*," she says emphatically, "not the business."

"Amen, sister."

Then she drains the Bieler's Broth and screws the lid back on, shoving the jar into her purse violently. "Maybe it's fame that people want to look pretty for."

"Fame's for dorks," I say offhandedly. "Only idiots wanna be in *that* club."

Her mouth drops open. "I had my own TV show! I was on the cover of *Time* magazine!"

Oops. I gather my books and crouch by the branch door. *Ummm . . .* "You didn't buy your own hype, did you?"

She freezes, then cracks up. "You're right," she says, laughing, "fame's for dorks."

We have a problem with people "buying their own hype." Not just famous people, but everybody. We accuse lots of people of doing this. We *love* to accuse people of buying their own hype. "Fame's for dorks," she chuckles again, crawling toward the branch door. When she gets there, the knees of her pantsuit black with mud, she looks up at me. "If my wig blows off on the way to class, you'll catch it for me, right?"

I step outside and lift the branch for her. "I'm not your butler."

"Old bones," she mutters, straightening.

"I think you're pretty fucking spry, Aunt B., scramblin' around on your hands and knees like that."

Betty grips her books and purse in one hand and puts her other arm around me, squinting into the sun and wind. "I *am* pretty fucking spry!"

My uncle brings his new boyfriend, True, over for dinner. True is wonderful—as gentle and funny as my beloved uncle. *Now I have two uncles!*

After dinner, we all watch *Masterpiece Theater.* It's disturbing: jailed suffragettes are fed by tubes to end a hunger strike.

In bed, I can't shake the image of the poor, suffering women. What if someone force-feeds my mother and hurts her throat with tubes? I can't fall asleep; I cry and cry, imagining Crane as a suffering suffragette.

True appears in my bedroom doorway and asks me what's wrong. When I tell him, he sits on my bed and holds me, rocking gently. As I fall asleep, he repeats over and over again, "Your mother's not a suffragette, your mother's not a suffragette, your mother's not a suffragette . . ."

The class Betty and I are taking this afternoon is Native American Mythology. Dude is our professor. When we walk into the classroom, he crosses his eyes, pushes his lips out, and puffs up his cheeks at us. Betty rolls her eyes. "That guy is so immature," she sighs, dropping her books on a desk.

"Just ignore him," I say out of the side of my mouth. Betty worships Dude.

When the other students have taken their seats and the class is settled, Dude walks to the window and leans against the sill. His eyes are so blue they look white, like holes in his head, the light from the window shining through them. As sun and shadows race across his face, he tells us that we're all going to try deep relaxation.

Oh, god, I can't do that. Sitting in a chair is hard enough. I raise my hand. "I'm not a *strong* meditator, sir."

"I *know* you aren't a strong meditator." He addresses the class. "When Kristin was four years old, we were living in the woods—" I shake my head wildly and he stops midsentence, looking confused. Betty glares at me.

If Dude hadn't made me take his courses, I would never have known that he uses stories from my childhood in his lectures—mostly embarrassing ones. In my opinion, this is an invasion of privacy. Dude disagrees. "You're my kid," he said when I objected. "I own you and I own all my stories about you. They're mine to tell." This is bullshit, of course; I own me and I'm *in* the stories. I have to keep a close eye on him.

Betty thinks it's "wonderful" that Dude puts me in his lectures. I keep telling her it's not, but she won't listen; she likes to hear stories from my childhood, says they're sweet. "You're lucky to *have* a father," she scolds.

I don't think it really counts as a "story" if my childhood was just a minute ago—it's just something that happened—but you can't argue with Betty. She thinks being old makes her right about everything, and when she can't pull that off, she becomes conveniently deaf.

". . . uh, so anyway," continues Dude, wisely skipping the trip down memory lane and into the commune, "deep relaxation is merely the first stage of Active Imagination, which is a Jungian meditation technique wherein one's perception is opened to the unconscious, allowing images free rein. There are many ways to reach both the personal and the collective unconscious, of course—most of them not cool in public—but hopefully, in this relaxed state, images will begin to communicate with your conscious minds, uncensored. We're trying to reach the you that is without ego, without boundaries, without worldly concerns: the waking dreamer.

"This can be a lonely place and that's okay," he continues. "I'm hoping to give you a taste of psychological isolation and, paradoxically, psychological freedom. Please, no freaking out, though; that gets messy and gross." Students are beginning to shift in their seats. They exchange uncomfortable glances.

"Because I can't throw all of you into holes in the woods," he says over nervous giggling and chatter, "we're going to try and reach your inner voices and images by quieting your conscious minds. I think you all can handle it." Jocks crammed into sweatshirts and young women in pressed blouses look at each other nervously. "If your tribes were here to help you begin the journey into adulthood—"

"Ha!" guffaws Betty. She's proud of being old.

Dude smirks at her. "—then you would be prepared to go hungry, to be stalked by animals, to face your deepest fears: loneliness, mortality, no TV. But you'd still have to be careful: as you know, a power vision describes what is essentially you, at this moment, and this is often a *hidden* reality. If this truth is something you aren't ready to handle, it could be unsettling, to say the least. A telegram from your psyche doesn't necessarily tell you what you want to know. It tells you what you *need* to know.

"It may speak in images that are outside of your comfort zone, in voices that you can't un-hear. In other words, *be very afraid*," he says ominously. The class chuckles but no one looks happy. "I don't imagine you will have power visions per se, but hopefully, as your mind's chatter dies down, your unconscious will be given the floor. And speaking of the floor, I'd like you all to lie down on it."

"The floor?" asks Betty, looking at me fearfully.

"You're *spry*, remember?" I whisper. I can't believe Dude can make so many people afraid of lying down—myself included.

Dude tells Betty she can opt out if she wants. "But you'll need a note from your doctor and it's too late for that," he says. "Sorry, it's out of my hands. Mostly because I think your unconscious is itching to get a word in edgewise and I, for one, would like to hear what it has to say."

All the students lie on the floor, even Betty—eventually—who lies extra close to me. "Okay, waking dreamers," says Dude. "Go!"

"Why is it hard for *you* to lie down?" I whisper to Betty.

"It's getting up that hurts," she whispers back.

♋ day glo

my silver lining:
this isn't anything

getting up is what hurts

Dude deep-relaxes the class by having us progressively relax all our muscles. By *tensing* them, of all things. I know immediately this isn't going to work because mine won't let go; they just stay tensed.

Minutes go by. I can feel the relaxation vibes spilling out of the people around me. I don't understand how they can just slip into stillness—is everyone always tired? *Maybe they're all hungover.* I open one eye and look at the other students. They sure do look peaceful, lying there. The hairdo chick to my left looks freakin' comatose. I imagine that her ego has stopped chattering, freeing her unconscious mind, which will soon spew forth the eloquence of a psyche released.

My unconscious mind is silent, repressed. Probably pouting. My brain chatters away, mostly yelling at my muscles to settle down and shut up before it slaps 'em upside the head.

Dude knows I'm a spaz—how can he do this to me? Lying down doesn't come naturally; I feel like a contortionist. Mentally, I place each limb in position, over and over again, to get them to stay still. *This is ridiculous.*

Dude reminds everyone to breathe. This sends me into another tailspin—one in which oxygen, the lack of oxygen and hyperventilating figure prominently. Chests rise and fall around me, slowly, deliberately. Hungover or not, these people are all goddamn yogis.

Soon, I have no idea how to breathe anymore. I can't remember *ever* breathing right. *What is it? Back and forth? Up and down? I think I'm breathing sideways . . . that's wrong, isn't it?* Dude's calm voice directs the class members to embark on their hypnotic journeys and then falls silent. I guess by now the students around me are all having out-of-body experiences, creating vivid daydreamscapes.

The industrial carpeting underneath us is itchy. Why doesn't that bug anyone else? I try again to relax my muscles and mind. *Maybe if I tense my muscles more, they'll give up and let go.* But there's no such thing as muscles that are more tense than this. My father's the teacher; I should be a star pupil, teacher's pet. Instead, I'm just a rigid little unenlightened tangle of tension.

More time goes by: days, I figure. Maybe weeks. It's all I can do to keep from leaping up and jogging around the room. I'm like a caged animal; I wanna jump out the window. And I can't keep my eyes closed, so I watch Betty. After about a month, she feels me staring at her and opens her eyes, looking wiped.

"What?" I whisper. "Did you have a power vision? Are you gonna get a new name now? Can *I* name you?" Dude invites everyone to sit up slowly. They stretch, murmuring to each other. "You can be Pretty Dirt."

Then I notice that Betty actually looks ill. "I was back in Michigan. I was a little girl," she says in a croaky voice.

Oh. "That's bad, right?"

"One of the women in our building was screaming, so I ran into her apartment." She stares glassy-eyed at the ceiling, takes a deep breath. "She was having a baby. I ran for the doctor and led him to the woman in labor, but the baby was stillborn." She pauses. "The doctor was disgusted. He handed it to me and told me to 'take care of it.'"

Wow. Grabbing her hands, I help her sit up. "Jesus, Betty, is that a memory or a dream? Did that really happen?"

She shrugs. "How should I know?" Her pallor is off—she's a ruddy gray. Dude begins making the rounds, talking quietly to small groups of students.

"Well, it's Active Imagination," I say. "So maybe you imagined it. Would that be better for you?"

She nods, looking into my eyes but thinking about something else. "What did *you* imagine?" she asks, her voice heavy and thick.

I think for a second. "I imagined that we were all lying on the floor." She nods again. "I'm not very good at this." She shakes her head. *God, she looks bad.* "Are you okay?" She looks like she's about to faint.

Dude walks over slowly and kneels down. "How did you guys do?" he asks.

Betty puts her face in her hands and rubs it, then tries to clear her eyes of the awful vision by opening and closing them a bunch of times. "I don't want to talk about it," she says.

"You shouldn't have made her lie on the floor, Dude," I tell him. "Look at her, she looks . . . blurry. She had a *dark* vision."

"That bad, huh?" he asks. "I'm sorry. But, you know, bad is good in Active Imagination. Bad is very good. I had a feeling your unconscious had some splainin' to do." He takes Betty's arm and helps her to her feet. As we sit back down at our desks, the last Deep Relaxation stragglers take their seats and Dude stands in front of the blackboard. "Good job, waking dreamers," he says gently. "A-pluses to all of you who managed to freak the hell out." He smiles at Betty.

I lean over and whisper in her ear. "That guy is *so* immature."

"Tell me about it," she says quietly, hunched over her desk.

"Can you still come to the show tonight?"

She looks very pale. "Wouldn't miss it for the world. . . ."

♋ shark

```
this afternoon
your back's not so straight
your eyes aren't too clear
```

The band is really flying tonight. No, not the band. The room and the crowd and the songs are flying; it's all become effortless. Something between everyone, crawling around in the rafters and across the floor like mad smoke, is making music happen. We're *all* just buzzed enough to feel each other's pain. Even the drunks get un-stupid tonight, wrapped up in the noise.

In fact, you can't really tell who's who out there. It's as if the junkies and the hippies and the painters and the psychos and the musicians and the knitters are all mixed up, have all become the same. So, it isn't us playing instruments that makes music happen; it's all those people caring about what's happening in this dank, dark room *right now*.

The song heat would be unbearable if it weren't so enthralling, like lying in the middle of the street in the middle of summer, enveloped in a calm danger. When heat like this soaks you to the bone, you become it, so it doesn't hurt.

It definitely makes you yell, but not in pain. I yell to drive the song into my head and everything else *out*. Which sends the band into a fury of intense playing. Which makes audience members yell along: a whole roomful of people, happily freaking out together.

Tonight, everybody yelling together is so *smart*—ugly beauty—that it becomes vividly clear that the song is the point and must be disappeared into. So I let myself be engulfed by evil and heat, let Doghouse tattoos glow, crawl down into wretchedness, past memories and muscles and guts, then down to bones 'til I'm nothing. And *that* you don't have to apologize for. No shame down there in nothingland, 'cause everyone's the same there— no me's, just us.

This is fun, of all things. I don't care if we *are* spinach, the Muses are the most happyfying spinach I ever had.

☽ solar dip

it was so easy to fly

I guess this is as close to meditation as I'll ever get—becoming nothing. That's meditation, right? I'm not lying on the floor, but I *am* nowhere.

As a chord rings out at the end of a song, I bend down to change the setting on a pedal and see Dude, Father McGuire and Betty standing in the back of the room. Dude catches my eye and grins. Betty waves, yells "Sparkle!" and laughs. She doesn't look pale anymore.

Beige Mark is in the front row, braving the spaz cases who congregate there. He shouts something at a huge thuggy-looking guy next to him, who laughs hysterically. I smile and he pulls me to him, shouts in my ear, "This is poetry!" I laugh and stand back up, ready to disappear again.

Maybe Betty's right, maybe this *is* falling in love. I didn't know what she meant. She meant: in love with the moment. We're all in love with this moment.

A junkie died last night. One of the painters finds me on Thayer Street putting up flyers for next week's shows and tells me, so we walk to the park together, afraid of what we'll find. He doesn't know which one it is—nobody knows their names.

Carrying my stack of posters, I brace myself; figure it'll be the funny one, the "husky boy" who took death on as both a mission and a joke. I watched him stick his head in the oven at a party and say, "So *how's* this s'posed to work?" Then he told me that if I made friends with junkies, I should prepare to be alone. I thought he was being melodramatic.

But when we get to the park, I see him; he's on the ground, sitting very, very still. It looks like they're all there except for the blond kid and the little girl who dyed my hair blue. As we approach, I see the blond kid lying down, his face covered in tears and snot. So it must be the girl. "Shit," I say. The painter won't look at me. This is so sad.

The blond kid was her boyfriend. He wails a silent scream that I think is gonna make me throw up. But you can't turn away—it isn't fair. That's why the funny junkie's sitting so still.

It was fascinating that she was alive. And it's boring that she's dead; it's dumb. And so fucking boring. Poor little thing was so sweet. "Blue is where it's at; don't let it fade." Sometimes a body just can't handle it, I guess.

The painter and I sit down with the others. It's a surreal funeral; people are playing Frisbee nearby. The only time anyone speaks, it's in response to whatever the blond kid wants to say.

"I killed her."

"No, you didn't."

But he did kill her.

"She was crying."

"She's numb now."

And this quiets him 'cause he doesn't hear how sad it is.

We play a game called "Coyote." We think we invented it,
but no one remembers having done so.

We all know the rules: the game must be played at dusk
and cars are to be avoided, since headlights can zap you
as they go by. The last coyote standing wins.

As darkness falls, so does each coyote. We tire and
collapse. The last to give up running around and hiding
in the bushes embraces a comfortable death alongside his
or her companions.

Eventually, the moon is out and we are all lying on the
ground, exhausted.

The first thing I see when I wake up is a snake, just out of the corner of my eye. When I reach for it, it disappears in a flash of shine.

I slept on Jeff the painter's floor last night. Soon after he took the Animal to the face, Jeff began filling his basement apartment with pets, and he doesn't believe in cages. Birds fly around the kitchen and perch on the counter eating crumbs, lizards scatter as you walk through the living room, hamsters live in the couch. I haven't really kept track of his pets 'cause it's hard to keep up. He buys a lot of them and they also die a lot, so I guess he isn't the best pet owner. Yesterday afternoon, I gently suggested to him that he either stop buying animals or stop killing them. "You know you have to *feed* pets or they don't live, right?"

Jeff's glasses make his face seem expressionless, but he still looked wounded. "I know that. I feed them."

"Not these, you didn't." I held up two dead lizards I found in the corner. Jeff reached out excitedly and grabbed them both, then carried them into his room. I followed in spite of myself. When I peeked in the door, he was squeezing glue onto their bellies. I don't know what I'd expected him to do with the lizards, but it hadn't involved glue. He pressed the lizards onto the painting in progress on his easel, stepped back to look at them, then jumped forward again to shift the lizard on the left up an inch. The poor lizards. They were still squishy.

"Stop that," I said. He paid no attention to me, just kept jumping backwards and forwards, shifting the lizards up and down. Clearly, I am one of the pussy musicians the painters make fun of. I leaned against the wall and sighed. "You know, that isn't gonna work."

He grinned at me. "Whaddya mean? It's great! Dead lizards!"

"I know it's dead lizards, but soon it won't be anything. They'll degrade and then eventually disappear." I waited. "And it's already gross. It's only gonna get grosser."

"Grosser's not a word," he murmured, staring at the canvas. "I guess it could be a photo essay . . ."

Yuck. "A little heavy-handed." He said nothing. "Did you buy those lizards just so you could have some dead ones?" But Jeff wasn't listening. He was digging around underneath the easel, tossing tubes of paint and rags all over the floor. Finally, he found what he was looking for: a small can. Opening the can with a screwdriver, he squinted at the canvas, then dipped a fat, fluffy brush into amber goo, which he then slathered all over the lizards' bodies. I sat down on his bed to watch. "Is that varnish? Are you shellacking those lizards?" He dipped the brush in and then ran it back and forth across the lizards' backs, over and over again—it was hypnotic. "Are you gonna shellac the birds when they die?"

"No." He was really enjoying his work. "It'd gum up the feathers. I'll dip 'em in acid first and then shellac their skeletons."

I laughed, then realized he was serious. "Geez, really? People'll get mad at you. People *like* animals."

"I shellacked a cat skeleton last year. Nobody cared."

"Bet they don't talk to you anymore, though." Jeff just kept brushing. *Christ.* I decided to leave him to it and go for a walk.

When you walk down any street on the east side of Providence, you get handed a fistful of pamphlets. Well-meaning—though copy machine–challenged—college students line the sidewalks to blab and thrust fuzzily printed booklets at you. Like many things in life, it's annoying and hilarious. For one thing, their causes just slay me. They can't seem to come up with anything you haven't heard a thousand times before:

"Save the what now? *Whales?* Why? What are whales for?"

"So . . . war's . . . *bad?*"

"Are you saying Republicans don't *like* me? Why not?"

I've found that if I take their pamphlets and appear to be listening to their spiels, they eventually run out of steam. Plus, the pamphlets make for entertaining reading back at Napoleon's.

This particular walk was interrupted by a kid on Angell Street with a tie and a cherry-red mohawk who stopped me to talk about "killing God." I was intrigued. Killing God is way better than saving whales. I definitely had not heard this a thousand times before.

And this guy was on *fire*. His mohawk twitching, he started right in. "Did you know that religious wars kill more people than political ones?" I didn't answer; I wanted him to hurry up and tell me how to kill God. "Well . . . they do. Historically, that is. And it's because we as a species have yet to rise above the church and take responsibility for our own actions." I waited. *Kill God, c'mon.* "For example, say you're a smack freak—"

"A smack freak?"

He looked down at me suspiciously. "A heroin addict," he said slowly. "You'd blame society for your problem." I nodded. "Which is understandable because you're hurting, but that's not taking responsibility for your own drug use."

"No, it isn't." I thought about this. "So . . . do heroin addicts . . . start religious wars?"

"We all start wars!" he yelled. I leaned back; spit was flying. "Throughout time, we humans have fought terrible wars against each other in the name of God!" He wasn't stopping to breathe. "If you take God out of the equation, we're all on the side of humans again!"

That sounded nice. Even so, I bet killing God is a hard sell compared to, like, fighting cystic fibrosis, which is what the girl on the opposite corner was selling. He'd probably had a hard day. I smiled. "That'd be great."

Finally, he took a breath and his shoulders dropped a little. "It would. Because no one is in charge but you." Pausing, he looked at me intently. "I bet if you were in the Holocaust, you'd blame Hitler, right?"

In the Holocaust? "If I were . . . you mean World War II? Hmmm. I never thought about it." He deemed this answer unacceptable by continuing to stare angrily. "Uh . . . I'm gonna say yes. I guess I'd blame Hitler for the Holocaust. If I was . . . in it."

"That's the problem," he sighed. "It's your Holocaust too, whether you're a victim or a perpetrator."

"It is?"

"Yes. When you hate Hitler, you hate everyone."

"I do?"

"Yes!" He grinned. He was enjoying himself now. I wondered if I was the first person who ever stopped to actually discuss killing God. I'm not sure what he said then because I was busy studying his face. He had thick, dark eyebrows and wicked cool crooked teeth. They looked like they were in backward. *I've always wanted teeth like that. My fourth-grade science teacher had backward teeth and she was beautiful.*

A mustache'd be good, too—the lady kind of mustache, just a little shadow on my upper lip. Or a big shadow on my upper lip, I don't care. I'd feel lucky to have any mustache. And a huge butt so I could sit anywhere as long as I wanted, and ride my bike forever. I hate my bony ass.

I need new hair, too; real is a dumb color for hair. Blue was good, but now that the junkie girl's dead, blue hair makes me sad. Can't say I like cherry-red much. This kid's hair makes your eyes jump around—it could cause seizures.

Crap, he's still going. Boy, do these guys like to hear themselves talk.

". . . say you were unemployed because you didn't graduate from high school. Most people wanna blame the government for unemployment. But it's *your* problem!" He pointed at me. "You can't blame the government; they aren't in charge, either."

"Can I blame God?"

He suddenly became agitated again. "There *is* no God!" he yelled.

Geez. "Oh. I'm sorry. I don't follow. Who do you want to kill?"

"Our perception of a God!" *Goddamn it, I knew it.* "I used to think there was a God, too, like a big father up in the sky. Then I realized it was my own father I saw in the sky. A fragile human being with problems of his own, just like yours." I took a second to picture Dude in the sky. "Nobody makes the rules and nobody's gonna take care of you. You have to kill that idea. Your way is your way, your path is yours to follow—you can't follow anyone else's." *Kill an idea of God. That is so boring.*

He was trying really hard, though, and I appreciated that; spiritual responsibility is a good cause. It's just that I was getting showered in spit. I decided to cut it short by taking his pamphlet. The guy looked sincerely grateful, took both my hands in his. "Read this and we can talk again to-morrow."

I took it but felt guilty, making a mental note not to walk down Angell Street tomorrow.

Every morning, I look for an angel in the kitchen.

I try to surprise it by tiptoeing in and suddenly
swinging open cabinet doors. I'm not sure what I'm
looking for, but know I'll recognize it when I see it.
Silvery glowing steam, maybe, or a tiny Christmas
ornament with a halo, hovering near the wheat germ.

One of the hippies sees her all the time, so she must
be there.

I figure I keep scaring her away or picking the wrong
cabinet, though, 'cause the angel never appears.

Jeff was in his kitchen talking to his jazz roommate when I came back. They were having a polite argument about how much the guy's jazz band sucks, it having already been established in their last argument that it *does* suck. We all know this 'cause they practice in the kitchen. "How's it going?" I interrupted.

Jeff looked over at me and his roommate took the opportunity to sneak away to his room. "How's what going?"

"Your lizards."

"They're dead."

"Mind if I take a peek?" I asked grimly.

"It depends. You have issues? You a vegetarian?"

"No, sir. I'm *into* animal murder."

"Then be my guest."

On the way to the bedroom, I tossed the mohawk guy's pamphlet on the counter, just missing a bird who was pecking at some crumbs. "Watch it," Jeff said, "or I'll have a new skeleton to shellac."

"You know, that's not even funny. You're seeming a little . . . mad scientist today. Maybe 'cause you live in a basement."

Jeff flipped through the pamphlet. "Garden-level apartment."

I peeked at the lizards, glued to the canvas in their varnish sarcophagi. It was pretty awful; they looked like giant scarab beetles. When I came back to the kitchen, Jeff was grinning, clearly enjoying Cherry-Red's mimeographed rant. "Who *is* this person?" he asked.

"Red mohawk," I answered. "On the corner of Angell and Thayer. Kinda hyper."

Jeff kept reading. "Wow. Was he fun?"

"At first. He had cool teeth. Then I felt bad for him. He actually raises an interesting point."

"That God should die?" he asked, laughing.

I shrugged. "Well, yeah."

"Hmmm. I thought he was *already* dead." He frowned, then pushed the pamphlet aside. "I found you a pool."

"You did?"

"The Brown University pool," he said. "I got you a student ID."

"Really? That's very nice of you. That makes you an enabler, you know."

"I know. But I want your name to be Kevin."

Had a feeling there'd be a catch. "It's a boy ID?"

"Wear a hat."

I played guitar like I always do before trying to go to sleep, but I just messed around, playing nothing. Nothing's good: no heat, no electricity, no noise or voices, just colors. It's comforting to play a fake song. This one was canary yellow and bright blue.

The only words floating around were Cherry-Red Mohawk's, so I wrote a dumb little song about smack freaks, unemployment and holo-causts. It was only a minute long 'cause I got bored, but it was funny.

♋ hate my way

i could hate god and blame dad

After a while, I put the guitar back in its case, grabbed a blanket and lay down on the floor to watch creatures skitter around under Jeff's bed.

I spend a sunny morning on a raft with a vague hippie
chick named Carol, poking my fingers into the water,
trying to catch water bugs, while Carol discusses various
life issues like feelings and trees. I'm just getting
drowsy when Carol suddenly jumps up and points toward the
riverbank, the raft tipping dangerously to one side.

"Kristin . . ." she says woozily. "Look at all the
ostriches with their heads stuck in the sand! There must
be six, seven, eight . . . nine . . ." she trails off,
still counting, as I scour the riverbank, desperate to
see something that isn't there.

I stand on tiptoe, squint, shield my eyes from the sun
and still I can't see any ostriches.

Maybe they're really small ostriches? Hiding?

I see the snake before I'm fully awake. By the time I sit up, it's gone. *You gotta be quick with a snake.*

Then I see it again out of the corner of my eye. Shooting my hand out, I reach for it. For a split second, I see something that looks like an X-ray of a snake, but all I feel is the cool wooden floor. I stare at my hand, flooded with adrenaline. *There is no snake.*

My mind races. What's the vocabulary for this? *Hallucination, a neuro-chemical imbalance, stress, sleep deprivation, repressed memory, a false impression, a fiction, Jung called waking dreams "visions," the motherfucker called dreams "wishes," careful what you wish for, we're permeable membranes, somebody slipped me something, concussion, brain damage, songs, paint fumes, toxicity, turpentine, shellacked lizards.*

Cherry-Red's song swells up in static, *but that's a fake song,* then fades.

Burning with shame, my skin flushed and prickly, I lower myself back down on the blanket.

Jeff's face appears over the edge of his bed, looks at me a minute too long. "Rough morning?" he asks.

I look back at him, feeling like I shouldn't move. "Sorta."

"If you got a buck fifty, I'll take you out to breakfast."

"Okay. Not the Town Chef, though," I answer carefully. I'm scared I'll throw up if I talk. "It's too smoky."

"Town Chef it is," he says, stretching.

"Asshole."

So glad I'm not alone right now.

♋ america

follow the road
swallow a snake
find shoes in the corner
run away

I watch my dog sleeping. The muscles in her face twitch and her feet paddle the air.

"She's chasing rabbits," Dude says.

I pat her head to try and calm her down. "Zoë's never chased a rabbit in her life."

"Right. So she chases them in her dreams."

I'm falling into a hole in my head—been tripping over my brain not working, a mess.

I wouldn't go back to the Doghouse, so it came and got me. Crawled through the sewer, lifted up a manhole cover and jumped me. One minute, it was beautiful: fast heaven. Then heaven took a dive and hell was waiting.

I knew that once you go to hell, you have to go back. I just didn't realize it was true.

♋ doghouse

i'm in a doghouse
leave me alone

The snake is a flashing light. I see an X-ray of its tail as it disappears underneath parked cars, behind trees and around the corners of buildings.

I'm falling so fast.

Falling *up*, on a high that's spun out of control. A wacky fucking tornado of heat, electricity and energy. Music follows me around, blasting my ears, its colors steaming into my brain one after another, mixing and swirling in a war of churning rainbows.

That goddamn witch. I was a kid on a bike; music only played when I wanted it to. Then she took her Chevy and jammed this lightning rod into my head and I can't get it out. Now music plays whenever *it* wants to.

The noise is brutal: songs crashing into each other, soaked in static. Separating one from the other is impossible. Chords layered over more chords, congested melodies and lyrics that've become a jumble of confused syllables. *I can't think*.

My hands fight back—they can't play all those parts at once. And I can't make sense of the words that're flung into me through the sick orgasm of color. I smash my hands over my ears and the music plays louder.

♋ mania

eyes is spirals

Cherry-Red Mohawk's song finished itself and it didn't turn out funny at all. It's only funny in a sick way, *macabre*. The fake part attached itself to a piece of Doghouse evil and took off, came back horrifying. All the songs are horrifying now—fractured, disjointed and harsh. About atomic theory and reincarnation, crashing cars, soap and ice, McDonald's murders, child abuse, slides and puzzles; it's sad to me how strange they are. The strangeness has a life of its own: unpredictable and out of control, impossible to measure because it won't sit still.

∞ hate my way

a boy was tangled in his bike forever
a girl was missing two fingers

Music's making me do things, live stories so I can write them into songs. It pushes my brain and my days around. A parasite that kills its host, it doesn't give a shit about what happens to a little rat girl as long as it gets some song bodies out of it. It's a hungry ghost, desperate for physicality.

I'm not writing songs anymore; they're writing *me*.

♋ close your eyes

i'm sliding really fast
my hands are full of snow

i don't understand
i don't understand puzzles

And every time a song is done, it whispers, *you can go now . . . you aren't needed anymore*.

Sound body, sound mind.

Every time I think I'm done, I pick another song out of the chaos in the air. The songs're keeping me alive so *they* can be alive.

Once you pick music out of the ether, once you discern its frequencies, you can't un-hear it. Maybe it alters your cellular structure, a cancer, I don't know.

I do know that the musical lightning rod sticking out of my skull is on fire.

♋ mania

electrify your head

Tendrils of industrial noise wind their way through the blast of songs: cracking, clanging, droning like broken bells in white noise. It creaks and moans and swishes. I've heard this before, but never like the wild phantom it's become.

When someone talks to me, it's through this din, which makes it even weirder to be around people than usual, so I avoid them. This new busted creature I've become is genuinely ugly, anyway; no one could ever like it. The creature is a body, certainly, and I live in it, but I don't think it's me.

I call it "me," call its parts my parts, like I'm steward of a broken ship, but I'm not the one animating it; I'm not in control. It sails along madly, cutting its own path regardless of wind direction.

♋ america

i'm losing my person

Hot muscles wrapped in buzzing skin tense of their own accord. They move and don't stop moving or they freeze in solid tension, gripping nothing. They can't find enough work to do to stay calm. My face is flushed in the mirror at the Y, my eyes bloodshot. I can't run away 'cause I'm not stuck anywhere but inside this hot-pink skin.

I was all about running away.

All I can do is try to beat this red, paper-thin body into submission, wear it out so it can't fight me.

♋ hot pink, distorted

it'll take much more than water
to fix my hot pink, distorted face

I don't even look like a nice girl anymore. I look like the songs sound because I *am* like the songs sound.

♋ diving

dive into ice water

Cold water is a punishment now. I hate it. My hair is yellow dreads from the continuous dunking in chlorine and salt water—and swimming doesn't even *work* anymore. I cut furiously through the water for hours, grimly aware that burning energy will still keep me awake into the night.

♋ ellen west

i'm awake with a vengeance

I can't sit still long enough to write in this diary for more than a few minutes.

I should never have researched music, should never have dissected it to learn its secrets. Bad chemicals, poorly mixed, blowing up in my face—music's a Pandora's Box of nightmares, and I'm too shrimpy to close the lid or fight the monsters that crawled out of it.

♋ pandora's box

inside that pandora's box
was a can of worms

I know most people haven't noticed songs banging around in the air, but clearly, songs do bang around in the air; I've heard them. If I could measure and publish my findings, then other people could participate in this discovery and I wouldn't seem so antisocial.

So I sit under Fish Jesus, making endless copies of the Muses' demos and stuffing them into manila envelopes along with our press kit. My hands are fast, busy, driven.

I made the other Muses hear what I hear. Now we can make everyone else hear it.

I mail the demos and press kits to record companies, radio stations and journalists. I know it won't work, but I do it anyway.

⚘ styrofoam rattlebox

if i could grab the man on the street
with my raspy rataplan

my only personal property:
a raspy, whispered plan

Today, while I worked, a bee flew in Napoleon's window and circled around me. Then another bee. I closed my eyes and saw them joined by hundreds more, swarming around me in double helix formation. When I opened my eyes, the hundreds of bees were there for a second, then transparent, then they disappeared. *My imagination isn't imaginary anymore.*

They weren't realistic bees; they looked fake, like little robots. As if someone had created tiny, metal bees and injected them into my retinas. I watched the bees fade and then stared at the empty space in the air where they had been. When I shut my eyes, I could see them again.

There used to be people here at Napoleon's. Where did everybody go?

♋ call me

something's gone
something's over

I walk. Often, all night long. Out of the light, out of the sun. The days are hot and too vivid, but the nights are gentle.

♋ `walking in the dark`

`you own a question`
`it's a body`

The snake is here. Sometimes I see it out of the corner of my eye, but I don't reach for it. Then an X-ray of the snake fades to static and disappears.

♋ winter

'cause shadows haunt you
in your headlights

I abandoned my beloved Silver Bullet by the side of the road one night
because I thought I hit a dog. I mean a wolf. It was not something anyone
else would have seen. So I pulled over, cut the engine, left the keys in the
car. I don't drive anymore.

I'm uncertain as to what world this is, where you might see something . . . pretend? magic? invisible? And so I'm uncertain as to who might live in this world. Not Betty, not Mark, not the Muses. Not me—that person is over. I'm not in here anymore.

The only thing left in this body is shame. And the only shred of self-preservation I have left is this thought: "Please, no *more* shame."

So I keep my distance from everyone. *Stay cold and they won't feel the heat.* I don't go to school, book shows or schedule rehearsals. I don't see anyone except the people I walk past on the street.

I don't belong on this planet. I'm not good enough.

♋ colder

i'm losing my friends
and my young dreams

The snake and the wolf are merely glimpses, so I can't stare them down. I see a flash of light and I know what it means.

It's like Coyote, the game we used to play when we were kids. Light zaps you.

♋ flood

flood my eyes with light

I can feel the wolf growing dirty and sick, gaunt and broken. At night, her eyes glow.

My music paraphernalia is scattered around this room: picks and strings, cords, bios, guitars, demos, pedals, posters, wire cutters, press, screwdrivers, tuners, notebooks, string-winders—it used to mean something. All of it was infused with potential.

Now it means nothing. It's garbage.

I'm finally numb. *That's something, anyway.* I achieved the junkies' goal all on my own and it didn't cost me a dime. Just one more step in this direction and I'll have achieved oblivion.

☞ fuchsia wall

an offer:
oblivion
forever

I hear the music around me, but I don't listen to it. It's indistinguishable from the white noise anyway, doesn't even bother to scream anymore; it just moans and swishes, playing to no one.

Music hasn't noticed that I'm not listening, or else it doesn't care. The songs play on, erratically, torn sails on a lost ship. *If they're outside of me, they'll fly away, but if the songs are inside of me, they're trapped.*

I take a razor blade out of Napoleon's medicine cabinet, sit down on the floor and cut the songs out of me.

♋ cathedral heat

sick as a dog
shaking like a leaf

you have to look close
to see what this disease has done to me

Carefully, I lift the barbed wire away from the barbed
wire directly below it and squeeze my head in between,
facing away from the barbs. The sharp metal scratches my
face anyway; my hair catches and tangles in it. I wanna
be in the open field just beyond, though, so I wipe the
blood off my face and let the barbs pull a chunk out of
my hair.

Twisting, I can see our little green house behind me, but
I can't go home—not with a beautiful empty field just
beyond. I have to be alone so I can run.

When my head is through, I bend over and squeeze my other
body parts through, one at a time. My jeans catch, so I
free them by tearing a hole in them, then I'm in.

I'm alone. I can run, I think, straightening up and
looking around.

Six cows are lined up in front of me, staring at me
in silence.

"Imagine that you're being reborn. Birth is a painful process, but a positive one."

♋ vitamins v

```
this lukewarm catastrophe
is a recipe for rebirth
or so i overheard
```

Mental health professionals all speak the same language and convey the same message in their conversation. This is the gist of their message:

"Sometimes chemicals go all haywire and send confused signals. This isn't your fault; it's just twisted chemistry. And maybe some hurt feelings."

This is a good message. A well-thought-out argument and a loving one. The mental health professionals are soothers who come and go, their faces indistinguishable from one another, their conversations melting into each other . . . but they're always saying something like that. It's really nice of them.

"Do you have racing thoughts?"

I try to think about my thoughts. "Sometimes and sort of. I mean, they might race. Maybe I can't tell because I race alongside them."

"Are your thoughts jumbled?"

Again, I try to think about thinking. "They *were*. The first time I saw the snake." I try to remember that while simultaneously trying not to remember that.

"Snake?"

While I never even gave these buildings a second thought, just walked by them over and over again, these people were cooped up inside, under fluorescent lights, helping other people stay here. My god. What a mission.

So I can't help but try and rise to the occasion of the soothers' impressive energy and investment—I keep telling the truth. Which is humiliating. "The *songs* were definitely jumbled," I offer. "They raced by and I couldn't keep up."

"Songs?"

♋ same sun

i can't lie
some bitch gets through
and tells the truth

But the funny thing is, the thing I can't say is: I *did* bleed out the noise.

It worked.

For a while, I was schizophrenic. The woman who first told me this looked terrified as she spoke. I felt for her, but the full-throttle numb I had going on kept me from caring very much; "schizophrenia" just sounded like a word.

Later, my sentence was reduced to manic depression. *Huh*, I thought.

"But it's not called that anymore," she said.

Huh.

"You couldn't be still?"

I think. "I *could* be still, but I wanted to run away."

"From what?"

"I don't know. I wanted to escape my own skin."

"Snakes shed their skin."

"Yeah."

So I'm not me anymore; I'm *bipolar*. No matter how okay I feel right now, I'm *not* okay and I never will be. Apparently. Which means I gotta take drugs, just like hippies and junkies and Betty.

If they say so. They're awfully nice.

A soother tells me that numb happens. That when stress becomes too great, a manic-depressive will shut down. "You shut down," he says sympathetically.

Huh.

It's difficult to know what to do for comfort when you can't handle comfortable, or who to turn to for help when you're shy. *Why do you all care so much? You don't even know me.* These people seem almost aggressive in their desire to help.

This may be the real medicine they offer and it's powerful. I watch them administer both their drugs and their kindness and the kindness seems just as effective to me, if not more so. Chemicals in the form of medication are interesting, ham-fisted tools, but humans themselves engage in myriad processes we haven't yet measured. We really are a deeply social species.

"This music you heard—"

"I heard noise that *thought* it was music."

"When you heard this noise in your head—"

"It wasn't in my head."

I listen carefully and try to learn the soothers' ludicrous vocabulary. "Drug cocktail" is the best—who needs euphemisms?

According to them, it wasn't the Doghouse that did this to me, it was actually my fault ("which isn't your fault"). Same with the witch. She was some old lady who happened to run me over; nobody cast a music spell on me. So songs're my fault, too.

I guess. Maybe none of 'em have ever seen a witch before, so they don't know what one looks like.

"Are you sure you've never been depressed? Maybe you thought you were just sad."

"I've been sad. Is that depressed?"

Get this: I coulda been happy in hell. The soothers tell me that most manic-depressives *enjoy* their time in Up Land. *My god.* The fact that I had a problem with it indicates to them that I may have been both manic and depressed at the same time. Something that really shoulda worked itself out, if you ask me. Either that or I was just so sped up that I spiraled out into oblivion.

I thought manic depression was a mood disorder—people who got real happy and real sad. Turns out you get real *fast* and real *slow*, and how that manifests is determined by your frame of mind. A fast brain fills in blanks in your visual field, makes stuff up at you. A slow one can't even cope with what's already here.

But they can both make you want to die.

They also say it didn't happen suddenly.

"Are you sure?" I asked them. I went to sleep on Jeff's floor and then woke up broken. That's pretty sudden. But *they* say I've spent the last couple years living with symptoms like . . . well, like my entire personality. I might not even be a spazzy guy. According to them, hyper is a symptom and it goes away. "So you get better? 'Cause I *feel* better."

"You'll feel better, but you won't *get* better. If you don't take medication, you'll experience further episodes and you may not live through the next one. Manic depression is deadly—one in five manic-depressives commits suicide. And like an alcoholic is always an alcoholic, you will always be manic-depressive. But it's not called that anymore."

Okay . . . but high and low, fast and slow? How is that not life? This planet gets very high and very low; it moves so fast sometimes and then so slowly. Sometimes it resonates intensely, sometimes it's all so strange, it leaves us in the dust. How could it ever be appropriate to feel less than too much?

I guess you just have to learn to deal. You gotta keep secrets, keep functioning. Gotta keep showing up.

"You could be heading into a depression right now. Depressions often come on the heels of manic episodes. Do you feel sad?"

"I feel nothing."

"Well, that's close."

The soothers feel very strongly that suicidal people are sad. I understand this point of view, but I still think, *well, not necessarily.* Couldn't we just be finding solutions to our own personal equations? Writing the end of our stories?

Night swimming is mania, wanting to learn everything and live everywhere is mania, feeling warm all the time (*the poor band must've been so cold*), hearing songs, restlessness (my inability to lie on a floor or sit in a chair), a disregard for the future, seeing things that aren't there, insomnia, racing out into storms, needing to fuzzify the world in order to focus, the Doghouse episode, hating buildings, ranting all night about how bad bad radio is (*the poor band must've been so tired*), thinking I have a calling, that I'm on a mission . . . these are all symptoms of a long-term manic state. How embarrassing. So what's left? What's "me"? Anything?

I'm gonna find out by doing these drugs. That's probably funny, but I don't feel like laughing right now.

"Drug cocktail" actually means "no easy answer." No one knows quite what to do about brains and chemistry, so they try all sorts of recipes and weigh benefits against side effects, trying to get the combination and dosage right in order to prevent the next "episode." This takes a lot of time and a lot of soothers and a lot of blood tests and a lot of appointments and a lot of bus rides 'cause the Bullet is gone.

No drug is a cure, though. Drugs are just big pieces of tape they stick over warning lights.

I wonder if the junkies know drugs are pieces of tape.

☺ civil disobedience

here's a big fat aspirin
maybe you'll choke

that's not funny

It's a little frustrating, 'cause I feel like I *found* a cure: you just bleed a whole lot. You can bleed out noise, heat, visions and speed. This is frowned upon by the medical professionals, however. They say cutting yourself open is a symptom, not a cure.

And also, it can make you die. They're pretty upset about me trying to die. Soothers're *really* big on staying alive.

Which is weird, 'cause every one of their drugs wrecks your body in order to save your brain. *I guess if I have to choose one over the other.*

Did you ever see *"The Brain That Wouldn't Die"*? This is like being a severed head in a metal tray, trying to make friends with a monster who could go apeshit at any minute. I gotta be a cold brain, talking patiently to a monster body. And I can't die.

"Do you have trouble sleeping?"
   "I have trouble sleeping. And breathing."
   "Breathing is important."
   "Yeah."

It sounds to me like manic depression is . . . soul sickness. Like sometimes your soul is too big to fit inside you and too magic to follow earth's rules. *Clairvoyance* is a symptom of mania, for example. How do they explain *that*?

   And then sometimes your soul is too small to find. Too small to fill your sad little outline.

"St. Francis was bipolar."
   How do they know that? "St. Francis of the Sissies? Alright . . . he was great."
   "And Abraham Lincoln."
   "Wow . . . cool."
   "Vincent van Gogh, Dostoyevsky."
   "Geez, what a list."
   "You're in good company, anyway."

Soothers see their patients as suffering from exposure, standing out in the pouring rain with no protection, so they rush outside with drug umbrellas to try and protect them from the elements as best they can. Then everybody waits for "therapeutic levels" to kick in. When they do, the soothers say it'll be wonderful—better than ever before. "Therapeutic levels" is like the chorus to the mental health professionals' soothing song. They all sing a different verse, and then chime in on the "therapeutic levels" chorus.

I listen 'cause I want to trust these caring people, but I can't sing along until I understand what's going on. My head's still sitting on a metal tray, trying to imagine what it'd be like to care enough to make friends with a monster.

♋ mania

i need an umbrella
if i'm gonna stand in the rain

All I do now is ride buses to and from Napoleon's, keeping appointments, bloated with medication, the snake bag on my lap. The snake bag was my idea. It gives me an in-between, a tiny little bit of control. It's a homemade-looking hippie bag I bought at St. Paul's thrift store so that I'd always know where the snake was: in this bag where I can deal with it. It's allowed to exist, so long as it doesn't jump out and *surprise* me anymore. The noise is gone, and the speed, but I feel like the snake could show up at any minute and start the whole thing all over again.

The soothers don't think the bag is helping me get better—believing in "magic" is another symptom of mania—but so far, they haven't come up with an antisnake pill, so I thought I'd take matters into my own hands.

It's definitely superstitious sacrifice to carry the bag around, but I believe in the snake and the soothers don't. I almost tried "just because you can't see it doesn't mean it isn't there," but stopped myself. They've probably heard that before.

I know the wolf is there, too, even though I can't see her. She just *is*— it's hard to explain. And the songs are there whether I hear them or not. And the bees. I believe in them.

Anyway, lots of people carry bags. This one just happens to have an invisible snake in it.

And it keeps me from losing. You can't say I'm winning, either, but I *am* trying to stay here, and that feels like flexing muscles I haven't used in a while.

On the bus, as the sun and shadows flit across the backs of seats, I stare out the window at a world that looks pretend—a human habitat version of reality.

Oddly, the buses I ride are full of people who seem much more likely to see robot bees than me. They look incapable of flexing trying-to-stay-here muscles. I mean they're seriously nuts. I know what normal looks like; I've been looking at it my whole life. Normal's on TV, for christ sake. I know how to imitate it. How do these people forget to act normal? And when did they stop keeping secrets? They're not even *trying* to deal. Do they feel no shame? If so, I envy them.

♋ listerine

```
i couldn't wait to come down
there's nothing here but the ground
```

The soothers said I was being reborn. But really, I'm still here.

I sit on the examination table watching the doctor's
eyebrows. They look like hair tubes, or little animals
crawling across his face. These are really spectacular
eyebrows, sticking way out from his forehead . . .
mesmerizing.

The doctor jokes nonstop and I get none of the jokes.

"I'm a bear," he growls. "Open your mouth!"

*He's not a bear. Why does he think he's a bear? Maybe
'cause of his eyebrows. Why would a bear want me to open
my mouth anyway?*

I open my mouth.

"This is a tongue depressor!" he announces, holding up a
tongue depressor. "My goodness, you're a lousy tongue!"
he makes it say to my tongue. "I'm so disappointed in
you!" Then he asks, "Is your tongue depressed yet?"

What's his problem? He's disappointed in my tongue?

Crane, sitting in the corner of the room with a magazine
on her lap, chuckles. "Just laugh, Kristin. You can
pretend to be normal."

On the bus, I sit with shavedy-headed, tattooed punk-rock girls in kilts and black boots, their backpacks full of comics and chocolate, but also old ladies, lonely and chatty, sometimes a little batty. I keep my snake bag on my lap and listen to my seatmates talk. The shavedy-headed girls are comforting; they come from the world of sweet goth knitters who hang in the back of clubs. But the old ladies I *love* 'cause they remind me of Betty. I'm sure that if I had any feelings, one of 'em would be Missing Betty, but I'm not ready to let her see me yet.

I'm in limbo, straddling the strange and the mundane. I *do* wanna live here, with these great old ladies who never seem bored. I wanna be like them. They have enough time in their day to look around and be impressed or disgusted. They think something about everything. And these women can *talk*.

"I had *four* husbands. *Four!* All named either Carl or John. That's my type, I guess. Some women like tall, dark and handsomes, I like Carls and Johns! Carl was a real piece o' work, though. What an asshole!" She whaps me on the thigh, laughing, and I laugh with her. "Honey, you think you know what's goin' on, you don't! You don't *ever* know what's goin' on!" She's beautiful. She laughs again—hoots, her jet-black curls quivering. "We had the prettiest flower garden, though. We lived on Broadway; you know where that is?"

"Yeah," I point out the bus window. "Right there."

"Mm-hm!" She looks grave. "Nobody on Broadway has a garden, but we did. I grew daisies and black-eyed Susans. People don't like daisies—Carl didn't care for them, but I grew 'em anyway 'cause I *do* like 'em. And they grow. I tried roses and tulips and they died."

"Dandelions grow pretty well," I say as we drive past a bright yellow yard full of them.

"Yes, they do. So they call 'em weeds!" She admires the dandelions going by. "Those pretty yellow flowers! It's a shame." She shakes her head.

"At least they don't know they're weeds. They don't speak English."

"No, dandelions *don't* speak English." She stares out the window and then says matter-of-factly, "That house burned down. The whole thing. At night. I got the kids out of bed and we all watched. It was cold outside, too. The neighbors woke up and made coffee and brought us some blankets to wear. Stuff was explodin' inside, and people would scream every time stuff exploded.

"Then the newspaper came and took a picture and the police and firefighters were all there. It was burning in the paper the next day, but in real life? It was covered in ice!"

How awful. "Wow. I'm sorry."

"Mm-hm. The cat ran away from the fire and didn't come back, but the refrigerator didn't burn."

"I'm ninety-five! Ninety-five years old!" a woman yells at me, her textured face cracking open in an enormous smile as she takes her seat.

Wow. "Well . . . that's a lot!"

"It's a lot of years," she agrees, her dark eyes shining. "Ninety-five today!" she exclaims.

"Happy birthday."

"Thank you." Smiling sweetly, she turns to the other passengers. "I'm ninety-five!" she announces to the bus at large, and then says it again to each new person who boards the bus. She repeats "I'm ninety-five!" every couple of minutes for the entire bus ride, shaking her head like she can't get over it.

Everyone on the bus is grinning; no one looks annoyed. I wonder if she did the same thing when she turned ninety-four or if it's just the round number that impressed her when she woke up this morning.

Each passenger waves and calls "Happy birthday!" to her as they step off the bus. So do I as we pull up to my stop and I stand to leave. Then she looks up at me, glowing, swelling with pride, and grabs me by the arm. "Once, I was a little girl," she breathes. "It's miraculous. A miraculous miracle."

♋ walking in the dark

i could glow
i could glow and swell

i could, well, grow

I want old ladies to look the way they do on *The Andy Griffith Show*: change purses and cotton dresses, straw hats with netting, my clunky black shoes. Adorable and creepily religious. They really don't, though. They can be adorable and creepily religious, but *I* dress like an old lady—*they* wear polyester. Polyester space suits sometimes, lots of gold and silver. And baseball caps, with running shoes on their feet.

It must be because clothes fall apart now. Old people on *Andy Griffith* dressed the way they always did because they still *had* those clothes—they were made to last. But our old people don't dress the way they did when they were young 'cause by then, planned obsolescence had kicked in. So they're forced to buy *new* clothes and they put them together weird. Lots of "sport wear" and "active gear," when all they're gonna do is sit. It's incongruous.

Mayberry dresses were *made* for sitting. Sitting on the front porch shelling peas, sitting in church praying for sinners, sitting on the bus talking shit.

A tiny old woman's tearful eyes flit nervously from passenger to passenger as we drive away from her stop. She wears a baseball cap over her pixie haircut and enormous baubles on her ears. I offer her the seat next to me, which she stares at suspiciously, then, with the motion of the bus, falls into against her will. Smiling weakly, she is attempting to settle herself and her purse when an involuntary noise from a man with Tourette's sitting in the back of the bus makes her jump spasmodically. She thumps back down on the seat, panting, hand on her heart. When the man makes another sound, she flinches, squeezing her eyes shut, and covers her mouth with her hand.

It does sound like the Three Stooges are sitting back there, but the other people on the bus are used to it. This lady looks like she couldn't get used to *anything*. As the bus moves along, she continues to twitch and jump with each sound the Tourettic man makes, over and over again, then looks at me, exhausted. "The Lord smiles on him," she says gravely.

"That's good," I reply, " 'cause the bus driver doesn't." Each time the poor man makes a sound, the driver looks at him accusingly in the rearview mirror.

"He sinned and the Lord made him sick," explains the woman. *And then smiled at him? What a messed-up god.* When someone behind us sneezes, she squeals, then drops her face into her hands.

"Are you okay?" I ask her.

"No," she says, her voice shaking.

"What's wrong?"

"I have to go shopping." Her eyes are red and swollen.

"Oh." *I know how she feels.* "That's too bad."

"Yes, it is," she nods. "You see, I never, ever leave the house."

"Never?"

"Nope," she answers defiantly, shaking her head, lips pursed. "Never have, never will."

"Oh." *Interesting.* "Not even to . . . take a bus somewhere?"

She continues shaking her head emphatically. "I won't do it and nobody can make me."

I shake my head along with her. "Why not?"

"Well," she looks around the bus like she has a secret, then leans in close to me and whispers, "*Look what they did to Jesus!*"

℞ gazebo tree

bless my baby eyes
don't you know jesus died?
i'm better off inside

One old lady *dies* on the bus. She isn't sitting next to me, but I can see her across the aisle. I watch her finish a bottle of something and go to sleep. When we get to the bus station, there is an ambulance waiting for her, but she's already dead.

The bus driver looks sad; the other passengers, alarmed.

"Canary in a coal mine . . ." says one.

℞ hook in her head

i saw this lady close her eyes
the bottle slipped between her fingers
and slid along the aisle

I sit on my grandparents' porch in the dappled
Chattanooga sunshine and play records I found in their
attic: *Sing-along Folk Songs for Children*.

Pressing thick plastic disks of bright red and milky blue
over the spindle on my little portable record player, I
listen to people who're probably dead now sing
scratchily:

"Hi-ho, the dairy-o" . . . "A kid'll eat ivy, too" . . .
"Pop goes the weasel" . . . "The cheese stands alone!"

I'm stunned. *This is the music regular kids listen to?*

It's insane.

I'm still.

Not "outer peace," not pretend-still-ready-to-explode, but soft, planted. "Therapeutic levels" are not the happy ending the soothers implied, though. This state of being is more like a failure of some kind—a failure to thrive. I'm pressed down and ill and that makes me "calm."

The pills make my hands shake so bad I can't play guitar, they give me crashing headaches and zits, they make me throw up and pee blood. I'm a different shape now: swollen, and I can smell the toxic compounds on my skin—but I'm here. You're supposed to stay here, right? And play by the rules? That's the polite thing to do. And I imagine I'm not alone in this. There must be thousands of us, sorta messed up, trying to be like other people instead of how we are.

♋ vena cava

we come
gray and hopeful

Really, I take the pills because if I disappear, then the band won't get to live in a van and play every night.

The white-noise bells still play sometimes, but I hardly notice them. They keep me occupied while I stare out the bus window, these tones and wind chimes, whistling and waves, that sometimes fold themselves into innocuous melodies. That's music now: an interplay of gentle noises, still wholly other than me, but now it's vague, dreamy. Like it was before the Doghouse: floaty angels. Not real pressing or vivid or evil. Arrangements are easy to hear and understand; they're stretched out and subtle rather than racing by. Syllables slip past unobtrusively. Sometimes I feel like memorizing this gentle music, sometimes I let it float away.

Pills can't make it stop altogether; that's sort of encouraging—*a miraculous miracle.* I listen because I no longer need to smash my hands over my ears when it plays.

I'm still too numb to care about much, but the drug cocktail type of numb is kind. Pills pat your hand and let things be as they are, just like the soothing mental health professionals who prescribed them for me. No cure, just Band-Aids. And acceptance.

They should call these magic beans "shame reducers."

But then, I guess, everybody'd take 'em.

♋ candyland

```
don't look for shame
you're better off without it
```

Standing at a pay phone in the pale yellow light of a summer evening, I call each band member, one by one, just to hear their voices. It's medicine, listening to them talk on the other end of a pay phone—everything they say is sweetness washing over me.

I need it. This has been a bitter month.

⚛ silver sun

only sweetness
that's all
to shake off the bitter

And it sounds like my bandmates've been talking to each other in my absence, 'cause they all say the same thing: they tell me they wanna quit school and focus on Throwing Muses. *They must've thought I disappeared 'cause I was losing interest.* "I'm cool with that," I say. "I don't have a lot going on right now."

When I hang up after the third phone call, I stand, staring at the phone, wondering what "focus on Throwing Muses" means exactly. So I start all over again, calling each band member in turn.

"People're always telling us we're wasting time in Providence," explains Tea. This is true, people do tell us that; I never knew what it meant. But by the end of six phone calls, we're moving to Boston, where, apparently, no one wastes time.

We'll go apartment hunting together and I'll call whatever we rent "home." *I can handle that,* I think. *I'm still now.* Turns out there's just a fine line between belonging everywhere and belonging nowhere anyway.

I used to see my bandmates as my allies in evil, the best devil's angels our religion could create. Now they seem to clear the air, make everything clean and good—*regular angels*, forgiving me for the blast of heat I injected into our lives and our sound. 'Cause there's no devil's breath in *those* lungs: Tea, Dave and Leslie smite the disease right out of religious disease and leave only religion. Their energy is forward movement, not downward spiraling.

I watch my shaking hand hang up the phone. *Oh, yeah. Lithium tremors. I can't play guitar anymore.*

Sitting on Jeff's floor, I run painstakingly through Throwing Muses songs, one after the other, begging my twitchy hands to straighten up and fly right. I've been avoiding the guitar because of its creepy powers and I *don't* wanna ask for trouble; I just gotta know I can still play, for the band's sake. When I took the guitar out of its case, I promised myself that the minute I felt charged or evil, I would put it down and walk away.

Turns out I was flattering myself, though, 'cause evil wants nothing to do with this screwed up monster body. My hands shudder and fumble their way through mild approximations of the songs, sticking to the strings, then slipping off the strings, muting ringing tones and then letting ugly notes ring when they should've been muted.

Syncopated rhythms are particularly embarrassing; they just sound like stuttering fragments. They trip, slip and fall. Eventually, I put the guitar back in its case, wondering why the devil hast forsaken me and how I feel about that. "*Goddamn it*," I mutter.

Jeff is sitting on his bed, reading and eating pastry out of a box. The lizards are frozen forever on their canvas casket above his head. No one ever bought that particular painting. "Done?" he asks.

"Nope. Finished." I lean back on the guitar case.

"That all sounded funny," he says helpfully. "Maybe you do too many drugs."

I sigh and talk to the lizards instead of him—it's hard not to look at them. "Yes," I answer. "Yes, I do."

Jeff nods, chewing. "Want some?" he asks, holding out the pastry box.

I shake my head, still staring at the lizards. "I have to learn to play guitar and do drugs at the same time."

"It can't be *that* hard," he says, finishing the pastry and closing the box. "Some of the dumbest guys I know do it."

My brother and I sit in the backyard, trying to build hay bales out of grass clippings, mimicking the real hay bales we see beyond the barbed-wire fence at the edge of our yard.

It's frustrating. The hay bales themselves are perfect: tawny, bristly boxes stacked in pyramids. Our grass bales are all different shapes, none of them nice. They look like something a cow spat out.

"Make your fingers work," my brother says accusingly. "Then make *my* fingers work."

The summer people out the window are glistening. Cars shine, even the sidewalk shimmers. This bus is taking me to Betty's house, or thereabout. Wherever I feel like hopping off, I can find my way to Betty. 'Cause I know the island by heart, but also 'cause it's not a very big place. As long as I'm willing to melt on the shining sidewalk with the tourists—it's hot out there. I'm glad I'm not Burning Me anymore; I'd be catatonic in this heat.

Betty has a party every Fourth of July and I figure this is a good opportunity to deliver what she might see as bad news. Throwing Muses moving to Boston will not make her happy, but at parties, Betty's surrounded by admirers and in sparkle mode, so it shouldn't make her too *un*happy. It's foreign to me, this desire to have a bunch of fawning party guests hover around you, but that kind of loving attention is something she seems to crave. Probably Hollywood asserting itself again. Betty loves to adore and be adored.

I haven't seen her in such a long time. I'm a bloated, vague, shaky me, with zits and a goddamn snake bag, but I gotta see her; I miss her. I'm lonely without her. And loneliness, I'm thinking, may be a sad little first step toward recovery.

♋ summer street

one lonesome body
one lonesome song

no lonesome body
no lonesome song

Betty lives in whiteness. Her walls are white, her sofa's white and her carpet's white. Betty's *hair* is white tonight. And the flowers she's spread everywhere. It's a blinding lifestyle that she lives. She says it's "calming." I think it looks like a dentist's office.

The front door is open, so I step inside. When Betty sees me from across the room, she wells up, walks slowly toward me and envelops me in a long, tight hug. *Does she greet all her guests this way?* She says nothing, just steps back to look at me, holding my hand, then walks into the kitchen, wiping her eyes. Betty is so Betty.

She often does a slow degrade at parties: sparkles and then collapses. It'd be nice if the party-guest love drug would keep her blood flowing with self-esteem long enough for her to feel happy forever, but I know she'll be crawling her way back up to okay tomorrow, praying for fans to hide from.

I have to wait out the initial blast of Entertaining Betty and then grab her for a conversation before Collapsing Betty kicks in. Sitting on one of her white couches, holding my bag, I watch her flit from guest to guest, laughing, hugging. When I notice her moving from stage two (flirtatious) to stage three (humming), I know I have to grab her before she starts singing, because the songs she sings will trigger memories and those memories will trigger collapse. Quickly, I take her aside and tell her I'm moving to Boston with the band, that she'll have to do school alone next year. She covers her mouth with her hand, looking horrified: horror-movie horrified. She stares at me like I'm the Blob. "But sweetheart!" she cries. "Oh no, you can't!"

I'm alarmed. "It'll be alright," I say gently. "Father McGuire'll buy your coffee." Tears pour down her cheeks. *How does she do that?* "Oh no!" she gasps.

I'm not sure she ever did quit drinking. She sure seems drunk; I hadn't planned on her making a scene. Nervously, I glance around the room. People with cocktails in their hands glare at me suspiciously, like I'm hurting their queen.

Maybe she isn't making a scene so much as doing one—it's hard to tell with her. I don't think she's lying when she's acting; she just sort of becomes what she thinks she should be—in this case, heartbroken, mortified. She must have an internal director that hands her a motivation and she just runs with it. I'm sure it feels like feeling to her; it just *looks* a little bigger than you see in most people.

"Look, I'm not trying to bum you out." I have my spin ready. I try to appear grave as I tell her, "The band is doing *so* well, we feel like we're wasting time here, you know? I have to . . . plan for my future or I won't have one." *She'll never buy it.*

Betty breathes deeply and dabs at her cheeks with a cocktail napkin. "Oh, I know." She sighs and smiles a sweet little smile. "And you thought you were gonna live in a van!" she says mischievously. I say nothing.

Suddenly, she lunges for me. I clutch my snake bag to my chest as she grabs me in a murderous bear hug—*god, she's strong*—and doesn't let go for a long time. In fact, she moves me around the room by the neck, introducing me to confused party guests. "Krissy's my little girl and she's moving to New York! She sings!" Betty kisses my cheek and starts crying again.

"Boston," I say in a strangled whisper.

"Careful what you say around her," she warbles. "She'll write a song about you!"

"No, I won't." She drags me to the next group of people.

"I knew this would happen! I'm so proud!" she dances with me, then wells up again. *God, she's just a big, sweet psycho.* "Broadway, Krissy! I'll visit you. I'll take the train in the snow and we'll go out to dinner. I can watch your rehearsals, make sure you remember to *string 'em along*!"

I hope she doesn't take any train to New York without calling me first, but I'm not sure she'll remember any of this on the fifth of July. *I'll send her a postcard from Boston. She'll figure it out.*

The fireworks are wicked, lighting up clouds and making the night look even blacker than it really is. Betty's white living room frames the explosions cinematically, color splashing on the walls and furniture, then fading. I decide to sneak out during the finale to avoid any more weepy hoopla. The lights are out and the party guests are all staring at the sky; it seems like a good time to leave.

On the front porch, though, I look over my shoulder and see Betty following me to the door. "Krissy?"

I smile. "Hello, psycho."

"Hush," she says over the crackling, popping fireworks. "I wanna talk to you."

"Okay." She doesn't seem drunk anymore, just soft. Maybe it wasn't alcohol in her bloodstream, but good old-fashioned sparkling. Betty does like her parties.

The finale ends and the guests cheer. Suddenly, all softness leaves Betty's face. "Don't disappear," she says as people yell and clap.

"I have to go. I promised the band."

"That's not what I mean." She looks mad—the porch light illuminates half of her angry face. "Don't use a strange city as an excuse to disappear inside yourself. Don't spiral down into that hole again: that hole is a grave. You know what I'm talking about." I do know what she's talking about, but I'm surprised *she* knows what she's talking about. "Don't leave people alone. It's unkind. Don't do that to me again."

What? "Unkind?" I say defensively. "I had no choice. I didn't do it *to* you, I did it *for* you. To keep it away from you." She still says nothing. "You weren't alone, anyway."

"How do you know?" she growls. *My god, she's pissed.* "What about us? We were supposed to stick together."

I don't know what to say. I'm in shock. *I don't need this. How can you yell at somebody for getting sick?* "We weren't us anymore because I wasn't *me* anymore." We look at each other in silence. Clearly, she's the dominant dog. She's actually being loving right now, it's just . . . scary love.

"You'll end up dead." She looks like she's gonna start crying again, but she's also really angry.

"You always say I'm gonna end up dead." I try to smile. The lights inside the house come back on; people begin talking and moving around. I wonder if Betty'll thaw a little, but she stays rigidly still, glaring at me.

"This time I mean it," she seethes. "Do you know how worried I was?"

"No."

"Listen. Once I saw Picasso unveil a painting of the darkest, ugliest death mask a woman is capable of wearing. I thought only Hollywood could create an image that skeletal, that awful. I know that's what Picasso thought, too, because that's where he found the ugliness that modeled for his painting—like a soul torn from its body. He horrified Hollywood that night by showing them their own ugliness, the darkness they had created in the name of false beauty and greed."

Huh? Picasso? I stand there, staring at her. She told me to listen, so I'm listening. I just have no idea what I'm listening to.

She keeps going. "*I* was a soul torn from its body, you know! When I left Hollywood, I never thought I'd have to see something so frightening ever again. But there are all kinds of hells! I saw the same death mask on *your* face. A young girl, of all people, going to hell. And then . . . you disappeared. You didn't even give me a chance." Her voice shakes in fury. "*Never* do that to me again." She slams the door.

I stand on the porch, stunned. *Jesus, weepy hoopla doesn't seem so bad now.* *"Death mask,"* slam! What am I supposed to do with that?

Listen, I guess. I put my snake bag over my head and around my shoulder, then turn and walk down her front steps in the dark. It occurs to me that Betty might be a wise and secure old person after all.

♋ clara bow

with sunburned lips
i can bitch
about another stupid summer

Another game of Coyote is winding down. No winner has
been declared. My friend and I are the only animals left
  standing, our brothers having fallen in the gaze of
          headlights long ago. He looks tired.

The little kids lie on the ground, staring at the stars,
      quietly saying inane things to each other.

"There's only one Martian in the whole universe, but he
doesn't live on Mars," whispers his little brother. "He
      lives on a bench near the movie theater."

      "I know," whispers mine. "I've seen him."

My friend and I lie down on the grass and call it a tie.

Rats run past my feet while I sing. The little ones are frantic—they scurry by, neatly avoiding my shoes. The bigger ones lumber through the room, taxed, going methodically about their business.

We're recording demos in a studio in Roxbury where the "vocal booth" is an enormous loft next to the control room. The loft is dark everywhere except for my spotlit microphone. After we record each song instrumentally, I come in here alone to stand in the spotlight and put down the vocals. Because we work at night, the rats are awake and surprised to be intruded upon, though not so surprised that they stop doing whatever it is rats do at night.

So we hang. They keep busy, I scream and yell, they run across my feet. The rats are here for a few good reasons: to eat and breed and not die of exposure. That's a valid existence for an animal.

Apparently my wolf had no reason to exist. When I found myself picking a pretty song about a she-wolf out of the air on a warm afternoon, I knew she was walking away.

℅ and a she-wolf after the war

this is the future
after the war
and i don't need any more

Then a gentle little song about the bees sent them buzzing in wider and wider circles, their buzzing leaving with them.

℅ buzz

don't worry
the bees
they buzz around me

So I guess my animals are me seeing sound. But the snake has not yet set itself to music. I actually have a song with the word "snake" in it, but I'm still waiting for the wolf and the bees to call the snake back to wherever they all came from. Maybe its work isn't done here yet.

Of course, it *isn't* a snake, just a remnant of a particularly virulent chemical bloom. I'm no longer sure what "real" means, but the snake flickers in and out of existence, soaked in static, like a busted TV. It's here even though it has no good reason to be; it doesn't eat, breed or die when exposed. It makes me like the rats.

♋ mania

rat, rat, rat, rat, rat, rat

The band struggles to stay awake all night, lying in a pile together on the Universal Couch or the red shag carpet, reading comics, eating organic Froot Loops and drinking burned coffee. When we're playing, they're okay; it's the downtime that hurts 'em. And there's a ton of it.

Comic books help keep them awake. Underground comics're our new passion, our greatest discovery here in Boston: a whole nuther world, fighting the good fight. I'm jealous of the form; it has everything—light, shadow, line, landscapes, bodies and speech. And lordy, how we feel for the artists in this genre. Whereas our Corporate Satan is Top Forty music, theirs is what? Marmaduke? How do they get up in the morning?

Most of the time my poor bandmates just cuddle the comic books, though, having dropped off somewhere in the middle. I watch them sleeping and realize that we are no longer the clean, healthy beach kids we were a few months ago. Boston seemed so ugly and dirty at first, but we've settled into grime as a way of life. In fact, we're comforted by it. I think we've become genuinely dirty—the kind of dirty that doesn't wash off in the shower. Crumbling walls and stained carpet match our own shittiness, mean we belong in a place. I hope it's because we're pure of heart.

When it's time to play, I speak their names quietly and touch their shoulders gently, so as not to startle them. I feel sorry for my tired friends— they're asleep only because they don't happen to be bipolar—but they're touchingly game. They shake off sleep like dogs shaking off bathwater. "I'll make breakfast," says Dave groggily.

"Is it misty in here?" asks Tea.

Leslie stretches and puts an arm around me. "And how are the rats this evening?"

No amount of tranquilizing can make me sleep, so I like having an excuse not to do it. This studio has no windows, which makes it feel like Las Vegas or a biorhythm experiment, sending me into a kind of suspended animation in which I feel no physical sensation at all, just a pleasant hum. And the sound! Explosions and flowers. Like coughing up your liver and seeing that yeah, it's slimy, but it's also sort of beautiful. We've become floating emotional responses, ragged and charmed.

Our producer is a vigorous, eloquent guitar player named Gary. He's artful, sweet as mutherfuckin' pie and only a few years older than us, though we're pretty sure he's a grown-up. He's more together than we are and already has his own road mythology.

We knew we loved Gary when our band opened for his and we heard him use the word "silly" when talking to the soundman. We all snapped our heads around to look at each other, open-mouthed. In our opinion, only individuals capable of tremendous import use the word "silly." Plus, Gary wanted to produce a demo for us and that seemed ultracharming, if a little masochistic. Luckily, we like both of these characteristics.

He thinks we need something to sell at shows, to beg record stores to carry, to get reviewed in the local music press, etc., and, in his opinion, our demos to date are nothing to write home about. "Not representative," he said kindly.

So not only is Gary making us sound good for the first time, he's also gonna use the artfulness that drips from his pores to package our cassette in such a way as to make it something more impressive than your average demo tape. I told him I always just wrote *Throwing Muses* in magic marker on demos and he made a face. "I'm gonna go graphic designy on your asses," he said.

So Gary picks us up in his van and takes us to the studio every night, bewitching us with road stories the whole time. He's trying to get a message across, it seems—a message about how awful touring is. How awful and how *rawk*. We focus on just the *rawk*, which gives us something to look forward to. He hasn't really sold us on the awful, anyway.

"No, you don't get it!" Gary cries, finding it difficult to keep his eyes on the road in his enthusiasm for the story he's telling. "The promoter and the bartender and the bouncer *and* the soundman were all hitting on us! Like our whole band was s'posed to *sleep* with them before we got *paid*!" He thinks. "Which pretty much makes me a hooker," he says primly.

We're impressed. "Wow! Your band slept with the club?"

"Oh god, no. They just wanted us to."

"Oh," says Tea, disappointed.

I'm disappointed, too. "So you aren't really a hooker."

"You were just *invited* to be one," adds Dave.

"I could be a failed hooker!" Gary says defensively.

Leslie giggles. "I think you at least have to have sex."

Gary thinks. "Okay. So I'm not a hooker at all. I would like to retract my last statement concerning me selling my body."

We drive in silence. I look over at him. "At least you aren't a *failed* hooker. . . ."

When recording songs instrumentally, the band plays in a circle, making almost constant eye contact. That makes it easier to guess exactly when and where the next beat and note are going to land. I never really noticed this before, but each song sounds like two or three unrelated songs put together. Plus, our chords are unusual and the time changes unpredictable—it's like racing down stairs juggling. Live, it flies, but recording's nerve-wracking. Exhilarating but nerve-wracking.

My eyes dart from Tea's pick to Leslie's fingers to Dave's foot on the kick pedal. We're fucking up this . . . well, sort of a bridge. It always starts too fast, then gets too slow before going into the next section. We're after abrupt changes, not wishy-washy noodling, and our timing here is mushy.

It could be my fault. My bandmates're often following me and my hands still shake so bad. We've really had it out, my hands and me. I seem able to override the shaking when I'm in release mode, but it's hard to sustain that for an extended period of time, and it's *always* a struggle. My fingers eventually realize they can't keep up and sort of collapse into stored-up tremors. *Goddamn lithium.*

From the control room, Gary speaks into the talkback mic, interrupting our fucking up through the headphones. "Is it possible that the shift *into* the change is tripping you up?" We all start talking at once, but no one has a microphone, so all he hears is babbling. "*What?*" he asks.

Dave leans into his snare mic. "Yes."

"Okay. Let's try the second half of the third verse into the shift into the change." We all talk at once again. "*What?*"

Dave leans over. "Okay."

"Or is that silly?" Gary knows not to overdo it. He won't allow frustration to enter the picture and we have to play it right, so Gary has to remind us to "identify our curve." Which means, essentially: when you start to suck, *stop.*

Once, we started sucking enough to have to take an actual sit-on-the-couch-and-do-the-math break. It was my fault: the timing in that song was so complicated, we hadn't *ever* understood it and now that oversight was being captured on tape. "There *is* a logic to it . . ." I ventured.

Leslie looked at me. "Do you know what that word means?" she asked.

"Well, there's a *flow* to it," I said.

Gary watched us sing our parts at each other on the couch until we had figured out how they were supposed to mesh; then he placed a book of photographs on my lap. I stared at it. "What's this?"

"It's a book."

"Oh." The photographs inside were disgusting and breathtaking. Roadkill, body parts, lab specimens, all lit like movie stars: warm and glowing, with crazy colors you don't see outside of death and injury. I stared at a picture of a severed hand for a long time. It was hard to turn the page— horror is hard to look at but harder to turn away from. And it was just so damn beautiful.

I found that the longer I stared at each picture, the more enchanted I was. My eye would eventually remove all emotional coloring, leaving only admiration for texture and form, for DNA and the fragility of those made of it. A severed hand is graceful, exquisite; a liver really *is* pretty. "This is cool," I said to Gary.

He nodded. "It's you guys."

"Thank you." I looked at him, then turned another page. A dead rat floated in a jar. It looked like it was sleeping—not distorted or injured, just . . . unusually still. And lovely. Each one of its hairs had to form itself out of cells, minerals and will. Life seems so unlikely when you look at it up close.

"Thank you," I said again to Gary, this time not for the compliment but for helping me see why a person might *want* to make the noise we make.

A music paper here in Boston described one of our shows as sounding like "four people playing four different songs at the same time." The writer meant this as a compliment and it's probably what we sound like to people, but it isn't really fair. Playing different songs'd be easy; it's playing the same song *differently* that's hard.

Recording this demo with Gary has helped us become just self-conscious enough to not sound like total freaks. We noticed, for instance, that some of our songs are deeply, inherently anxious. In order to play them right, we gotta play on top of the beat, ahead of the drums. In others, if we don't sit solidly behind the kick, we sound like a giant spaz; to cement Dave's rolling, we have to hit our notes a breath after every kick beat, even if the passage is racing by at a hundred miles an hour.

And they do race by at a hundred miles an hour. Whether they're screechy or rollicking, our songs don't meander, they *run*. Gary calls the rollicking ones "country punk." I've never identified them as such; we just call these the "fun" songs, the ones that make audiences hoot and holler in relief after we play screechy songs at them.

Those screechy ones're so intense that when we play them in the studio we're only good for about three takes. We're used to live—when you're allowed just one—so while we're loving throwing ourselves into careful abandon rather than just abandon, it takes something out of us. We "identify our curve" fairly quickly when a song is soaked in nervous energy. Lately, we've been trying to downplay that nervous energy just to make the band sound less annoying.

Of course, when I sing, the band only gets *more* annoying. I open my mouth and horrible things come out: strange words, guttural noises, squashed-bug squealing. And then screams . . . you wouldn't wanna meet that girl. Me and the rats hang together for a reason.

I can't believe I can still do this, muted by medication. The songs still fly out, inflatable words, intense as ever. Even though personally I don't seem to have a shred of intensity left in me, a vocal will still shake me apart, like a midair explosion. Then, as the song ends, the distortion fades and the dust settles, I float back down to the ground, tame again.

"Are you okay?" Gary asks me in my headphones after a particularly yucky take.

"Whaddya mean?" A young rat stops and looks at me. "*I wasn't talking to you*," I whisper to it.

"*You weren't?*" Gary whispers back.

"*Yes.* I mean no, I was."

He pauses. "No, you were?"

"What did you mean, am I okay? Did it sound bad?"

"It sounded terrible," he says. "In a good way."

"Well, then, I guess I'm okay."

♋ sugar baby

what did you mean am i okay?
what did i do?

It's strange to sit on the Universal Couch at 2 A.M. with a bowl of Froot Loops and hear this crap. My Froot Loops get soggy as I stare at the speakers, wondering why they're talking that way. I never figure anything out, just move down to the red shag carpet and keep staring. Sometimes I try lying on the floor, twisting my head around like a dog, trying to understand, but the music is still . . . baffling.

First the walls disappear, then the Universal Couch and my friends are blotted out by colors and shapes. Long strands of blue whole notes speckled with dotted green eighth notes, like buckshot over sky: a turquoise A minor, at once staccato and an extended exhalation. A blocky, red, syncopated E major becomes moody burgundy squares when the A flat within the chord gives way to a violet G. Black swathes of snare hits cut through the lines and dots, each one fading before the next one appears.

My bandmates listen, talk, read and sleep. Gary bobs his head, like he's enjoying himself. When a song ends, I'm usually standing behind him, still staring at the speakers, cereal bowl sideways on the rug, forgotten. I know this sound is what I have to offer, so it shouldn't feel foreign to me. It's the sound of my heart or my bones or . . . I don't know, it still sounds strange. If the song was a minute longer, I'd have my face pressed up against the speakers, as confused as ever.

♋ mania

that is how i pray

On the way home every morning, I ride shotgun, snake bag on my lap, so Gary can point out significant Boston architecture to me. Gary is restless, too; he never seems tired, refusing on principle to sleep more than four hours a night, so he's always up for a conversation. He's also taken it upon himself to make me stop disagreeing with buildings and he's doing an excellent job. I went from "Those're big and gray, alright" to being able to identify dozens of different architectural styles. Gary loves architecture even more than he loves music. We discuss various movements and their originators, buildings' details and quirks. His enthusiasm alone is beautiful. "Architecture," he says, "is the *first* art form you should try and wrap your head around. Buildings illustrate artistic concepts concretely."

"'Cause they're made of concrete?"

He smirks. "Sometimes because they're made of concrete, as concrete is a malleable substance capable of both strength and delicacy. *Sometimes* because 'structure' is a fundamentally similar concept in any artistic venture."

"Comics are better. I had no idea they were so great."

Gary doesn't like to change the subject when we're talking about architecture. "Only *great* comics are great."

"Yeah, well, the form is beautiful. I used to think sound had everything."

"Sound has *an* everything; nothing has *the* everything."

I laugh. "'Nothing has the everything.'"

Gary looks at me sideways. "Buildings have an everything, too."

"Yeah. I don't have to go inside them, though, right?"

"Yes! Yes, you do. You have to see terrazzo floors and crown moldings and carved wood mantels and *doors*! Wait 'til you see doors . . ."

"I've seen doors."

"No," he shakes his head. "No, you haven't."

While I think about doors, I notice that the leaves on the trees that're whipping past are just beginning to turn. I love fall. "Is architecture art or science?" I ask him.

"It's both. Which is why you need to go inside buildings."

"Okay. I don't like art a whole lot, though. I prefer science."

"Why?"

"'Cause it's pure. I get tired of art. So messy. And pretentious."

"*People* are pretentious," he says, "not art. And pretentious people don't make art; they merely imitate it."

I watch the leaves go by: green, red, orange, green, yellow, red, orange, yellow. "I've noticed that. They're jerks." *That's how people end up with ass-holes for heroes.* "And they don't just imitate art; they *succeed* by imitating art." I stare out the window at the empty sidewalks. "But they're still just jerks. They never do anything but fool the easily fooled."

"Which gives us all a bad name," he agrees. "Then people who aren't fooled, like you, think that *all* artists are pretentious."

"Mm-hm." I nod. "We should quit. I'm willing."

"Nope. You're not allowed."

"Aw, c'mon, fire me."

Gary stops at a stop sign and stares ahead. "Sometimes you have to crucify yourself for your work. If you accomplish what you set out to and your output is valuable, well . . . somebody thinking you're pretentious is part of your crucifixion."

"Part of my *crucifixion*? Geez, Gary." *I think I still prefer science.* "Do scientists crucify themselves for lab experiments?"

"Of course they do. And pretentious scientists are *way* pretentious. And ego-driven. Money figures into the equation. You would hate that world. Purity is purity, and pretense is pretense, regardless of the sphere it's in." He leans forward to race through an intersection, whipping his head from side to side, looking for cars. "I don't see how you could ever tell art and science apart," he says. "Maybe you're trying to differentiate be-tween craft and inspiration."

I think. "Science is something you can measure, art is something you can lose yourself in. I mean literally: lose your *self*."

Gary sees a cop and slows down, then drives, saying nothing, for a good minute and a half. "That may be true. But I wouldn't discount your ability to lose yourself. You're very good at it."

We're almost home. I turn around to look in the backseat. Tea, Dave and Leslie are all asleep again. "*That* is an embarrassing talent," I say quietly.

"I imagine it is." Gary pulls up on the sidewalk in front of our house and turns to face me. "But it'll keep your standards high."

My bandmates stumble out of the van. I wave goodbye to Gary and walk up the front steps with them. In the early morning, our neighborhood smells like laundry and diner. Dave struggles sleepily to unlock the front door as Gary blows us a kiss and takes off into the pink and orange sunrise.

I lie under the water with my friends, staring at the sky
through the surface of the ocean. Both the water and the
sky are perfectly clear. Bubbles escape our lips and rise
to break the surface.

Suddenly, a huge wave rises up beside us, its foam
spreading in great mounds. It crashes down, churning the
water up like a funnel. Up is down, sand looks like sky.

We twist and somersault, spin and roll.

Bleary-eyed, my bandmates fall onto their beds for a few hours of sleep. I drop my snake bag at the foot of my bed and then lie down. *Christ, look at me!* Not that I'm gonna sleep, but I can lie on my bed and stare at the ceiling . . . and I don't even explode.

I really thought it was a bad idea to live somewhere, to be trapped, to belong in only one place. But the other Muses have made the word "home" safe. And someday we'll get to live on the road in a van: the Silver Bullet Two. Then I can be home and moving at the same time.

For now, when the band is allowed to play every night, music absorbs all the heat and energy my body can create. I don't feel trapped because I'm truly spent. This is due in part to the brain-fuzzing drugs I take, but they're clumsier than music. Plain old sound rides over and through medication to do its own biochemical revamping. It's an elegant, enchanting process— I'm wiped out but *right-minded* under music's spell.

I know drugs keep my soul from expanding and contracting unecessarily. I know they slow down the body monster and the clanging static, but they seem to keep me from thinking what my brain wants me to think. And my brain still refuses to die.

We live on the first floor of a house near Harvard Square with a bunch of other people. The neighborhood's adorable: blue collar plus old people. We get flyers asking us to attend block parties and town meetings where they discuss issues like litter and barking dogs. The house itself is crappy, just like the houses around it. Colorless on the outside, chalk-white inside, it's been painted so many times the windows won't open, and the mantels over fireplaces that no longer exist are soft and squishy.

The apartment is actually a long hallway with vastly different rooms shooting off of it, culminating in a dingy kitchen. Open one door and Vicky the painter's colors leap out at you. We brought a painter to Boston with us for good luck. Like all painters, she makes sense of chaos but she also makes chaos. Old movie posters and records hang crooked on her walls, toys and paintings are strewn around the floor, brightly colored dresses hang from lamps. She has no window and has made up for it tenfold with Day-Glo psychedelia. Vicky's room makes you squint. Fun fact: Vicky is the person who painted "The Doghouse" on the Doghouse door.

The next room is Leslie's Zen Den. This room has the opposite effect: dimly lit and empty, nothing but a futon and a sewing machine. I helped her pick up this sewing machine from an elderly aunt who told her to "*Use it!*" and Leslie does. She kneels like a monk and sews for hours, a cup of bark tea at her side. I don't know *what* she sews, exactly; I've never seen her finish anything. It seems to be the act of sewing that's important to her. Her den is that Zen.

Dave's room is right off the kitchen. It's dark and squeaky 'cause I gave him a mattress with mice in it by accident. I mean, I gave him the mattress on purpose—I just didn't know there were mice living in it. I avoid Dave's room because of the mice. Mice aren't rats; mice're uneasy, and they like to be left alone.

My bed is jammed into the corner of what was originally a living room; my sister's bed is against the opposite wall. We use the mantel of our busted fireplace to display Vicky's cartoons and paintings (the paintings are funny and the cartoons sad, for some reason). We also have a bunch of dusty plastic fruit up there. It was probably there when we moved in. I don't remember buying plastic fruit.

Every morning, Tea and I make a fist as soon as we wake up. That's the first thing we say when our eyes open; we yell it, trying to catch the other one out. "*Make a fist!*" Try it; it feels awful. Though, if you can do it, it's probably a good, proactive way to start the day.

At night we lie in the dark, talking. Tea talks and then sleeps. I talk and then wait for sleep, which occasionally comes. A streetlight and a tree cast cool shadows on the wall then. We wanted to trace these shadows, but were afraid of losing our damage deposit, so we traced them in pencil to be on the safe side. Every night, our pencil drawing is filled in with light and shadow that matches it perfectly. Its beauty actually lulls me to sleep.

Trying to sleep in the bright morning, though, even after playing all night, is all but impossible. Tea says from across the room, "If you lie really still and pay attention to each part of your body, you realize that you're always in pain."

Geez. "What do you mean?"

"Well," she answers, "part of you is always hurting."

"Why do I want to know that?"

"Just do it; it's cool." I try it: forehead, arms, knees, ribs . . . she's right. Everything aches. "Did you try it?" she asks. "I'm right, right?"

"Yeah," I groan. "How'd you figure that out?"

"You know how, on the island, when a party ends, the whole party walks everybody home?"

"I love that."

"Well, once, me and this girl were the last two people walking home and she told me that we're always in pain; we just don't sit still long enough to notice." *Maybe sitting still isn't all it's cracked up to be.* "I bet it's what old people do. They sit around feeling all that."

"And then whine about it. I would. This is a bitch."

"Mm-hm." We lie there, sun slanting into the windows, lighting dust particles in the air. Tea turns over and goes to sleep.

We have a gaggle of roommates. None of us knows how many; we can't tell them apart. They're nice enough, but they all seem interchangeable and, I suspect, actually do change—subletting their beds to friends who look and act just like them. We call them "the aliens."

I guess we could learn their names, but they think we already *know* their names and we don't want to hurt anybody's feelings. Once I went to the grocery store with a few aliens out of politeness—thought I could learn something about them. They all bought cereal, then took it home and ate it.

The pantry shelves might've helped us understand the aliens, but they only ever buy cereal. I find the Muses' food more interesting, and proof that none of us will ever grow up. Tea buys party food for very small parties: miniature boxes of petit fours, little jars of Vienna sausages, tiny pieces of toast. Dave eats only spaghetti and chocolate-chip cookies. I see him wandering the aisles of the grocery store with a cart full of normal food, but by the time he gets to the checkout, it's all morphed into spaghetti and cookies. Leslie says he's gonna die.

I eat the hippie food I was raised on, as if I'm still a toddler on a commune. And Leslie somehow subsists on ziplock bags filled with leaves, roots and sticks. This *might* be grown-up; I have no idea. Grown-up in the woods maybe, like a grown-up gnome or something. She says these plants have medicinal properties. "Why do you need medicine?" I asked her once. "Are you sick?"

"It's a Santa Cruz thing," she said. "You wouldn't understand."

The aliens don't bitch when I play guitar, which is good. Unfortunately, they also play guitar and they do it badly. And in the kitchen. I know now that playing guitar isn't the same thing for everyone. Like yawning during sex, they sit with their feet up on the table, strumming boring chords and playing pointless covers. It's fascinating to me.

I bring them coffee in the morning and beer at night so I can grill them on keys and such, just to get them talking about music. "What song is that?" I ask them. "Why are you playing it? *How warm are you right now?*"

The aliens are friendly and they like to talk, though we don't really have conversations as much as I interview them and they pontificate. I offer up no personal information; these talks are purely for my own research and they're truly fascinating. The aliens' eyes scan our dismal, gray backyard through the paint-spattered window, the shelves of records we keep in the kitchen, the penciled messages on the wall by the phone. I keep my feet on the linoleum and my eyes never leave their faces. I'm not making fun of them—I'm jealous.

Their feet are invariably on the table when they play. "Why do you put your feet up when you play guitar?" I ask.

"I'm just kickin' back." *Wow!*

Dave says the aliens're "normal" people, but I like them anyway. They're so . . . easygoing. Here's a basic outline of my research findings: (A) No change occurs in an alien's electrical charge when he plays guitar. (B) Ditto for his body temperature. (C) Double ditto for his emotional state. In fact, nothing changes at all. He might as well be sitting there doodling.

Like all apartment buildings in Boston, this one's infested with roaches and snotty Harvard students. The Harvard guys're half preps, half drunken louts and they treat us like shit. They seem to be under the impression that we're retarded whores, which is actually an intriguing idea. I'm just not sure where they got it. Is it because we aren't rich? Lots of people aren't rich. It doesn't mean we're so dumb that we *forgot* to be rich. And it doesn't mean that rich boys can *have* us.

The week we moved in, a thug in a Harvard sweatshirt leaned out the second-floor window as I stood on the sidewalk, fishing around in my pockets for my key. "Hey, group homie!" he yelled. "Wanna get it on?"

I squinted up at him and my snake bag slipped off my shoulder. "Nope!"

"Whatsa matter, reta'd?" he leered. "Lost yer key?"

"Dick," I muttered, picking up my bag. But he was right, I had lost my key. *Maybe he's right about the retard thing, too.* I looked up. "Hey, Dick! I have an idea: first you shut up and then you let me in."

"I'll let you in if you . . . *come* . . . upstairs!" *Ew*. "Wanna get it on?"

"Why do you keep saying that?"

He laughed and a thin line of saliva lowered itself from his lips to the ground in front of me. He did this on purpose. I watched, entranced. His face and the brown grass below shared the same slime for a second, then he let it go.

I was impressed. He was a champion spitter, really world-class. How do you control something that viscous? He must get a lot of spitting practice with all us peasants around. "Wow," I said. "Did you just try to spit on me?" He grinned. "Didn't you just say you wanted to *sleep* with me? Dick?" There's gotta be something wrong with a person who spits on the people he wants to go to bed with and vice versa.

He laughed again. What a happy little rich boy. "My name's not Dick, reta'd!"

I walked up the front steps and looked under the mat for an extra key. "My name's not *reta'd*, Dick!" *How did this guy get into Harvard? Spitting scholarship?* I checked both mailboxes. No key.

He was still hanging out the window, staring at me, so I walked down the steps and into the bushes to bang on the front window of our apartment. An alien waved from inside, then came out to the sidewalk to flip off the Harvard thug and let me in. "Some people are just too fucking weird to talk to," he said.

Whenever we're mad at the Harvard guys, we open our apartment door wide and slam it into their expensive bikes. Then we yell, "Sorry!" up the stairs. The alien did this as we went inside. Their bikes were pretty nice when we moved in. They look like crap now.

Joseph Campbell, the mythologist, is staying with us
while on a lecture tour. Sitting by the fire while my
parents make dinner, he and I discuss cats and dogs.

"I was a dog person first," he says. "When I was little,
like you, I loved dogs and hated cats. But now I'm a cat
person. I love cats and hate dogs."

It has never occurred to me that you might like
one animal more than another. I tell him I like both
dogs *and* cats.

"But which one do you like *best?*" he asks. "Which one would
you invite to a party?"

I have no patience for ambitious musicians; ambition is a really embarrassing tap dance to watch. Uptight and self-conscious, posing for pictures with anyone who might be able to help thrust them into a spotlight: *look at me!* And no reason to do this, nothing of substance to show us when we turn around and look. They aren't even real musicians; they're just show-offs, "performers," who can't get people to watch them do anything else, so they dress up and play fashion sound. "The blind ambitious," Dave calls 'em. They're Boston's mosquitoes.

But the musicians who make noises for noise's sake fascinate us. Their vocabulary is slamming joy and desperation, lethargy and force. These musicians are funny people who're serious about something and sad people who're happy about something: they're kind. They seem to wanna be just buzzed enough to feel what others feel, too.

We didn't even know what we were looking for when we found this scene, but here it is, filling in a bunch of blanks; a subculture within a subculture.

Late afternoons, I grab my guitar and snake bag and walk to sound check. The city smells like smoke then, and sounds like roaring The crush on the sidewalk, tired people going home as my workday is beginning, is unself-conscious at this hour: hungry, honest, work clothes wrinkled and askew. Lost in this shuffle is a good place to be.

In the clubs, we get lost in a shuffle of humanity, too, and it's lovely. A show is an opportunity for people to get base together, take a ride together, a group high. The bands are in the audience until it's their turn to play, when the band onstage becomes a part of the audience in order to watch the next set. It's such a celebration. No one seems to headline; bands just pile up, watching each other and cheering when somebody throws another log on the fire of *real* music. As if together we can make enough healthy noise to drown out the blind ambitious.

```
☜ caffeine

the radio keeps playing
the radio keeps saying
"nothing lost and nothing gained"
```

Every generation *thinks* its music is low and dirty, but you can always get lower and dirtier. People looking to expand their horizons are hungry for a body depth or a mind mess. Whatever floats your boat, I guess.

There are an unbelievable number of clubs in this city, but rat people like me (there are others, as it turns out), come to the Rat for low dirt. Short for "Rathskeller," it's a sweaty pit that is actually underground, and it's the epicenter of this subculture's subculture. It smells like beer and dark.

♋ devil's roof

i love the smell of beer
the smell of dark

Tonight, we're playing the Rat with three other bands who all sound like themselves. Music that doesn't imitate other music—imagine that. And the audience *likes* it. They wait in line on the sidewalk at all hours and spend cash money just to be allowed to crawl down into the airless Rat and sweat over expensive cheap beer. And listen to bands who sound like themselves. I find this very moving.

Plus they . . . well, I'm not sure what they do; it's like they're playing along. They get it. When music walks into the room, we all know it. It isn't delivered to an audience by musicians, it happens *between* people.

♋ pale

and when the music starts
it goes straight to your head

Gary peeks in the dressing room after sound check, beaming and holding a cardboard box full of our new demos and starts handing them out to the other bands. I grab one out of the box and look at it. It doesn't look graphic designy to *me*. "This isn't art," I say to him. "It's a picture of us."

Gary peers at it over my shoulder. "It's art," he says. "See how it has colors on it?"

"Colors?"

"*Nice* colors. Don't you think it looks a little Warhol?"

"Well . . . there're colors on it."

"Yep. But you hate pretense. So it's an unpretentious picture of you. 'Cause you guys are adorable."

I look at him. "*I'm* not adorable."

"No, you're awful. I meant *them*," he says, pointing to my bandmates. "*They're* adorable."

Tea, Leslie and Dave study the cassette in silence. Suddenly, Dave grabs a fistful of beers out of the bin and gives one to each of us. We all stare at Gary, waiting for a speech. The other musicians in the dressing room notice and grow quiet. Gary looks around the room and holds his beer in the air. "To not sucking!" he says to polite applause and a quiet hoot or two. I clink my beer against his and then go out into the room to watch another band sound check.

According to Massachusetts law, because we're too young to drink, we aren't allowed anywhere in the building during business hours except the dressing room (where all the free beer is) or on the stage (where the rest of the free beer is). So if I wanna see a band play, I have to either watch them sound check in the afternoon or hide behind the drum riser during their set, where no one but the drummer can see me. Hiding behind the drummer is wonderful—my ears ring all night, like the hangover that's part of the high.

A full–body onslaught, better than a hurricane, music is the only nature I've got here in Boston, and it's wild.

♋ flying

```
if I'd known leaving every home would get me here
I would have gone sooner
```

I settle the record gently on the turntable like Dude taught me, pull the lever to start the turntable spinning and delicately place the needle on the smooth part of the disc where there is no music. I know that a record is like a brain: smooth means no information, lines and ridges indicate stories.

I sit on the floor, only barely prepared for the rapture to come. In seconds, the room is full of bursting color.

But today there is no sound check to watch; a film crew is setting up their equipment on the stage instead, placing tripods between amps and holding cameras up in the air and on their shoulders, trying to set up the best shots ahead of time. *Damn it, I forgot.* While the bands play, they'll race around, crawling between our effects pedals and standing over us, shooting from above. They do this a lot and it's sort of terrible. Not that they're in the way. Our crap didn't make the move to Boston, as we'd gradually lost our enthusiasm for setting up lamps and carpets and legs and then tripping on them. So we're just a band on a stage now, not a band on an obstacle course; the film crews have plenty of room to run around. The problem is that they *show* us what they shot.

Yesterday, the filmmaker that's shooting tonight invited us to his apartment to watch footage of ourselves. We didn't wanna go but couldn't think of a nice way to get out of it. "Keeps you honest," Dave said, staring sadly at the video monitor, when the guy left to make coffee.

I squinted at the screen in misery. "Well, no it doesn't. It keeps you self-conscious. I was honest *before*."

"Yeah. Being in the moment doesn't look good." He pointed at himself. "Watch the face I make whenever I do this fill." He grimaced angrily both on film and in the room. "I wish I didn't do that."

Hmmm. I glanced at Dave. He looked sick.

"Well, geez, look at me," I said, pointing at the screen. "I really *don't* blink." We watch. "Golly, that's creepy." I knew I stared into space when I played; Betty never stopped giving me shit about that. She *should* have been giving me shit about the thing I do with my head. It swivels from side to side in a figure-eight pattern while I play. *What the fuck?*

"I think of it as an infinity symbol," said Dave kindly.

For most of the set, I stand rigidly still, except for the head thing and my twisting left shin. That part of me was broken in half when the witch hit me with her Chevy and it seems to have some leftover resentment, 'cause it just goes *apeshit* when we play. My foot bends over itself, maniacally keeping time, squirming and straining to release the song. Then the head swivel and shin twisting spread into the rest of me: my shoulders roll; an arm'll fly out suddenly, then go back to playing guitar like nothing happened; my trunk stretches, twists, then straightens. I sort of . . . writhe. It looks like a seizure, or at least an elaborate tic.

I figure it's what I gotta do to get the déjà vu syringe to work. When memories in the songs are stuck in my muscles, I need to release them.

That's what it feels like and that's what it looks like. But I already knew how it felt. I didn't know how it looked.

I turned to Dave. "I didn't need to know this."

"Tea and Leslie look good," he replied airily.

I nodded. "They do. Maybe we should hide behind them when we play."

"I *do* hide behind them. It's not working."

When the excited filmmaker returned, Dave and I took our coffees and smiled politely. "Wow," said Dave convincingly. "Just beautiful."

"I know." The filmmaker smiled proudly. "Didn't it come out great?" *It'd be better if we weren't in it.* "Yeah, that was fun," I answered. "Good work."

"You guys make it so easy," he said. "I can't wait to shoot you again. I think I'll use a wide-angle lens to shoot you tomorrow night."

"Mm-hm." I jammed my face into my cup, trying to imagine my reflection in the coffee through a wide-angle lens. *Shoot me.*

As we trailed sadly out of the filmmaker's house, he waved happily. "See you tomorrow!" he called after us as Dave and I exchanged grim looks.

In the dressing room, Leslie fishes around inside her backpack for set-list paper and a marker. "Got a handful of narcs coming tonight," she says offhandedly. Some record company employees are actually forced to listen to demo tapes, as it turns out—*poor sons of bitches*—and apparently, we have a "buzz," so they send representatives to shows to check us out, see if the buzz is anything to get excited about.

I wish a buzz was really a *buzz*: a humming whine that everybody could hear, whispering the names of bands. The record companies are just hoping that local hype will grow into a scene that could then be marketed nationally, with *big-ass* hype. In other words, they ask "What's cool?" and try to be the first to come up with the answer. Then they sell that to people who are also wondering what's cool and would like to be told by someone else. So record companies perform the questionable service of telling people what to think while reaching into their pockets for cash. "Yeah. We're going to dinner with one," I tell her.

"Oh, good," she says. "I'm hungry."

Food is really the only reason to go out to dinner with one of these guys. The reps we've met are all good people, but none of them are looking for good bands. They want *cool* bands. We aren't cool and never will be. Cool bands are different from us—they have an eye to the outside, an impression of the impression they make. It's the opposite of being lost in your own world the way we are. We only appear to be hyped because music writers like us and they like music. Fashion is where you find cool, though, and fashion is not music.

"How could you possibly sell what we do?" we ask the reps and are met with blank stares.

"Don't you think your band is good?" they ask.

"Sure we're good, but that doesn't mean we *sound* good."

"But you know you're special."

We laugh. "Yeah . . . *short bus* special."

We don't tell these people that they're in the fashion industry, not the music industry, 'cause that would be rude, but it seems obvious to us that music is timeless, fashion ephemeral. Our orientations are necessarily opposed. It'd be like trying to sell paintings as wallpaper; people would hate that, it'd hurt their feelings.

Really, record companies are in the *marketing* industry. Fashion probably wasn't evil before marketing people got involved and tried to invent it themselves and then sell it to America's youth by convincing them that the rest of America's youth were already partaking. Fashion probably began as a groundswell of beauty: the tribe enjoying the way buildings look and music sounds, right now, in this moment. That's valuable, because it allows for substance to shift styles. But marketing'll do anything to *avoid* substance and engage *only* in style. No longer beauty that falls from trees like apples, fashion becomes shiny, scary chemical candy, unnatural and unhealthy.

There's no way we could play that game even if we wanted to. We'd suck at it; we have no ambition in that world. Our ambition is limited to the next song, the next show. If someone wants to listen, we're touched; if no one wants to listen, we figure they're missing out.

Which means we're too up our own asses to be marketed nationally, big-ass hype or no. I can think of so many bands that'd jump at the chance to play along with the entertainment industry, to use cool to sell records. So we hang out with the reps, eat dinner with them and then gently suggest that their company sign one of *those* bands instead of us.

Tonight we're having dinner with one of the old guys, the coke guys, the VIPs with orange tans and tinted glasses. VIPs are not the reps in the rock club trenches—they're far removed from everything musical. Oozing out of the moneyed world of limos and palm trees (*really!*), they personify the tragedy of errors that is the music business. VIPs are always expensively dressed (Gary once tallied one of their outfits at a few *thousand* dollars; the clothes I was wearing that day cost thirty-five cents), they are never women and they all have a creepy, fake peacefulness that comes from both feeling safe because you're rich and wanting people to think you're self-actualized.

All VIPs have a stylish, articulate assistant to speak for them and help them do things like *move*. Because they seem partially dead. As if they're just dying one piece at a time, their money holding up what's left of their corpse with various . . . treatments. They're fascinating in a yucky way, but you can't spend too much time with them. It's like going to Vegas—not funny enough.

The VIP and his assistant take us to a coolly beautiful restaurant where a coolly beautiful hostess seats us at a round table with a white linen table-cloth. I watch fish swim in an enormous fish tank set into the wall while the VIP orders three bottles of wine and name-drops old musicians we either haven't heard of or don't care about. When he forgets our names, the assistant steps in and addresses us personally. "David, I'm guessing you must be a Who fan, am I right?"

Dave smiles. "Can I have another Coke?" he asks.

When the VIP leaves to go to the men's room, his assistant smiles at us. "He's legendary," he says. "A brilliant man." We all watch the lumpy figure shuffling across the restaurant. "He can make or break you," the assistant hums admiringly.

When the legendary, brilliant man shuffles back to the table and sucks down another glass of wine, we order all the food we can and then watch his face melt. VIPs' faces melt when they drink. I don't know if it's face-lifts or tanning booth abuse or maybe hair transplants slipping down their scalps, but it's freakin' weird.

While his face is melting, the VIP tells us he can give us money to make a record—answering our prayers, fulfilling our dreams—and we sigh and eat more. Hearing this is sad and boring, because we would *love* to make a record and we *don't* have the money to do so. But three things have kept us from doing a deal with a record company:

1. Once you sign, they can drop you whenever they want, but you can't leave.

2. They tell *you* how your record will sound.

3. They don't have to release your record, but no one else can either (not even you), because your record is essentially *their* record. They paid for it, they own it. You aren't even allowed to re-record your songs and release the new versions—your songs are gone.

I'd sent out all those demos and press kits before I knew this. See, we're nobodies and nobodies have no rights. And in order to be somebodies, we'd have to sign a nobody deal, sacrificing our firstborn song babies in the process. It just isn't worth it. We know they could never sell what we do; they'd just make us suck, then drop us. Living in a van's the dream and living in a van'll stay the dream. We'll just have to keep playing until we can afford a van.

So we voice our concerns halfheartedly and I'm sure the VIP and his helpmate have more to say when we do, but we can't listen 'cause we're too busy eating all we can and watching his waxy skin drip like the candles on the table.

♋ mercury

this meeting with old ladies
on tremendous amounts of coke

Our press is increasing exponentially: the more people write about us, the more people write about us. We do a fistful of interviews every time we play. The four of us sit in a row on a Universal Couch and talk for hours during the other bands' sets. I can't sneak off to hide behind the drum riser and listen because I stand center stage when we play. This, to journalists, seems to imply a willingness to mouth off. Apparently, to them, "lead singer" means "person who won't shut up."

It's so lousy to know that we're missing all that music. We feel left out, listening to fuzzy thumping through the wall as writer after writer points out that we're teenagers and three of us are female. We never have answers to these nonquestions. "Teenager" just means stupid. And is there a difference between male and female people? *Is* there? Seriously. I have yet to identify a single character trait I would attribute solely to one gender or the other.

Tonight one of the sexist journalists is a woman who's angry that Dave is a man. "Why didn't you hire a *woman* to play drums?" she asks me accusingly.

I'm at a loss. "Because Dave's not a woman," I answer. "I didn't 'hire' him anyway; he doesn't get paid."

"I'm a volunteer!" Dave chirps happily.

She gives him a blank look and then turns back to me. "Surely you would agree that you play female music."

"*Sometimes* we play female music," I say. "But not any more often than men do."

At first, it's easy to be patient with these writers because it's clear that they don't *mean* to be so wrapped up in stereotypes, but . . . by the time the fifth person comes in and asks us something to the effect of *why did you decide to be girls?* I sorta lose my cool and end up mouthing off in spite of myself. "We aren't girls on purpose; we're girls by accident! We're *musicians* on purpose. I mean, do *you* treat men and women differently?"

This poor guy happens to be really nice; he just didn't know not to ask that particular question. He shakes his head uncertainly. "Well, it'd suck if you did," I continue. "I don't see how gender could inform anyone's character; it's useless when it comes to predicting behavior. Except for idiots' behavior—'cause thinking you have to act male or female instead of human makes no sense."

He looks so tense that I begin to speak more gently, but I don't stop, which is what he would like me to do. "What could gender possibly have to do with how your hands work?" I ask him. He shrugs. "Women's hands work on typewriters but not guitars? Or are we only allowed to play acoustics 'cause electricity's too *bitchin'* for girls?" He nods along, then shakes his head, trying to agree with me. "For god's sake, didn't we all grow up with *Free to Be You and Me?*"

"Yes!" he says heartily. "I did!"

Even *I* wish I would shut up, but I don't fucking stop. Music pounds through the wall and I blame this guy for making me miss it. "We all know there're bigger differences *within* the races than between them, right? So substitute 'gender' for race, *duh-uh*. I thought we already did that!"

He opens his mouth, but I interrupt him before he can say anything. "Not to mention the infinite shades of gray inherent in the whole *concept* of gender. Gender is a spectrum, with no clear division between the poles. Hetero and homo are just scratching the surface of sexuality . . ."

This is when the exhausted journalist moves warily on to another band member, writing in his notebook next to my name, "outspoken feminist."

I'm building a snowman in my front yard when a plow comes laboring down the street, spraying snow into the ditch. When he sees me, the driver slows down, then stops next to my house, cutting the engine. He stares at my snowman. I stare at him.

"Is that a boy or a girl?" he asks.

"It's a snowman," I answer.

"Looks like a snow lady."

I look at my snowman. "No it doesn't."

"Oh," he says. "My mistake." He starts the engine and continues down the road, waving goodbye over his head.

"Self-expression," says a woman with glasses, her army T-shirt bunched and sweaty. She holds her tape recorder out to us. We look at it.

"What about it?" asks Dave politely.

"Let's just talk a little bit about self-expression," the woman says.

Leslie looks at her. "What, just 'talk about it'?"

"How important is it?" she asks, squinting thoughtfully.

"Self-expression?" says Dave. Tea and I just sit there.

The woman begins to rethink her impression of us as articulate. She turns to me and puts her tape recorder under my chin. "Tell me your thoughts," she says slowly. "Regarding songwriting and expressing your-self."

I'm confused. "My *self* ? Why would I wanna express *that?*"

Leslie peeks out the dressing room door. "The next guy's a grown-up!" she says incredulously.

"What?" asks Tea. "Why?"

"I can't imagine," answers Leslie. "Maybe he's a newspaper."

I look at her. "Maybe he's a newspaper?"

"Shhh . . ." Leslie opens the door with her biggest California smile and offers the guy a drink. The Newspaper is indeed a grown-up. He has a trim beard and a tweed jacket. He looks more like a professor than a newspaper to me. Or like someone auditioning for the role of "professor." I guess he could be a newspaper.

The man declines Leslie's offer of a drink and gets down to business. Placing his tape recorder on his lap, he begins to talk about art and com-merce. It's his feeling that a musical genre begins with a select few, in a period of intense energy and chaos. In time, the movement both picks up steam as it's popularized and loses focus as the energy dissipates.

"I'll buy that," I say. "That's why 'legendary' means 'overrated' in Top Forty and 'where are they now' in underground music."

"Right," he says. "When a band comes along who can adopt the es-sential elements of a genre yet lose the idiosyncratic chaos associated with the groundswell period, essentially imitating the style and smoothing out its rough edges, it's funded by the recording industry with the aim of popularizing this sound, which will eventually be considered mainstream," he says.

"Sure," says Leslie.

"I don't think you guys are that band," the Newspaper says carefully.

"No," answers Tea.

"No, I wouldn't think so," agrees Dave.

"We're the chaos people, aren't we?" I ask.

The Newspaper nods.

"You guys play a lot of notes really fast!" says a young guy in a T-shirt with the words *Candy Time* written on it. He's enthusiastic to the point of hyper.

Leslie laughs. "A lot of notes really fast?" she repeats.

Candy Time looks at us and laughs uncomfortably, thinks Leslie might be making fun of him. We just smile. "Yeah! You're untrained," he says, "but you can still play fast. It's cool."

Leslie stops laughing. "Untrained?"

"Yeah . . . you just play whatever comes into your head, right?"

"I guess that's what we do," answers Tea. "Isn't that what everybody does?"

"No, that's the thing," he explains. "*Professional* musicians take lessons to learn how to play by the rules, but you guys just play whatever you feel like playing!"

I can feel Leslie bristle next to me on the couch. "Are you implying that we sound the way we do because we don't *know* the rules? That we don't know *how* to sound like other bands?" Candy Time realizes his mistake, but too late. "What gave you the idea that we were 'untrained,' anyway?" she asks him, but she doesn't give him time to answer. "You know how hard it is to play this way? Try it sometime! There *aren't* any lessons to teach you how to do this!"

The more Leslie talks, the angrier she gets. "And do you know how *easy* it is to sound like everyone else?" Candy Time blanches. Interesting how often a journalist is afraid of *one* of us. They just have to hit a nerve in order to get an ax ground on 'em.

I'm enjoying this, but Candy Time looks ill. "I'm sorry. I didn't mean to offend you," he says.

Leslie shakes her head. "I know you didn't. Just don't think that any-more; it bugs me."

"Yeah, it bugs her," I add.

"It doesn't matter how many notes you play or how fast you play them," Tea explains. "You have to play the *right* notes."

"And no one can help us figure out what those are," says Leslie. "It's hard to learn something that no one can teach you." He nods and looks down at his notebook, hoping to come up with a better question.

"What's *Candy Time* mean?" asks Dave in an attempt at friendliness.

The guy looks up, bewildered. "What?"

A goth-y chick with straight black hair in cutoffs and ripped tights balances a beer on her knee, holding a notepad and pencil. "Why," she asks us suspiciously, "are you guys the *only* band my mother likes?"

There is a gentle, tattooed boy next to me on the couch, hunched over his tape recorder, his eyeliner smeared with sweat. He requested an interview with "the lead singer," so the other band members gleefully took off, leaving us alone.

When the door shuts behind them, the boy stares at his knees. "Whadda you do," he asks slowly, "when you wake up on the wrong side of the lithium?"

Aw, geez. I wince and he smiles, but his eyes look sad. "Sorry. Bad first question?"

"Yeah. I was thinking maybe favorite color? Dream date?" I lean toward him conspiratorially. *"My favorite actor is Daffy Duck."*

"What's your favorite color?" he asks.

"Green."

"Whadda you do when you wake up on the wrong side of the lithium?"

I'm trying to read him. *Is he asking for help? Or is he gonna make me sound crazy in his article?* "It doesn't matter," I answer. He looks at me intently. "The music we play isn't craziness. It doesn't need lithium."

"What about you, though?" he asks.

"Well, that doesn't matter, either."

"Why not?"

" 'Cause I'm just one guy in a sea of people," I say. "Plus, if something gets you where you're going, it'd be wrong to question it."

He thinks about this. "What if you can't come back?"

"You mean if you just went nuts?" He nods. "That's the risk you take, I guess. I mean, if that could happen, you're probably already nuts."

Chuckling, he looks down at his knees again. "But . . . what if it makes you dead?"

"Well, dead's better than crazy."

"Which brings me back to my first question."

I look at him. "My favorite color is green."

"Do you need to be healthy in order to survive?"

"I don't know. There're probably a lot of okay ways to survive. You may need a passion, though. Or else you don't have any reason to stay here."

"Define *passion*." He turns his tape recorder toward me.

Some people from one of the other bands burst into the room, then notice the boy's tape recorder and shush each other, smiling at us. They grab beers out of a bin full of ice, then sit on a bench across the room, talking in low voices. One of them is a lady who looks as monochromatic as Mark. *I miss Mark.* She mouths "Sorry!" at us and I smile at her. Staring at her beige hair, skin, clothing and eyes, I remember what Mark said about poetry.

"I think you need something in your life that is both beautiful and necessary. A person or a mission or a place. Beautiful might not be pretty, and necessary might not be understood, but, still . . . I think caring, not death, is a passport to heaven."

We sit in silence while the band next to us continues to talk quietly.

The boy leans back against the Universal Couch. "Do you have to go to hell to get to heaven?"

This has never occurred to me before.

♋ heaven

this is heaven
and all my friends are there

After the show, we do a photo shoot outside the club. It's raining, and we try to protect each other's heads—especially Leslie's, 'cause her dreads almost drowned her in that pool drain in Santa Cruz. We all have our arms around each other, soaking wet with sweat and rain.

It's raining hard now. Autumn rain is different in Boston. Less . . . leafy. At home on the island, rain always smelled like leaves; here, it doesn't smell like anything but water and tires. At least in front of rock clubs.

I'm waiting for Gary to pick me up and take me home. We loaded the gear into his van and now he's settling the show in the back office for me 'cause he said I looked tired. I laughed when he said this. "Tired! I don't get tired!" but now I'm noticing that I actually do feel tired. Not sleepy— more like I just ran a marathon. Like no amount of rest could make a dent in this . . . weakness. God, now that I have a minute to think about it, I'm exhausted. *Is it my drug cocktail?*

I'm never sure what those crazy chemicals are doing. Keeping my swollen and shrinking soul inside my outline, I guess, but I'm seriously dulled. I feel like I'm living in a fake, soft world, my real dimension just beyond this one. I can remember it: it buzzed and my muscles sang with its energy. It was electric and frantic and hard and real. I was never tired there.

Boy, am I grateful for the coat Dave made me buy. Tonight, I'm hiding in it. It isn't a raincoat, though, so it doesn't *repel* water; it soaks it up instead, getting heavier and heavier. Wish I could lay it on the sidewalk and lie down on it. *Wow. That doesn't sound like me.*

Suddenly, I hear a voice over my left shoulder, speaking quietly into my ear. "On another night, there'll be another tree and it'll be raining again." I look up and see a dark-haired guy next to me, dripping in the rain. *Where'd he come from?* "I'll be there and you'll be there," he continues, "and then we'll both know."

"Know what?" I ask him, looking around. *I don't see a tree.* But he doesn't answer—just walks away in the rain.

I'm watching him walk away when Gary pulls his van up and pushes open the passenger side door. "Who was that?" he asks.

"Don't know." I ride shotgun even though it's too dark and stormy to see any buildings tonight.

While I'm arranging my wet coat around me, Leslie tosses a flat, shiny package onto my lap. "I got you a present."

I squint at the package in the dark. "What is it?"

"Well," she says, "you know how you always wanted a giant ass?"

"Yes!" *Aaaaah!* "You got me a giant ass?"

"I got you a *bigger* ass. Ass enhancement." Tea and Dave giggle.

I hold up the slender package. "There's ass enhancement in here, Les?"

"Yeah!" Her accent makes everything she says hilarious. Leslie can make the word *yeah* funny. And three syllables long. "It's black-girl stockings, booty included!"

I'm starting to be able to make out the figure of the beautiful booty-full lady on the package. I hold it up to show Gary. "Wow . . . I'm so sad I didn't know about booty-included stockings until now!"

"It's never too late to grow a booty, honey."

"Or fake one! Thank you, Les."

"That was awfully thoughtful," says Tea.

"It sure was. I'm gonna ride my bike all over the fucking place. I'm gonna sit on that bus like nobody's business." Rain splashes on the windshield, the wipers sending it pouring into my open window.

"Kris?" says Dave from behind me. "Can you close your window?"

"Sorry!" I roll it up and turn around to see how wet he is.

He's soaked. Blinking, he takes off his glasses and holds them out. They're spattered with raindrops. "It's okay. Can I use your new ass to clean my glasses?" he reaches for the package, but I pull it away, shaking my head at him grimly. Rolling his eyes, he cleans the glasses on his damp shirt.

"I can't wait to try 'em on," I say to Leslie.

"You're gonna look great, Kris," laughs Tea.

"Hope they fit," Leslie says. "Those're some big-ass stockings . . ."

Leaning back in my seat and hugging the package, I watch the rain outside. Gary switches on the radio. "Oh, good," calls Tea from the backseat. "I'm cold."

He looks at me for an explanation. "She means that we get mad at the radio and that warms us up," I explain.

He nods. "I get mad at the radio, too. But I *like* pop music."

"We like pop music. I think we *play* pop music. And we respect it." I point at the radio. "But they don't."

"No. I think when they say 'pop' they mean something else. Like . . . stupid."

"Pop's short for popular, right? Popular should mean smart. That would imply that we're all smart for liking it." I turn sideways in my seat to face him, pulling my coat around me, still gripping the panty hose. "But pop music's both dumb *and* pretentious. Don't know how they pull that off."

"By being dramatic," he says.

Dave leans up between us. "*Melo*dramatic!"

"Mmm . . . much worse," says Gary. "If you guys ever get melodramatic, I'll take you out back and shoot you."

"Deal," says Dave. His glasses are smeary from raindrops. I consider letting him use my new booty to dry them, as it's the only dry thing in the car, then decide against it.

"What happened to pop music?" moans Gary. "The radio used to move me to buy records. It was my life." This is a loss that seems to cause him pain. "Where did pop music go?"

"Underground," I answer. "Or else we just lost it somewhere between the *Joy of Cooking* and *The Joy of Sex*. I think the same thing that happened to food and sex happened to music."

"What's that?"

"Selling it. It's public and denatured when it should be personal and intuitive." I think. "Valuable and free. And healthy. But monetizing it and marketing unnatural facsimiles confuses people. So they're uneducated in their *own* responses—" *Wait*. I check myself. *Am I ranting? Am I embarrassing myself? Gary'll figure out I'm bipolar if I don't shut up.*

I learned from the soothers that part of learning to deal is knowing how people who aren't bipolar act. Sometimes all I can remember about this is *not like me*, and I draw a blank, lose my train of thought. Like now, I just freeze up. Luckily, Dave jumps in. "Bad people dumbing it down, trying to make wads-o'-cash off it," he says. "Lowest common denominator crap."

"The Joy of Music," Gary hums thoughtfully. "Corporate America wrecked it. Figures. They made that terrible bed and now they gotta lie in it." He stops at a stoplight. "And it's filled with money . . ." *Listen to Gary, all ranting about bad radio—and he's not bipolar. I don't think.*

I'm too tired to be manic, anyway. I bet we're just talking.

"You guys have to keep going," he announces. "You have to make popular music good again."

"We do?" I lean my head sideways against the headrest and my eyes close for a second. "But we play *unpopular* popular music," I chuckle into the seat.

"That's exactly what you play," says Gary, "because you're inventing something. You're gonna be hugely influential. You'll change the face of pop music."

I manage a tired laugh. *"What?"*

Gary is serious. "It's true!"

"It's true that pop music needs to change its face," I murmur, "but the Newspaper said we were chaos people."

"Huh?"

"I mean, pop songs should be witch doctors." *God, I'm tired.*

Gary leans toward me, confused. "Sorry?"

Maybe I'm not thinking clearly. "Micro and macro." I try to make sense. "Intimate yet worldly, and of indeterminate age," I slur. I slide down further in my seat and my eyes close involuntarily again. I struggle to open them, but they insist on closing.

Gary watches. "What's wrong with you?" he asks. "You sick?" I open my eyes and my mouth to answer, then close them both again before I can think of anything to say.

♋ peggy lee

in between midnight and sleep

I wake up when the van stops outside our practice space. Gary is looking at me accusingly. "You were *sleeping*," he says.

I'm amazed. "No!" He nods and walks to the back of the van, opens it, then begins piling gear onto the sidewalk. I follow him. "I've never done that before." I still have the package of big butt in my hand. Tea, Dave and Leslie start carrying gear into our space.

Gary raises his eyebrows like I've just confessed a crime. "I'm not here to judge. But there's something seriously wrong with you." When the gear is on the sidewalk, he picks up the kick drum, then holds a guitar pick in front of my face. "You can carry this."

I put the pick in my pocket and lift an amp, just to prove that I can, but it now weighs about twice what it used to. Putting it back down on the sidewalk, I look in the back to see if someone maybe hid *another* amp inside it. It's empty. So I toss the stockings in the back and pick it up, struggling into the dark building with it as my bandmates pass me in the hallway on their way back outside.

When I get to our practice room, I shove the amp on top of another one, then lean on it for a minute. Somehow the rest of the gear is already in there. My bandmates must be waiting in the van, ready to go home. *I'm moving in slow motion.*

Gary watches me heave my rain-soaked coat into the passenger seat.

The fur collar smells like wet dog now. "Maybe you're tired because you played a show," he suggests.

Sitting on the edge of my seat and staring through the windshield, I say, "That was, like, our bazillionth show, Gary."

"A bazillion's a lot. You could've hit a wall." He pulls away from the practice space and the tires splash water up in the air and onto the sidewalk. I fall back against the seat and stay there. "A musician is an athlete. And an athlete should be totally spent after a race, used up, or else he won't ever win. Some other athlete'll be there using everything *he's* got and beat him."

"Her."

"I don't like saying 'beat her.'"

"Oh," I answer sleepily. I watch Gary drive for a few minutes, feeling drunk. Then, all at once, I feel the weight of his charity. It hits me hard that we have nothing to offer. He keeps helping us, wasting his time and his money. I hate that we're such a burden. We are *not* gonna change the face of pop music . . . losing oneself isn't a marketable skill. In fact, we won't even last. Nobody buys ugliness; *why would they?* And there's no grant for this kind of art because we all know it *isn't* art. Painting is art, sculpture is art, antiquated musical styles are art, even avant-garde music is art, but not dumb-ass rock music. As soon as our sucky equipment dies, *we'll* die.

I feel like I should warn Gary that we have no future, that we aren't a safe investment. Tell him to go care about some other band—place his efforts in a nice successful basket of cool ambition, not the sieve of *right now, in this moment* that is Throwing Muses. Who *is* he, anyway? Some misguided angel. I don't get it.

I can't say any of this, though; I'm too tired. "Why are you so nice to us?" I grumble instead, without lifting my head off the seat. Gary doesn't answer; he just keeps driving.

When he drops us off at home, he looks at me suspiciously. "Get better," he says and pulls away, then sticks his arm out at the intersection and waves like he always does.

∽ pneuma

you're like a warped godmother
with your baffling love

Orange popsicle syrup coats my face and hands. Tipping
forward, I press my nose and palms into the sand, eyes
closed, and listen to the sound of the waves and the
screeching children playing near our blanket.

When I sit up, I imagine I must look very different and
amazing. I make my hands into claws and growl
terrifyingly at Crane, who lifts her head off the blanket
to look at me through big, brown sunglasses.

She does not tremble with fear. "Do you need a nap?"
she asks.

When I open our front door in the morning to get the paper, there is a bouquet of flowers on the porch, and a six-pack of beer. Our doormat often has something nice on it: a letter, a record, comic books, candles, an Easter basket, horoscopes, candy or a painting. I don't know where you find Easter baskets in autumn or how anyone knows our astrological signs, but we hang all the paintings, and the Easter baskets have replaced the plastic fruit on our squishy mantel.

This is what an audience does out in the real world. Delivers presents. They're like sweet, old relatives who forgot when your birthday is, so they bring presents all the time. Sweet, old, invisible relatives.

I put the newspaper and flowers on our rickety kitchen table and stick the beer in the fridge. I actually fell asleep last night when we got home and stayed asleep, *a miraculous miracle*, but I'm still tired. Taking a smudgy glass off the drying rack next to the sink startles two roaches, who scurry off the rack and into the drain. While I fill the glass with water so I can take my pills, I realize I don't want to. I look at the pills in my hand and recoil with nausea. *What? I never get sick.* Slowly, I walk over to the kitchen table and lower myself into a chair, taking a minute to admire the flowers and wake up.

The phone rings. I look at it and wait for somebody else to answer it. I'm too tired to move, but I don't really ever do phones anyway. Not unless I have to, like when I have an interview or someone says "phone for you" and holds it out to my face before I can slink away. *Phone for me.* There is no phone for me. I'm not good at them because of all the talking out loud you have to do on them. No expressions or body language. It doesn't seem like communication to me, just a trick to make you stand still.

My roommates gently bitch at me about this, as if I don't understand how the machine works: "You can't just pick up the phone, Kris . . . you have to say *hello*" and "Geez, they can't see you *nodding*!"

The phone rings and rings. I stare at it until it stops, then I study the wall next to it.

Our message wall is covered with penciled doodles, cartoons and notes. We do sometimes take normal phone messages for each other, so there are a bunch of *2:15, what's-her-name called, like/don't like/hate? can't remember*, or *wednesday the twenty-fifth at the paradise? there's $*, etc., but the majority of pencil marks are devoted to quotes from various phone calls.

In other words, if, when you answer the phone, the person you're talking to says anything interesting or confusing, you're encouraged to share it with others by adding it to the wall. Taken as a whole, this wall looks like an art project:

then EVERYTHING started falling!

I told her I had a dog and now she's coming over

Mr. Brownie is what I named the plant AFTER it died—before that, it was just "the plant"

tell him I wasn't, like, MAD, I was just in a loud mood

I do a lot of interviews standing here, drawing on the wall. Most of the music journalists I talk to are very bright, and I'm grateful for the press they give us. I like the idea of a professional music listener, so I do whatever I can for them. Unfortunately, what they usually want me to do is answer questions, and I'm not good at that. I start doing the math and always come up with: *how could anyone ever know anything?*

My bandmates are a tiny bit better at articulating responses, so I write questions on the wall and eventually they grab a pencil and answer. I have to tell journalists I'll get back to them as soon as the wall responds.

Q: "What style of music do you play?"
   A: "No."
Q: "Why are your lyrics so cryptic?"
   A: "Yes."
Q: "Do you mean that you have a fish nailed to a cross *in your mind*?"
   A: "You don't?"
Q: "What's your favorite color?"
   A: "Clear."
Q: "What's your favorite flavor?"
   A: "Plain."
Q: "Is this a dream?"
   A: "Yes."

I figure I've stared at the message wall long enough to try and take the pills on the table, but as soon as I swallow them, my stomach seizes and I have to run for the bathroom. The pills then throw themselves out of my stomach and into the toilet. *Geez, I really am sick.*

Dragging myself back to the kitchen, I can't think of anything to do but sit back down at the table, so I lower myself carefully into a chair. I'm wondering how soon a bipolar brain that doesn't take its medication starts making up its own rules when Dave walks out of his bedroom in a rumpled T-shirt and jeans. "*Mahnin*," he says.

"*Mahnin*."

He pads over to the table. "Guess what?"

"What?"

"Laundry. *Cleans* itself." *That doesn't sound good.* He pulls his T-shirt out to show me. "I left these clothes at the bottom of a pile of dirty laundry and now they're clean."

"Oh. How does laundry do that?"

"I don't know! Compression, I'm guessing . . ."

"Boy," I say admiringly, "that's some screwy logic you got there."

"No, really, it's true." He leans over the table. "Smell my shirt."

"I'm good," I say, turning away. My stomach's still shaky. "How're your mice?"

"Squeaky," he answers, sitting back down and yawning.

"Well . . . that's mice for you." I drop my forehead onto the cool table-top. It feels wonderfully soothing, so I leave it there.

"Kris?"

"Yep."

"Whatcha doin'?"

"Well . . . a minute ago I was staring at the wall."

"Mmmm. You okay?"

"Oh, sure." I pick my head up to look at him, but it weighs way more than it should, so I put it back down. "I feel kinda lousy."

"Why don't you lie down?'

"'Cause there's no way I could lie down low enough."

"You could lie on the floor," he suggests. I say nothing, just keep my head pressed onto the table. "Gary gave me passes to the aquarium last night. He says we should go."

I speak into the table. "What does that mean?"

"Well," Dave says, "I think he meant we should go to the aquarium."

"To look at fish?"

"Yes. Aquariums are for looking at fish."

I pick my head up again, but not very high; it's still so heavy. "Why?"

"Don't you like fish?"

"Fish're okay."

He stares at me. "Maybe it would cheer you up."

"I'm not sad. I'm sick."

"Are you sad about being sick?"

I think. "Yeah, I guess I am a little sad about that."

He stands up. "Get Tea and Leslie up and tell them we're going to the aquarium. I'm gonna shower." As he walks away, I lean up to smell one of the flowers from the bouquet left on the porch this morning. The flower is so nauseating that I have to run for the bathroom again, pushing past Dave in the hallway. This time I don't actually throw up, though, 'cause you can't vomit the scent of a flower. I just stare into the toilet, breathing hard.

"Anything I can do?" Dave asks outside the door.

"Throw away those flowers!" I yell into the toilet.

♋ caffeine

the best of us
puking

A few hours later, I'm chewing some of Tea's peppermint gum 'cause she said it makes nausea go away. My fingertips and forehead are pressed against the glass of a giant fish tank and I'm wondering if the devil is gonna rear up and grab my soul.

Anyway, looking at fish turns out to be pretty much the best thing ever in the whole history of the world. *Gary's so smart.* We've all been to this aquarium on school field trips but none of us remembers anything about those field trips except echo-y noise and lunch. We didn't remember the *majesty* of the fish.

Humans aren't creatures anymore; we're too out of touch with our own nature. We're just TV plus hair gel or something, but fish are still actual creatures. They can't lie, so they seem to have more humanity than us.

My bandmates and I can't talk to each other about the fish coolness, though, 'cause everything we say about them makes us sound like stoned adolescents. We tried when we first got here:

"Wow. They live *inside* the water."

"Air is their water and water is their air."

"And they fly in it."

Then we gave up and just watched.

A Buddhist monk is the guest lecturer in one of Dude's
classes. Dude has brought me along to hear the lecture
'cause he thinks all kids are Buddhist by nature.

The monk speaks on a patch of grass overlooking the
ocean, using the sea to help teach Buddhist principles.

"You must show compassion for water and the fish who live
in it," he says, and the students nod and smile.

"You must disengage from worldly attachments," he says to
more nodding and smiling. "You must fly the sky!" The
students stop nodding and smiling.

"You must throw a candy bar into the ocean!"

The students turn to look at Dude with blank expressions.
He leans down and whispers to me out of the corner of his
mouth, *"Don't litter."*

I'm leaning over a table in the dressing room at the Rat, trying not to heave into the beer bin, when a guy from another band grabs my arm and whispers excitedly that a "scout" is in the audience. "I know," I say. "I brought him."

"Oh god, it's true. Now I'm really nervous," he mutters, jamming his hands into the pockets of his army jacket.

There're record company guys in the audience *every* night; it never occurred to me that somebody might care. "Naw, don't be nervous. He's nice."

"I hope we play good," he says, shaking his head.

I laugh. "Not *too* good."

"Right. They don't like *too* good, do they?" He grabs a beer and opens it, then sits down on a grimy bench covered in graffiti. "How about cute? Should we play cute?"

"Maybe." It's so sad when people care about bullshit. It's like watching him pine for a bimbo, and he's not a bad guy. Of course, his band describes itself as "an A and R guy's wet dream." How embarrassing. These bands are incredibly adept at buying their own hype; Betty would hate them. Except that they're so good at showing off. What they do is sell counter-culture as approachable yet hip. Which is manipulative and extremely effective. People like that fool practically everybody. *Trying to be cool is so lame.* "Cute's been done to death," I say. "Smug is in; you could try smug."

He takes a sip of his beer and stares at nothing. "Smug," he sighs.

I smile. "You can do it!"

He turns to face me, narrowing his eyes suspiciously. "What's that sup-posed to mean?"

Oops. "I mean play nice. I've seen you play nice."

"Sounds like a euphemism for sucking," he grumbles.

"I thought you did that on purpose," I say.

"What, suck?!" he leans forward and some of his beer spills on the floor.

"Watch it," I say, looking around for a paper towel. I can't find one, so I grab a wad of Kleenex out of my sister's backpack and wipe up the spilled beer. He watches me clean up his beer. "Thanks," he says.

"No problem."

"Did you just tell me that I suck?"

"Did I? I don't think so." I toss the beer-soaked Kleenex into the trash. *I'm such a jerk.*

"I'm pretty sure you did," he sighs, taking another sip and staring at nothing again.

"That doesn't *sound* like me," I say pathetically. "I thought I said you guys played nice."

"It's okay." He looks at me, grim. "Honesty's important."

I sit down on the bench next to him. "No, it's not."

He stares at nothing again. "We do kinda suck on purpose," he says thoughtfully.

Gee, that's sad. And true. Nobody's more an artist than anybody else but bands like his pollute the impulse. It's mean to suck—it's rude. He's a good person; he should have the decency to be a good musician.

He can probably tell I think that, but, of course, I can't say it out loud. "You're lucky," I tell him. "My band's a *mutant*. Nobody'll ever like us. Y'all know how to sell yourselves. That's not a negative attribute; it'll get you far."

He quits staring at nothing to search my face. "You shoulda stuck with 'smug.'"

Unlike A and R guys' wet dreams, my band is very suspicious of its fans. We could stand to buy a little of our own hype. When people come to our shows, it confuses us; we can't imagine what they're doing there. We like Throwing Muses 'cause we *are* Throwing Muses. But why do *they* keep showing up?

We figure they gotta have some ulterior motive. The four of us stare into the packed bar from the dressing room, making guesses as to why the people in the audience are people in the audience and not people at home. Leslie turns around to look at us. "Thirsty?"

"Lonely?" guesses Tea.

"Lost?" I ask.

"I don't understand it." Dave shakes his head and shrugs. "We're *so* not fun."

We stare into the noisy room full of happy, sweaty people, trying to imagine feeling what they're feeling and reflecting it back at them. "At least we know they're buzzed," says Tea.

♋ pneuma

i tongue a socket
you feel the jolt

When we get home after the show, a three-letter word is written on the message wall in between cartoons and quotes: "IVO" with a twelve-digit phone number after it. I don't know what that stands for. *International . . . Voting Organization?* Can you vote internationally? I know we can't afford to call them back anyway; that's a ton of numbers. *The poor I.V.O.*, I think. *They don't know how far away they are.*

In the morning, the front porch holds a carton of cigarettes, a cinder block painted blue, a bottle of essential oil that says "rain" on it, and a flyer inviting us to join the neighborhood softball team. I place all this except the cinder block—which is gonna stay where it is—on the kitchen table and then try to face my pills again.

The roaches that scatter when I lift a glass off the rack have always intrigued me; I think of them as guys who know where they're headed. But roaches and nausea don't go well together. Their scurrying supercharges the nausea and I throw my pills away without trying to take them. When I do, I see yesterday's flowers sticking up out of the garbage.

The phone rings. *Who calls every morning?* I'm scared the ringing'll wake my bandmates and we had a late night. So I cross the room, take a deep breath and pick up the receiver, putting it to my ear. After about four seconds of long distance crackling, a man says "Hello?" in an upper class British accent.

I wait, hoping he'll hang up, but the crackling continues. "Hi."

"Oh, hello! Is this a member of Throwing Muses?"

Oh, shoot . . . phone for me! What're the odds? "Yes. This is Kristin."

"Oh, Kristin!" He sounds very excited. *About what?* "Hello!"

"Hi!"

"My name is Ivowattsrussell. I run 4AD Records out of London."

"I'm sorry, what did you say your name was?"

"Ivo. Watts. Russell," he articulates. This guy talks like the goddamn queen.

"Could you spell that?" I say, looking at yesterday's message on the wall.

He pauses, then starts spelling. "I-v-o-w . . ." *Hey, it's the I.V. O.! I don't remember sending any demos to England.* Ivo's still spelling. ". . . u-s-s—"

"Oh, it's okay," I interrupt. "I just meant your first name. It's written here on our wall. I've never met anyone named that before. I thought you were an international voting organization."

Silence for a few seconds. "Oh, I *see!*" He laughs, then pauses again. "Can you vote internationally?"

"I doubt it. Who would you vote for? King of the world?"

"Yes . . . well . . . it's nice to meet you."

I can't think of anything to say, so I nod, then remember that I'm not allowed to. "Yeah. Hi." I roll my eyes. *Brilliant.*

"I'm calling about your self-released cassette. I think it's really brilliant."

Hey, I'm brilliant after all. "Thank you very much."

"You should make a record that sounds just like it."

"Yeah, we should."

"However, I regret to say, I don't sign American bands."

"Oh." *What'd he call for?* "Well, that's too bad."

"It is, actually. I love your music. If there's anything I can do for you, don't hesitate to ask."

I laugh. "I'll try to think of something."

Silence again. "*Is* there anything I can do?" he asks.

"You mean right now?" I shake my head. "I mean, no. No, thanks. Sweet of you to call, though."

"Of course. Nice to finally meet you. Goodbye!" I hear a dull clatter, then the crackling on the line stops.

While I'm standing there, still holding the receiver up to my ear, Dave walks out of his bedroom. Seeing me on the phone, he drops his jaw in mock horror. "Who're you talking to?" he whispers.

"Nobody." I hold the dead phone out to him.

Dave nods, taking the tea kettle off the stove and filling it at the sink. "That makes sense, I guess. You aren't scared of the phone if nobody's on it." He turns to me and narrows his eyes. "But what do you and the phone talk about . . . ?"

"See this?" I point to the IVO on the message wall. "I talked to it. It's a man and it's English. From England. That's why the phone number's so long."

Dave frowns. "You'd think that if you speak the same language, they'd knock off a few numbers."

I shake my head. "Nope."

Ivo calls the next day, asks for me, and then tells me again that he has an English record company that doesn't sign American bands, expressing his regret that such is the case, given Throwing Muses' "integrity." The next morning, he calls to say that he's *still* enjoying our music and also doesn't sign American bands, which is a shame because he owns a whole record company all the way over there in England. Then he calls again the *next* day to say pretty much the same thing, asking if I'd thought of anything he could do for us. The next day, he doesn't call.

I find that I'm disappointed. I've had this flu for almost a week now, so during the day, I can't really do anything but feel crappy and talk to Ivo on the phone. I like trying to picture where he is, though all I ever come up with is a weird amalgam of Buckingham Palace and Monty Python sketches.

We always reach a dead end talking about music because he can't sign my American band and I don't know how to ask him for help. He probably wants to help us find an American deal, but we don't want one; they seem so evil. So Ivo and I talk about everything else. He's really fucking funny, especially with that accent. It makes everything he says entertaining, but he's also genuinely entertaining. And open, childlike. I picture him as a six-year-old with a bowler hat.

I'm guessing that he hasn't called because he's ready to move on to other, more English bands, when the phone rings. "I'm calling to tell you about a boil . . ." he says in his man-queen voice, a little breathless. Apparently, he had a boil on his neck that burst in a café and sprayed all over the wall. "It was lovely," he sighs.

"Sounds nice," I say. "Wish I could have seen it."

"Maybe you could picture it," he says. "It was like a verruca and a carbuncle combined."

"A what and a *what*?"

"Like a wart and a . . . uh . . ."

"It's okay. I'm a little pukey with the flu right now. I wouldn't wanna picture anything too gross."

"I had the flu myself, last week," he says. "Dismal."

"Maybe I caught it from you."

"Impossible. I caught it from a curry."

"Oh. I caught it from a rainy night."

"You know what you should do," he says. "Put your feet in hot water and put an ice bag on your head."

"Ice bag?" *I wish I had the queen's voice so I could use it to say "ice bag."*

"Or maybe it's the other way around . . ." He gets suddenly brisk. "Please give me a call," he says, "if there's any way I can be of help to you. You have my number, right?"

"I do. It's written on the wall here. But I can't afford to call it. Too many numbers."

"I see." He sounds serious. Usually he sounds goofy—well, like the queen in a goofy mood. "Is there anything you . . . need?"

"We need a cat," I answer. "We have mice but none of us wanna get into the mousetrap thing." I tell him that Dave's mattress has been squeaking at night even when he lies perfectly still, and that he and Leslie actually cornered a mouse that ran out of it, then tried to kill it with hair spray.

"*Can* you kill things with hair spray?" asks Ivo.

"No. It sneezed and ran into the toaster."

"Oh my. Then what happened?"

"Then they tried to toast it."

"Ah," he says. "Did they succeed?"

"No, they just singed its fur. I think all that hair spray protected it."

"You're lucky it didn't explode . . ."

"I know. Then they felt bad, so they let it go and it ran right back into Dave's mattress."

"I see," says Ivo.

"That toaster cost twenty dollars. So now we're talking about cats."

He thinks. "I have *two* cats," he says. "They're both rather nasty, but you can have the pretty one."

"Why's it pretty?" I ask. "What's it look like?"

"Well, like a big . . . *cat*," he answers.

"You mean like a cat, but big?"

"That's right. And I'll throw in some catnip. He's wild about catnip; makes him quite mad."

"Your cat's on drugs? Okay, we'll take it."

A few days later, we receive a contract from 4AD Records. "But he doesn't sign American bands," I say.

"Who doesn't?" asks Tea, reading it.

"Ivo."

She looks at me. "I-V-O? From the wall?"

"Yeah. He was gonna give us a cat."

This is Ivo's offer: to fund, release and work one record, then see how we all feel. That's the contract. *What the hell, doesn't he know how the music business works? Who is he, anyway? Another misguided angel.*

Behind the door in the shed is a box full of kittens. The
mother cat, wrapped around her babies, purrs loudly.

I've never seen this cat before; she seems to have come
out of nowhere, so I figure she must be an angel in cat
form, delivering all this happiness unto our shed.

Zoë lies near them, panting and smiling. My little
brother whispers, "They're named Jake. All of them,
except for the girl kitten. And she's named Jake, too."

A vial of blue fluid tells me I'm pregnant. The fluid is beautiful, aquamarine. The sun shines through it as I stare and stare. I'm in shock. So I don't have the flu. *I thought birth control worked.*

Some boys like little rat girls. Not many, but a few. I've always been grateful for the ones that did. Now I'm not so sure.

All us teenage females know that pregnancy is a remote possibility. So you get an abortion and move on. We all know that, too.

I stare into the blue fluid, hoping it can tell me more.

It doesn't, so I find my way to the bus station and buy a ticket to Providence. In the bus station, I make a deal with my brain: we will not think until we get to the beach. This is surprisingly easy. I stare out the bus window instead of thinking. Soon things start to look familiar and Providence comes into view.

At the Providence bus station, I buy a ticket home, to the island. *I'm so sick.* Then I look out another window until the view begins to look familiar. *And so tired.* From the bus station on the island, I walk to the ocean.

Now I have to think.

Sitting on a cement wall, looking out at the sea, I kick off my shoes and stick my feet in the sand. The water is beautiful, aquamarine.

I feel as if there is a light in my middle. One I shouldn't put out.

So much for our record deal. And everything else.

It's late September. The last few days of ocean swimming. I pull off my jeans and jump into the water in my T-shirt.

♋ 37 hours

like flying on fire

I listened when the soothers spoke kindly of wayward chemicals and I know they meant it when they decided my reality wasn't theirs, but now I need permission to stop taking pills. Brain-fuzzing is one thing, teratogenic compounds another—drugs could put out the light in my middle. And not taking them could make me manic again. Or depressed. I don't know what to do.

So I'm reading every psychiatry book I can find. They aren't written for me. Most of the books intended to help you help yourself are in the "self-help" section, and you *don't* wanna go there. You'd think helping yourself'd be a ballsy thing to do, but self-help's the whiniest section of all.

I went to a bookstore first. Everybody all glasses and sweaters and constantly asking if I need any "help." Well, obviously—if there was a "desperation" section, I'd be in that. They probably thought I was shoplifting; they *always* think I'm shoplifting. 'Cause I dress homeless, I guess. *Please . . . if I were shoplifting, I'd dress nice.*

I stood in this bookstore for about an hour, tearing through whiny books for whiny people who wanna learn how to whine more coherently, looking for information. I couldn't find any. It's so condescending to fill books with everything *but* information. Like us laymen can't handle it. It's fucking research, for christ sake . . . *share it.*

Soon I realized I wasn't looking to help myself; I was looking for someone else to help *me.* So much for ballsy. *I'm whinier than I thought.* So I thanked the helpful sweater people and left; went to the library, where they leave you alone. The library's full of panicky students cramming in cubicles. Still all glasses and sweaters, but these people are too preoccupied with their own stress to even look up.

Poring over reference books all afternoon, college textbooks and drug manuals, I've learned that the medications I'm supposed to be taking are, of course, potentially dangerous to a fetus. I already stopped taking them anyway; I can't keep 'em down.

I look down at my snake bag. An alcoholic is always an alcoholic—I am always me. Soon a manhole cover will throw itself off and evil will fly out and suck me in. So far, evil hasn't, though. I'm hoping this means that, for now, I can handle my own twisted chemicals better than the light in my middle can handle those that have been prescribed for me.

♋ silica

play a grown-up
'til you grow up

I've made an appointment with a psychiatrist to ask permission to stop taking the drugs I already stopped taking. If he tells me I'm not allowed to do this, then I know I have to have an abortion. It wouldn't be the first time that happened to somebody. But I feel like I gotta serve this light as best I can, give it every shot at living before I give up. Maybe that's stupid. But I haven't met the light yet; it could be great. Its existence is my fault, anyway, my responsibility.

This doctor has what looks to be a seven-syllable name, which I avoided trying to pronounce on the phone with his secretary, who also didn't mention the doctor by name. She used the name of the clinic instead.

Walking to the appointment, my snake bag on my shoulder, I feel heavy. The heaviness of guilt for bringing a potential being into the world who probably can't stay and the heaviness of responsibility to do everything I can to keep it here. If an abortion is smarter than bad chemistry, then I'm going to have to rise to that occasion. If the light can become a child, then I need to reinvent myself as its mother. Right away.

How's the band gonna live in a van? That's child abuse, isn't it?

Everything in this office is either brown or gray, including the psychiatrist himself, who is both brown *and* gray. A pleasant-looking Indian man, he leans back in his chair and smiles. "What are we talking about today?" he asks.

I sit in a brown chair on a gray carpet, hands folded, ankles crossed in front of my snake bag, and tell him my story, asking him if I can forgo medication for the duration of the pregnancy. I have no idea what he'll say. He is a soother, so, in my experience, he'll seem obsessed with both life *and* drugs—it really could go either way.

I feel so awful right now, it's almost hard to care. Don't know what's morning sickness and what's withdrawal, but I have my nails dug into reality right now, just catching glimpses of the world through a swirl of exhaustion and nausea. Abortion or pregnancy? I can't root for one or the other. They *both* seem like bad ideas.

The psychiatrist looks alert but thoughtful. "I think that we should look into other medications or possibly alter the dosage of your current medications, but not having met you before, it's difficult to say. Are you delusional? Do you have mood swings?"

This is embarrassing. Way harder than I thought it'd be. *Why is doing the right thing never the easy way out?* I talk to his left shoulder instead of his face. "No. I mean I only ever had the one mood swing: up."

He stares. "What medications are you taking?" I place the bottles of pills on his desk and he picks them up, one by one. Reading the labels seems to make him tired.

Staring at the pill bottles on his desk makes me tired, too. I waited trustingly for therapeutic levels to kick in, lived through sickness, shakiness and imitation calm. And now the pills seem dangerous. I mean, all that brain-fuzzing can't be cool, can it? "So what do you think will happen if I stop taking them?" I ask him. "'Cause I already did."

"Any number of things; I can't really predict." He puts his elbows on the desk and leans his chin on his hands. His tone of voice sounds like he's talking about the weather or lunch. "You may become manic again. You may experience a psychotic episode. It's also possible that you could become depressed, suicidal." We sit, looking at each other. Then he smiles. "Or maybe you got better!" he yells, throwing his arms up in the air. I laugh. "Did you at least taper off?" he asks pleasantly.

"No. Cold turkey. I can't keep them down."

"That can be extremely dangerous," he says, a wide grin still on his face. "And you'd like to remain free of all medication?"

"If possible."

His smile flattens. "Of course I'll take your feelings into account, but you should know that manic depression is a serious disease. It isn't called that any longer, by the way."

"So I hear."

"Many bipolar individuals commit suicide," he continues. "Twenty percent, in fact—that's a lot. Some, while in manic states, even die of exhaustion." He thinks for a minute, looking sleepy. "Most of my bipolar clients struggle with the depressive aspect of their condition, however. Given that you were in a manic state for such an extended period of time, I imagine your experience is quite different from theirs." He looks at me for a response, but I don't have one. I don't know any other bipolar people. "Let me ask you this: do you hallucinate?"

I glance down at my snake bag. "Not really." Looking out the window behind him, at the bright green and orange leaves blowing back and forth,

I wish feverishly that I was outside and not stuck in this brown and gray room. I like this guy, but his office doesn't match what happened to me this year. My experience of manic depression was so physically and emotionally intense that it's hard to relate it to a clinical setting. I know psychiatry is a science, but how do you measure a systemic effect like *soul sickness* in a cold, flat room? It was messy, huge; a muscular panic. It actually felt more like . . . art.

"I hear music sometimes," I say. "I think there's a snake in this bag. Even though I know there isn't. I mean, I know it isn't here the way you and I are here. I just believe in it."

Now he's awake. "Is it more of a dream image?"

"Sort of. I'm a musician and I suspect that it's a song image." He stares intently. "It's me seeing sound."

He looks down again and begins to write as he speaks. "That makes sense."

This was the last thing I expected him to say. "It *does?*"

"Yes." He looks up from his writing. "Art and dreams are very closely related and they're worth listening to, as long as your hold on reality remains intact." I sit, stunned. "It's also entirely possible that you hear music because you're a musician. It's certainly not considered normal, as you know. But at the present time, though you aren't asymptomatic, would you say that your symptoms are mild and not exacerbated by discontinuing your medication?" I nod. He hands me the piece of paper he's been writing on.

"Of course, you know it may be some time before the medications you've been taking are completely gone from your system. Do this for me: tell one friend, one family member and one work associate that this is what you're doing. If you show symptoms of any kind—a change in energy level, speech or thought patterns, any mood swings, visual or auditory hallucinations—you or one of your contacts must call me right away. We will try this as an experiment, but you should know that bipolar disorder may be as dangerous for a fetus as psychotherapeutic medications."

I glance at the paper. It's not a prescription; it has a phone number on it, nothing else.

"In the meantime, I will go over your medical records and speak with your obstetrician. Together we'll try to come up with a regimen that works for all of us. Please leave his or her contact information with my receptionist on your way out."

I'm so relieved, I can't even think. The light won't be put out. It doesn't feel like heavy responsibility; it's light, like spring landing in the room after a desperate winter. *I'll cross the living-in-a-van-is-probably-child-abuse bridge when I come to it.*

♋ hope

i saw hope in my backyard

"Any questions?" he asks.

I don't know what to say. "Yes. How do you pronounce your name?"

He laughs. "You don't! It takes too long!" Then he stands and walks me to the door. "Eat well and sleep. You're not very pregnant, I assume?"

"No. Hardly pregnant at all."

"Ah. Enjoy vomiting!" He laughs again and closes the door.

I leave the office, my head spinning. Finally, I'm outside with the autumn leaves.

So I really am pregnant—time to grow up. What're the rules here? Do I have to call Ivo and ask him to fire me? Do I quit playing clubs? Do I quit the *band*?

Wait, did he say "obstetrician"? I don't have an obstetrician. I gotta get one or I won't have a phone number to give his receptionist. How'll I pay for that? People say babies are expensive. Why? Are they expensive right away or not 'til they have to go to college? Do diapers cost a lot of money?

I better go back to the library.

My witch hat falls down over my face as I vomit into my
trick-or-treat bag. I am deeply disappointed by this. I
know that the green makeup which took my mother so long
to apply is smearing to reveal green skin.

My small companion, dressed as a hobo, smokes a plastic
cigar and watches me. "You done yet?" he asks.

I look up. "Almost," I answer weakly.

Moonlight fills the gaps on the sidewalk left by
streetlights; there is no place to hide. A small crowd of
trick-or-treaters gathers to stare. I continue to throw
up while Aqua Man, a princess, Gilligan and their basset
hound watch.

"She okay?" Gilligan asks.

The hobo removes the plastic cigar from his mouth.
"Yeah," he says. "She's just *really* drunk."

♋ ether

this gnawing emptiness
seeps in like a cold mist

Wow. Dr. Seven Syllables wasn't kidding. I lean against the tiles as the shower sprays my face. I've heard of projectile vomiting, but never seen it. It's like a special effect—it'd be cool if it didn't feel so terrible. "Morning sickness" turns out to be a misnomer, by the way. This sickness goes on twenty-four hours a day, coloring the world an intense palette of garish grays. I can't even keep water down.

This particular kind of nausea is a gnawing, icy hunger, like your blood is hungry and your *bones*'re hungry. Your bones and blood think they're starving. But somehow your confused stomach has convinced your eyes to recoil at the sight of food, your nose to object to any scent: *everything's poisonous garbage,* it says; *let's starve!* If you sneak a bite of food or a sip of water past your eyes and your nose, your stomach knots and spits it right back out again. So you wait . . . until the hunger and weakness are so overwhelming that you try to sneak a bite of something again. Then your stomach whips around, pissed off, and spits it back out at you.

This is my new job. The other Muses noticed, of course. They've never seen *anybody* this sick before. "And I know some dead people," said Dave gently.

So I sat them down on my bed, shut the bedroom door to keep the aliens from overhearing, and told them I'm pregnant. They took the news soberly, sort of like when I play them a new song. No one suggested that we not be a band anymore. Nobody questioned our dream of living in a van. They seemed more concerned about *me* than future career repercussions. "Are you happy?" asked Leslie.

"I have no idea," I answered. "I don't think so. But I'm not *un*-happy."

They all sat there, leaning against the wall, their feet sticking out over the side of the bed. I joined them. Leslie turned to look at me. "How about . . . one day at a time?" she said.

That made sense. Nothing has really changed yet and we don't even know how it'll change when it does. Since we have shows booked, we'll play shows. That's as far as we got. Our record is probably in jeopardy; I just don't know these rules and neither do my bandmates. One day at a time.

Each morning, when I wake up, it's clearly a day to be spent puking,

not breaking up the band. I don't actually know what it means to be
pregnant yet; I'm still sort of in shock. Didn't see this coming, you know?
Don't even know what it is, really. People grow inside each other? *Weird*.

The bus is now a major endeavor: a frozen and feverish sea of nausea, the
autumn leaves out the window my only relief. But it takes me to a fascinating place where I hang with a subculture I've never paid much attention to
before: breeders. I mean ones who're actually *breeding*. Like me, I guess,
but . . . on purpose.

I don't talk much at the midwife's office, mostly just smile and listen.
Everything the other pregnant women do is interesting to me, because
they're all two people, not one. Crazy.

Even more fascinating than the breeders themselves are the already-
born children they bring with them. Tiny, beautiful and disarmingly honest (they're even honest about lying), they're like little space creatures who
just moved here. The babies are so punk rock: bald and drooling, yelling
and grinning, learning how to work their new spaceships made of bone,
muscle and skin. And the toddlers are all far more graceful than their
mothers, even when they fall over, which they do a lot. All motor develop-
ment aside, gravity's a bitch goddess.

These tiny people aren't TV-plus-hair-gel yet. They seem to have the
built-in grace of animals—something their mothers have lost. Maybe because being alive is a child's reason to be here, since they aren't asked to
prove their worth in any other way. They're here, here on purpose and they
celebrate here by feeling it out, gravity and logic be damned.

Some of these children seem to keep feelings to themselves, but not
many of them. Impulsive is not the word—thoughts erupt, questions and
ideas fly out of their mouths the instant they're formed. These little space
creatures remind me of songs. They're offshoots, but they're super creatures; better than us.

♋ i'm alive

fan your flame and can your heat

As I sit in the waiting room pretending to read a *National Geographic*,
a little girl I'd been watching out of the corner of my eye sidles up

to me and holds out her fist. "Do you know what's in here?" she asks gravely.

"No," I answer, "what?"

Her mouth twists up. "Well . . . it *was* a secret. Are you a nice girl?"

"I'm pretty nice."

"Just don't tell *her*." She points to a woman across the room reading a magazine. The woman looks up.

"Why not?" I ask. "She looks nice enough."

The little girl leans in and stage whispers, "I took it out of her pocket." The woman's eyebrows shoot up.

"Maybe you should give it back," I suggest.

Confused, the girl opens her hand to reveal a piece of lint. "Do you think she *wants* it?"

I figure if you can't do one *day* at a time, one minute at a time still counts. Probably a good rule for almost anything.

Interestingly, the white noise couldn't do it at all; it whispered, then fell—a pregnancy casualty. No more waves, no more wind chimes. I still hear music sometimes, but one song at a time, quietly, clearly. As if Throwing Muses were playing next door.

My Brain That Wouldn't Die seems to have taken a backseat to the Body Monster, letting it drive for a while, 'cause it has a job to do. I don't hear too much from evil these days and I'm softer than I was before, gentle. It could be all the puking, but I feel okay: *peaceful*. Peaceful with a single-mindedness of purpose I've only ever associated with music.

The purpose is this: the baby's heartbeat. I heard it. A heart beating. A little light, unconcerned with this universe, having created its own. I'm not one person, but two.

Crazy.

෨ golden ocean

your baby takes your balls
and gives you back your teeth

your baby takes your balls
and lights a fire in your belly

On my shelf in the pantry now are prenatal vitamins and bananas, whole-wheat this and organic that; the fridge is full of wheat germ, yogurt and apples. I bought my first dozen eggs. I have to eat on this nausea planet, eat right through the threat of special-effect vomiting. I stare into the fridge wondering how the hell to keep my bone-deep hunger and suspicious stomach from fighting with each other. I can't even do hippie food anymore 'cause it has flavor in it.

"No, it doesn't," says Dave, leaning against the kitchen sink, eating a plate of spaghetti.

I look at him, surprised. "Yeah, you're right. I don't know why I said that. My stomach changed all the rules." Tea and Leslie make their dinners around us. It all looks and smells awful to me.

"Can't you tell your stomach what to think?" he asks. "I mean, you *know* hippie food tastes like a bowl of paste. Your tongue must know it, anyway."

"Don't knock hippie food, Dave; I said you were right."

"I'm just saying it seems right up your alley now. Don't you like to eat paste?"

Geez. "Don't say 'eat paste.'" He shrugs and goes back to his spaghetti. I'm so jealous of his ability to eat food and keep it down. "Pasta *means* paste," I tell him in my misery.

He holds his plate out to me. "Want some?"

Tea interrupts with her idea: Pepto-Bismol. Chalky, pink goo. She holds it out to me. "Are you high?" I ask her. "Chalky, pink goo?"

She gets a spoon. "Remember the commercial? It coats your stomach."

"With chalky, pink *goo*," says Dave.

"Yeah!" she says brightly. I shake my head at her. "Just *taste* it." She pours out a big spoonful and sticks it in her mouth. In a flash, her expression goes from encouraging to disgusted. She covers her mouth with her hand, trying to swallow, then gives up and runs to the sink, spitting the pink goo into the drain. Such a crazy color—it looks like something from Dr. Seuss. We watch her run the water and wipe her mouth, then take a deep breath. "Okay," she says, turning to me and grabbing the bottle of Pepto-Bismol, "now you."

Leslie stops her with one hand. "Not cool for pregnant chicks," she says. "I have a better idea." I warn her that I'm not going to do leaves and bark, no matter how cool Santa Cruz was. "How about flowers?" she asks.

"Eat flowers?"

Tea frowns. "Don't make her eat flowers, Les."

"I was gonna make them into a tea . . ."

Dave finishes his spaghetti and drops his dish in the sink. "You're gonna make her *drink* flowers?"

"Sure!" *She seems so . . . perky. Everybody seems perky now. Everybody but me.* "Hibiscus flowers!"

"I've heard of those," I say. "I thought you only ate magical forest roots."

She gives me a look. "I'm not sharing my magical forest roots with you. So, you want some hibiscus flowers? You've heard of 'em, right?"

"Well, I've heard of barbecue, too, but I don't want *that.*"

She sighs, disappointed. "Have you heard of toast?"

In the smoky clubs, I collapse. We work so late at night. *So this is how tired feels . . . ow . . . I hate it.* The other Muses scout out hiding places for me where the air is better, where I can lie down and have a clean place to throw up nearby. Then they surround me while I quietly pass out. They know I feel no pain when we're playing, that the nausea will dissipate during the opening chords of the first song, but they also know I'm completely useless until then.

Talk about jumping in with abandon. I feel like I've asked a lot of my bandmates this year and here they are, willing to do this with me, too: wrangle this new sick and tired me. They treat it like a fun project, like this is *our* baby.

My pregnancy is a secret outside of the Muses' tiny circle, so in the clubs, we tell people I'm tired or I have the flu. Both of these lies make people go away, which is good. For some reason, a crowd of people fills my eyes with humanity and makes me even sicker. I have no idea what that means. *Too much?* Somehow, the other Muses know this instinctively— smoothly, kindly, they keep people at bay.

When Leslie and Dave take off for the dressing room through the crowd, Tea stays behind, kneeling next to me on a red vinyl bench. I'm lying on my back, my feet resting on the snake bag, reading graffiti sideways. The club is noisy and full, so we're hiding behind a table, facing the wall, in order to avoid eye contact with anyone. Facing this wall is worthwhile, though, 'cause some of the graffiti is great: notes passed to faceless friends. "*Thoughts are empty, heads are full,*" I read.

"*Hurt bullies,*" says Tea.

"*I don't know, but I do care.*"

"*One dog barks, the others bark at him.*"

"That's a Chinese proverb," I say.

"What would make somebody write *that*?" she asks, disgusted.

"Write what?"

"Just *fuck you*. Can't they think of anything else to say?"

"I guess not."

She looks down at me and splays out her hands. "Then why say anything?"

"Does it hurt your feelings?" I ask her.

"Sorta."

"You shouldn't take it personally. Every wall says *fuck you* on it somewhere."

We both stare at it. "I don't take it personally," she says. "I just don't get it."

"It's kind of a tradition . . ."

"Yeah, but I'm tired of it. Aren't *they*?"

"Maybe they didn't write any of the other *fuck you*'s in the world, so they want one of their own."

The crowd of people presses in toward the table. Tea tries to rub the *fuck you* off the wall with her thumb. The wall bends in ominously. "Careful," I say. "That could be load-bearing graffiti."

"I don't understand," she says. "Are they trying to make us feel bad? Why? That's not nice." She thinks. "Should we feel *sorry* for a person who writes *fuck you* on a wall?"

We both look at it. "Could it be an ironic *fuck you*?" I ask. We continue staring. It doesn't look ironic. "Fuck just means sex, though, right?" I say. She nods. "So maybe they're talking about expressing love."

"Yeah, probably," she says. "Like, *love ya!*"

"Love ya lots!"

She pulls a folded piece of paper out of her back pocket. "Here's your set list," she says. I unfold it and read the long list of song titles. "Okay, I'm getting nervous," she says. "I'm gonna get a beer. You want something?"

"This is unpossible," I moan, still reading the list of songs, trying to remember all those messed-up chords and lyrics and tempo shifts and odd counts. I look up at her. "We do this all the time, right?"

"That's what I was thinking," she says. "How do we remember it all?"

"We don't always."

Tea shudders. "I need a beer. You okay here?"

"Sure."

"See you up there. Ten minutes, okay?" She disappears into the crowd. I can't stop reading the set list. It looks so hard—so many songs. Just an unbearable amount of effort and concentration, two things I feel incapable of pregnant.

Flat on my back on the bench, hidden beneath the table, I stare at the first song title on the set list for a full minute, trying to rehearse it in my head, but I can't remember the opening guitar line. It's the snake song: "America." We play it all the fucking time. *What the hell is the opening guitar line?* Pounding club music is making it hard to concentrate. The audience is getting noisier, too. *If I can't remember it now, I'm never gonna remember it up there. And we're opening with it.*

I panic, thinking I'm gonna screw it up and be unable to disappear— *that'd suck*—so I sit up and look around for Tea to ask her how the song opens. Or to get her to play one of her songs first. But she's long gone and there're people everywhere. I gotta make my way through the crowd to find her or I won't see her until we're on stage. Grabbing my snake bag, I know the snake isn't inside it.

What?

I freeze, rip open the bag. It's empty. The snake is gone. I mean, there isn't a snake, was never a snake, was never gonna be a snake. The wolf didn't "walk away," she was a dream. The bees were a moment—an image caught in a thought. What *was* I thinking? What was I *thinking*?

And the snake . . . the snake was nothing. I just got used to carrying a goddamn bag around.

Is my brain finally dead?

I fall back onto the sticky red vinyl . . . *holy shit* . . . *the soothers said I wouldn't get better.* The opening guitar line from "America" winds its way into my head and I exhale.

No therapeutic levels this time. No levels at all. I make a mental note to call Dr. Seven Syllables in the morning.

My parents take me to Woodstock. We drive and drive. Like
any toddler in a car, I'm so tired and bored that I'm
antsy, feeling trapped.

Suddenly, we're there. Or almost there—we see people
pouring over a fence. Dude says we should pour over the
fence *with* them because on the other side of the fence is
a big party: music and happy people.

♋ red eyes

i'm okay
i'm okay

"The snake is gone?" asks Dr. Syllables on the phone. I picture his brown and gray person in the brown and gray room.

"It isn't there. That's different."

"Hm. Yes." He doesn't sound brown and gray; he sounds animated, speaking quickly. "Very different. You don't believe in it anymore? Was the snake a song image, as you thought?"

"Maybe." I try to imagine that. The idea of turning a snake into sound seems like alchemy. *I couldn't do that.* "I do have a song with the word 'snake' in it," I answer lamely. "And I was thinking about it . . ."

"Okay." He pauses. "And your pregnancy? Are you taking care of yourself?"

"Yeah, I'm doing my best. Just the *thought* of food makes me sick, but I eat anyway. And I'm sleeping, for once."

"Good. The clarity you're experiencing could be a side effect of physical vitality. I see this sometimes when patients adopt a health regimen. Their predisposition to a disorder is more apparent in times of physical stress, and conversely, their symptoms are diminished when they feel more robust physically." *Robust? I don't feel robust. I feel pukey.* "Did you learn to say my name?" he asks.

What? Oh, right. What the hell is his name? "Uh . . . I'm *American*."

He giggles. "*Hee hee.*" He actually says *hee hee* when he laughs.

"I call you Dr. Seven Syllables." He stops giggling.

"I've never counted." Silence. I guess he's counting. "Do you still hear music?" he asks.

"Yes, but it sounds better. And it isn't . . . *invasive.* I mean, it isn't loud. The songs are just insistent. While I was taking medication, I could choose not to pay attention. The songs would sort of float away, but now they stick around."

"One piece of music again and again?"

"Yeah. Until I pick up my guitar and learn it. Then it stops."

"Interesting. And does another song begin?" he asks.

"Eventually."

He is quiet for a moment. "Is this better or worse for you than songs floating away?"

"Well the songs are no longer dimished, so it seems more . . . real."

"Well, I think that's better, don't you?" he sounds happy.

I laugh. "Yeah, real's good, I guess."

"*Hee hee hee*." He becomes suddenly serious. "You know, my brother plays an instrument and thinks about music a great deal of the time. He seems to daydream as music plays in his head. In our family, we laugh about this. No one has ever called it psychosis."

Hmmm. "You mean maybe I'm just a musician? 'Cause I agree. I don't think I needed those pills to mess me up any more than music already did." He says nothing. "Or am I getting better? 'Cause I feel like I'm getting better."

"That's not exactly what I meant." He pauses, then says, "In my experience, claiming not to be manic-depressive is actually a symptom of manic depression."

Oh, for god's sake. "Claiming not to be manic-depressive is also a symptom of *not* being manic-depressive, isn't it?"

"*Hee hee hee hee hee hee!*" He takes his time composing himself, then, abruptly, is quiet again. "There is maybe a stigma attached to mental illness that prevents you from seeking help. I see this often, even now that we're all supposed to be so enlightened in this regard."

"Maybe they have a point."

"Who?" he asks.

"The stigma . . . people. If your brain doesn't work right, it could be because you're stupid or because you're mentally ill. Either way, your brain's unreliable. If you broke your arm, your arm'd be 'stigmatized' because it isn't as reliable as a working arm."

"Okay," he sighs. "I wouldn't get very far in my profession supporting the stigmatization of mental illness, but it may explain why you don't accept your diagnosis. If you are bipolar, your mind is broken; if you are a musician, it's not."

"They didn't just tell me my *mind* was broken," I explain. "They told me my whole personality was broken."

"I see," he says quietly.

"I'm not being glib. Perception is deeply entrenched."

"Yes," he says. "This is why I told you about my brother, who has not been diagnosed anything other than 'dreamer.' The reason this is so is that he feels peaceful perceiving music the way he does. I believe you should ask yourself if you are *peaceful*. We should all do this. If the answer is no, you're being called upon to help yourself."

I'm stunned. *What a great thing to say.* "Peaceful is a good word to use."

"Thank you," he says. "I use it a lot. Let me know if this music you hear becomes distressing to you. Or if what you see or think is very different from what the people around you see and think. Or if you find yourself doing any activity to excess, even the most mundane. Like shopping, for example."

Huh? "Shopping? Shopping is a symptom?" *I knew shopping was bad.* He giggles quietly, but says nothing. "No. I don't shop excessively. Or at all."

"Fine. We'll try to keep your system clean for as long as possible throughout your pregnancy. But keep in mind that you are to evaluate your mental state continually. Do you have a friend, a work associate and a family member on call?"

I haven't actually done this; I've always kept this stuff from the people I care about. "Uh . . . I'll get right on that."

"It's important because you will not always be able to evaluate your own behavior. That's true of anyone."

I cringe. "Okay." I'm not into the sharing/caring thing; it seems rude and embarrassing. I hide wretchedness—*duh-uh*—doesn't everybody? Such a strange story. I don't *wanna* tell it; it'd just make me seem strange.

"How's the vomiting going?" he asks.

"Oh. It's not as much fun as it sounds."

"*Hee hee.* No, I'm sure it isn't. *Hee hee.*" He stops laughing abruptly again. "Vomiting can weaken you; therefore, when you're tired, you must sleep. If you have trouble sleeping because of excessive energy, it would be better to control this with medication than to have you staying up all night, right? So pay attention to that.

"And don't be afraid to take on partners in this. Regardless of the stigma associated with it, mental illness is an illness like any other and you need caregivers. People will understand. If you have no one, there are networks which can provide support. They can be very helpful."

Network sounds uncomfortable. "I'm not a group therapy guy," I say. So I guess I gotta confide in a friend. But this stuff is ugly and my loved ones are beautiful. They've always been my world without this ugliness. I don't wanna poison that world with this crap. "I think I can do this on my own."

He is quiet for a few seconds. "You do a lot on your own, don't you?"

In a bad way? "Do I? Maybe."

"Just be aware that thinking you are unassailable is a symptom of mania." *God, is everything a symptom of mania?* "Bipolar disorder and pregnancy are both valid reasons to seek support. You have a person other than yourself to consider now. Your unborn child may need the support of others more than you can know right now."

I guess. "Well, thanks, Doctor . . . Syllables."

"*Hee hee.* Call me Seven."

When I hang up the phone, I walk to my room, take the snake bag off the foot of my bed, fold it up neatly, and throw it away.

This is what Dave says when I make him my friend, family member and work associate, by the way: "Keep walking."

♋ colder

keep walking

I have to swing my guitar around to the side when I play now; otherwise I can't reach it. The weird thing is, at shows, nobody can tell I'm pregnant. They're shocked when I step off the stage and suddenly grow a huge belly. I don't understand this. Maybe facing me head-on you can't see it, or at the right angle the guitar blocks it? Maybe they just aren't looking at my middle. I'm disappointed; I want points for taking up more space. I *love* being size Big.

Aside from wanting to show it off, though, my swollen middle's making me even *more* introverted than usual, 'cause it's so much cooler than anything I could be paying attention to on the outside of me. It's such an *active* body part. My gut jumps around, of all things; it's very entertaining. I'm guessing beer bellies don't do this. Tiny heels push against my ribs, little fists pound away at my insides. My dancing gut wears my coat, sleeps, hiccups. It's almost a person.

When the band plays, though, the baby stays very still. Maybe because when I'm working, the baby's working—the physical form that is us is fully engaged. Or the music heat puts the baby to sleep? I can't imagine the *music* would put anybody to sleep.

The stillness is awful. A baby in your belly should make its presence known. I hold my breath, waiting for the kicking to start up again. It always does, but . . . it's terrifying every time.

For this reason, it seems, I no longer disappear when we play. I mean, I can't. Mothers shouldn't disappear, I guess; they need to be present, to keep watch. This is okay as long as we don't play for too long.

We looked it up: babies in utero are often asleep—they *are* babies, after all. And all mothers freak out when their babies stop moving. But Tea still worries that rock bands aren't good for them. "Maybe she's passing out from the noise," she says, turning her amp down during another rehearsal in our dank practice space.

"No, he's listening," says Dave. "Kris's baby is different from normal babies. He *likes* music."

Tea scowls. "*Kristin* doesn't even like music! Can't you play quietly?"

Dave holds his sticks in the air. "Do you know what I play?"

"Yes, I know what you play, *Uncle* Dave," says Tea, glaring at him. "Too loud! It's unnecessary; we're just practicing. You're hurting the baby. She's sad now." She leans over and pats my stomach, cooing, "It's okay, honey."

"He's fine!" Dave says. Then, to the baby, "Tell your aunt you're fine, slugger."

Leslie rolls her eyes. "Can we try that one again?"

"Yes," I answer. "Go. Please."

Tea looks at Dave and puts her finger to her lips.

I joined the Y, but not because I need a place to shower. And not because I need to swim songs away, either. I'm good with all of that these days (*a miraculous fucking miracle*). I joined the Y because my midwife says that pregnant women should exercise daily because we're "athletes in training." I don't know if I was supposed to take that literally, but I'm scared not to.

The lady who gave me my Y membership card and schedule looked like an upside-down triangle. A real swimmer: big and meaty and clean. Right now, I look like a right-side-up triangle. Or a snow man with legs. Anyway, when she handed me the schedule, she told me that it was "super important." I thought "super important" was a strange thing to say about a schedule, a thought that was probably reflected in my expression, 'cause she got very grave then and said, "No. Seriously."

So I stuck the printed schedule in my coat pocket and promised to study it so that I wouldn't try to swim laps during water polo or be given swimming lessons with a bunch of three-year-olds. I couldn't really think of anything else that might go wrong at the Y because of a scheduling mishap.

Here's what can go wrong at the Y: naked. They swim naked here. I did notice on the schedule that lap swims were gender segregated and thought that was unusual—a vestige of a more prudish time, maybe. Like they hadn't altered their schedule since the Victorian era and that's why it's so "super important" to them.

Nope. Men swim with men and women swim with women because they're all nude. When I stepped out of the locker room in a new blue bathing suit for my first lap swim, stretching goggles over my head, I thought all the ladies in the pool were wearing flesh-toned suits.

So tell me this: which is more embarrassing, swimming laps naked (and hoping you read the schedule carefully) or being the only person *not* swimming laps naked? I stood there pondering this in the echo-y room, some dumb-ass goggles stuck to my face, my giant stomach splashed by naked people, sucking in chlorinated air.

I haven't been able to tell Ivo I'm pregnant. We still talk on the phone all the time but it just hasn't come up. "What did you expect, Kris?" asks Tea, seeing me hang up again without having told him.

I sit at the kitchen table with her. "I thought he might mention baby booties. Or prenatal vitamins. Or his favorite fertility goddess—and then I could segue into it gracefully."

Tea folds up the paper she's reading and looks at me sadly. "Gracefully? Really? You thought you could do it gracefully?"

I shrug. "He's always talking about something . . . producers and studios and stuff. Plus, I'm nervous. What if he fires us?" Tea giggles and I glare at her. "Don't laugh at me!"

"Come here," she says, smiling. "Let me fix your sweater. It's buttoned wrong." I look down, but I can't see the buttons that're hidden under my stomach. "It's not your fault," she says. "You're just chubby."

I lean over to let her button my sweater the right way. "Thank you," I pout.

"You know what I think?" she says.

"What?"

"I think it's none of his business."

"Oh." *Duh-uh.*

She's serious. "Really. You don't believe that people have to quit life when they have babies, right? So don't imply that you do. Just make the record you want to make and be pregnant at the same time."

Wow. That sounds easy. "Yeah! And Ivo's so far away, he'll never know . . ." I squint out the kitchen window, trying to imagine such an impossibly simple solution.

"Even if he flew over here, he'd just think you were a little fat kid like everybody else does."

I look at her. "What?"

She shakes her head. "But he probably won't fly over here."

I like this. "You're right. Pregnant ladies can make records, right? I bet they do it all the time."

Tea looks at me. "If you can make a baby, you can make *anything.*"

ෞ night driving

if you can
you see it home

"Elizabeth June," says Betty luxuriously, flicking a sugar packet across the table at me. Then, fists in the air, she shrieks, "Touchdown!" The sugar packet glides off the edge of the table and topples to the floor.

"Oooh, so close," I cackle. Reaching down to grab it, I notice other restaurant patrons staring. They always do that.

I called Betty when I got up this morning and told her I was taking the bus to the island because I felt it necessary to take the bus to the island. "I just need to," I said. "Can we hang?"

"Are you homesick, sweetheart?" she asked.

"Not homesick, exactly. I just wanna go home."

"Because you're homesick."

"Really?"

"Yes. We should meet at the Creamery for coffee," she decided. "You can have decaf."

And when I got to the Creamery, Betty was . . . I don't know, she's always just so Betty. She sets the scene and performs the play and means every minute of it. She's pumped colors: engaging and engaged. "That's a beautiful name," I tell her. "Elizabeth June what?"

"Thornburg."

"Thornburg?" I ask. "City of thorns?" I flick the sugar packet and it flies up onto her saucer.

She looks bemused. " 'City of thorns.' I like that. School of hard knocks, city of thorns." She gets dreamy for a second, then snaps back into paper football mode, grabbing the packet of sugar and sending it ricocheting off her empty water glass. Her glass tips into the salt shaker, knocking it over and scattering salt everywhere. Then the salt shaker spins across the table and slides into my lap. Paper football is a rough game. "I was born Elizabeth June and I kept Elizabeth June out of show biz. Betty Hutton was a caricature. Ask my husbands."

Uh, no . . . I replace the salt shaker, then line up the sugar packet and flick it onto her lap. "And Judy Garland's name was Gum?"

"Well, not chewing gum, dear. And it was a surname. Parents don't name their little girls *gum*." Betty flicks the sugar packet with an overly light touch. It moves about two inches.

We stare at it. "You want a do-over?" I ask.

"Do you mind?"

"Be my guest. What about . . . Cary Grant?"

She eyes the packet suspiciously, then lines up her shot like a pool shark and delivers a perfect touchdown, smooth and controlled all the way across the table. "Yes!" she shouts throatily. "Archibald Leach."

"No. You made that up!"

Betty looks offended. "I most certainly did *not*. Cary Grant is a lovely man and a dear friend."

"You mean *Archibald Leach* is a lovely man and a dear friend."

"Yes. I imagine Cary Grant is a caricature, too." Old Hollywood is still very real to her, more real than this coffee shop, I bet. Whether she's loving it or hating it, it's not far away or gone. "He suffers from manic depression, too, Krissy." She says this as if he and I share a common hobby.

I grab the sugar packet and tear it open. "So . . . Elizabeth and Archibald are *real* people," I say. "And Gum was real?"

"Yes. And Betty and Cary and Judy were shiny packages."

"On purpose pretend?"

"On purpose pretend."

"Personas?"

She nods. "Personas."

I hold up the sugar packet. "This?" then stir it into my coffee.

"In a way," she answers.

I stare into the swirling coffee. So we're hating Hollywood today. "Shiny packages are easy for people to understand and swallow."

When I look up, Betty is smiling, her eyes shining. "Aren't movies wonderful?" she sighs.

What? We're liking Hollywood today? "Are they?"

"Beautiful people living beautiful lives . . ."

"For seven bucks? They're just pretending. I'd rather watch real people living real lives for free."

Betty twists her mouth up thoughtfully. "Real people don't buy their own hype as often, it's true. But real people could never be that beautiful; reality wouldn't allow it."

"Those faces aren't beautiful, Betty. They're just feature-free."

Her mouth drops. "Oh, Krissy, of course—you don't know! Cary Grant is just a name to you!" She reseats herself on the leather bench to introduce a new idea. "The movies they made when movies were great were *hyper*real," she says slowly and carefully. "They created a reality that *should* have been." She waits for this statement to make an impression. My face is probably blank, though, because she gets suddenly brisk. "I'll give you a list of movies you have to see."

"I'd like that."

She takes a tiny pad of paper and a pencil out of her purse, but instead of writing down any movie titles, she leans over the table. "How're you feeling?" she asks pointedly. Betty has a very businesslike attitude toward my pregnancy. She doesn't seem to think of me as a teenager any more than I think of her as an old lady; she just sees us as humans moving through time, bumping up against each life phase in turn.

"Great. Fat. Like a superhero, and my superpower is *stomach*."

She laughs. "The first movie you need to see is *The Miracle of Morgan's Creek*."

"What's that?"

"One of *my* movies," she says, writing it down on the notepad. "Watch it; it's good. I think you can rent it at the video store. It's about an unwed mother."

So listen to this: Betty turns out to have been an actual movie star. Dude told me this—reluctantly because he didn't want me to be weirded out. I *was* kind of disappointed. I wanted Betty's world to be Betty's world, not dumb ol' Hollywood. But no, she really *was* on the cover of *Time* magazine and everything else. She made blockbuster movies and had her own TV show. The movie stars she talks about were her friends, and Mr. De-Mille really did shoot close-ups of Betty's lovely face. Her invisible fans used to be visible, and she probably had a butler, too. Which is all really weird, but at least I *can* rent one of her movies.

The waitress appears with a coffeepot and asks us if we want any more coffee. We both decline. Betty declines by hiding her face and whispering "*No, thank you*." I guess she thought the waitress was gonna ask her for an autograph. "How's Boston, Krissy? You okay?" she asks when the waitress leaves. "Do you feel like a grown-up there?"

I laugh. "I don't know. What's a grown-up feel like?"

Betty smiles. "Well, do you still buy your underwear at the grocery store?"

"Uh, no."

"Then maybe you *are* grown-up!" She giggles.

"No. I still *wear* my grocery store underwear, so I don't need to buy any more."

Betty laughs hysterically, then wipes her eyes. "I don't guess I ever grew up either. And I *so* wanted to. It was a dream I believed would come true. I had this image of me and my husband—"

"Which one?"

She thinks. "Not any particular one. Just 'Husband' with a capital 'H.'

And we'd have a nice house and children, but my image was mainly just . . .
sitting on a couch together."

"Your dream was to sit on a couch?"

Betty looks at me accusingly. "*Your* dream is to live in a van!" *Touché.*
"We'd sit on the couch because everything else was okay. It was an image
of peace."

"Oh." I try to take a sip of coffee, but the cup's empty. "I get that."

Betty's looking wistful. I hate it when she looks wistful. "I think you
did better than sitting on a couch, though." I tell her. "I bet you have
'peace' wrapped up in your adventure somewhere."

"I *have* had an adventure," she sighs. She doesn't sound happy about
her adventure. "Krissy, how're your reviews?"

"They're good. They're positive, I mean. But they call us 'alternative'
rock. We think it's disparaging." She nods. "I mean, alternative to what,
real rock?" I take a deep breath; I don't want her to be disappointed in me.
"And most of them call me crazy."

"I was afraid of that," she says. "Did you tell them you hear songs?"

"I told some people. I gotta get better at lying, I guess."

Betty looks away for almost a minute. I sit listening to the clattering
restaurant noise while she thinks. "Sweetheart, I know the way you play
music is real," she says, "but to others, it may look like a caricature. That's
why they don't always treat us like real people." Show-biz advice. I take a
napkin out of the dispenser and fold it into a tiny triangle, then shoot it into
her lap. "You don't have a persona, so you *can't* keep yourself somewhere
else."

"Maybe I should get one. I could be Assumpta Tang. Or Pretty Dirt.
Or Gum Two. Or *Betty Hutton* Two: 'The Revenge of Betty.'"

She picks up the napkin and places it on the table. "It's a handy safety
net! A one-dimensional one, maybe, but people create them for a reason."
Carefully, she balances the napkin football under her index finger and lines
up her shot. "Personalities are more reliable, of course, even though they
seem to be . . . processes. Processes of building up and tearing down. Con-
struction and destruction."

What a cool thing to say. "I hope you know how smart you are."

"I know how smart I am. I hope *you* know how smart I am." She raises
her eyebrows reproachfully. "And if you have a minute of trouble, you will
call me before it becomes *two* minutes of trouble." She says this like a hyp-
notist, as if she's making it so.

"Yes, ma'am."

Betty tears off the tiny sheet of paper with *The Miracle of Morgan's Creek* written on it, pushes it across the table at me and drops a five-dollar bill next to it. Then she kisses me on the forehead and, pulling on her coat, walks out the door.

♋ elizabeth june

god left you here, too

"Reject Beach" is what they call the poor people's side
of this beach. The rich people hang out behind the rocks,
    near the country club, where we can't see them.

My brother and I build drip castle after drip castle in
"crabtown," where the tide pools are. Waves and crabs
            destroy them instantly.

We love the dripping and the castles and the crabs and
    the waves, the building up and the tearing down.

♋ crabtown

lost my head on reject beach
lost my heart

After Betty leaves, I race to the bookstore next door. I hunger for book-stores now; up-to-date pregnancy information is something researchers actually *do* share with us laymen. I can't afford to buy any books, though, so I stand in the pregnancy section reading as many as I can as fast as I can. My biggest health concern right now is cigarette smoke. The clubs we play are very smoky; fans in the front row actually blow smoke directly at me because it looks cool in the lights.

So I take a book with a black-and-white photo of a baby on it off the shelf and turn to a chapter called "Pregnancy in the Workplace." I figure there's no way I'll be able to use any of the information in it—they always say weird shit like, "Keep carrot sticks in your desk drawer"—but this particular book says: "Request fans that blow smoke *away* from you." I'm not kidding; that's what it says. For a minute I think the book is speaking directly to me. *You can request different fans?*

When I realize they mean fans, not *fans*, I close the book and replace it. *I'll just keep some goddamn carrot sticks in my guitar case.*

Leaving the bookstore, I think, *I'm still homesick.*

On the sidewalk in the cold, I stare at a pay phone for a second and then, on a whim, call my mother and ask her if she has time to take a walk with me before I catch the bus back to Boston. "Ooo . . . *yes*," she says. "Let's go freeze our butts off." So I sit on the curb and wait for her to pick me up and drive to the beach. We both love winter beaches—windswept and clean. It's goddamn freezing, but winter is a beach's secret.

When Crane pulls up, smiling, I notice for the first time ever that she looks a lot like me. I drew thousands of crayon pictures of her when I was little in which she looked like an enormous queen: diamonds and lace, shin-ing hair and sparkling eyes, crooked stars floating around her. I always drew myself as a little stick with a baseball cap, in the background. I had no idea we looked alike.

We drive in silence because the evening is so pristine and perfect. When we get to the beach and climb out of the car, though, shrieking wind blasts our faces. We both squeal, laughing. She wraps a scarf around her face and reaches over to put my fur collar up around mine. Then we lean into the wind to fight our way toward the surf.

The water is dark. Wild and foamy. "Only a few more months," she calls through her scarf, patting the baby through my coat.

The pink and orange sunset, shot with deep blue, is like every other sunset that's ever been since my grandmother held Crane and Crane held me and this baby here came to life. And like every other sunset that's ever been, it's shockingly beautiful: a snowball on fire, the flames spreading across a field of dove-gray and navy. "Look at that!" I say, stopping to look up. *Yet another miraculous miracle.* So clean and full. *I miss this.*

"It's un-freakin'-believable!" she shouts over the combined roar of ocean and wind. "Takes your breath away!" I nod, grinning. "I can't believe," she yells, "the magic that happens every single day!" Crane puts an arm over my shoulder and a hand on my stomach, her smiling eyes crinkling over her scarf.

♋ buzz

```
my limes make a baby healthy and wise
i cut lemons and lemons and limes
```

I can't believe I have to spend money on food now. It's expensive stuff. Especially the good kind of food. A hundred grams of protein a *day*. Do you know how much food that is? And how much money? I would so flunk foraging. All I wanna eat is lemons and limes and grapefruit, for some reason, and there's no pregnancy book that says *that'd* be okay.

So after swimming naked laps, I stomp through the snow to Bread and Circus, the straw-scented health food store here, and hang with the braided and bearded to read labels and compare unit prices and protein grams and RDA equivalents. Gotta get vitamin E in me somehow (helpful hint: it's impossible), plus all the B's (and they have to be balanced), C *and* its cofactors the bioflavonoids, iron (but not too much! and never with vitamin E, which you can't get anyway!), balanced amino acids (there're unbalanced ones?), vitamin A (note: the wrong kind is *dangerous*. Also, too little is dangerous—oh yeah, and too much), omega 3's for essential fatty acids, calcium (lead-free! and *only* with D and magnesium!), trace minerals, acidophilus, enzymes, and did you know there was a vitamin K? *Aaack.*

And then there are the don'ts: no caffeine, alcohol, preservatives, artificial sweeteners or colors, molds, palm oil, refined sugar, refined flour, pesticides, herbs, spices, seafood, raw food, deli food, *smoked* food, saturated fats, *hydrogenated* fats, tap water, corn syrup, painkillers, antibiotics, cough medicine, cold medicine, *any* medicine, potential allergens or carcinogens . . . it's exhausting.

This afternoon, I've given up scanning shelves and reading labels and have lapsed into a vague stare when a—what's a nice word for wan and anemic? willowy—a *willowy* health food store employee glides up behind me and offers help. I'm clearly dazed; this is a pity move on her part. "I was just looking at protein powders and got lost," I tell her.

She grabs one off the shelf and holds it up. The label has a picture of a himbo with bulging muscles on it. "I use this stuff," she says.

You do? You aren't a very good advertisement for it. I take it from her and read the ingredients. Whole lotta herbs, and I can't remember which ones are supposed to be good and which are supposed to be bad. "Some herbs are contraindicated in pregnancy," I say.

"Oh, you're pregnant? I thought you were just fat." She giggles. I wait, smiling politely. "Herbs are *good* for you," she chirps.

"What about this, though?" I say, pointing to an artificial sweetener.

She squints at the list of ingredients. "I can't even *say* that!" she laughs. *Sigh.* Then she takes another can off the shelf. This one has a picture of cookies on it. "This is whey protein powder. It's for people with soy allergies. Do *you* have a soy allergy?" she asks hopefully.

"No."

"Oh, well, this has *whey* in it."

"What's whey?"

"Like *curds* and whey?" she screws up her face.

"What's that?" I ask.

"You know, Miss Muffet and the spider?"

This is not helpful. I read the ingredients. "Oops. It has caffeine in it," I say.

"Caffeine wakes you up!" she squeals.

I think I hate her. "Yeah . . . still, though . . . I *am* pregnant." I put it back on the shelf. *I'm tired.*

"I can't believe you're having a baby; you're just a baby yourself!" We look at each other, then turn back to the shelves. She points at another can. "Can you eat strawberries? This one is strawberry."

I give up. "Yeah. I'm sure it's fine," I take it and toss it into my basket. "Thank you for the help. That was really nice of you."

The hippie chick looks at me thoughtfully. "You know, maybe protein powder isn't what you're looking for. Like, you should maybe just eat meat or something."

Huh? "Can't you get fired for telling me to eat meat?"

She laughs. "I just mean that if you were, like, living in a jungle? You probably wouldn't be shopping for protein powder?"

She's trying—I can't hate her anymore. "That's true. I'll pick up a leopard steak on my way out."

She leans over and yells at my stomach, "Hey there, baby! Mommy's making leopard for dinner!"

Geez. "Okay, thanks!" I laugh, backing up. She covers her mouth with her hands, giggling.

Crazy hippie chick.

Finally, I leave with a brown paper bag full of the most valuable foodstuffs I can possibly afford, too tired of even the idea of food to eat it.

At least I can keep it down now, so when I do eat, it doesn't go to waste. It goes toward making eyelids and shoulders and tiny lungs, somehow. As far as I know, I can't make those things, but I've seen a bunch of little baby parts on the monitor at the midwife's office. She puts some goo on my stomach, turns on a TV, and shows me a little space creature, dancing around. A universe, complete with eyelids, shoulders and tiny lungs. We're both quiet as we watch the universe dance.

Do you know what a sonogram is? It's seeing sound. So other people do this, too.

At shows, I wear the big cotton Mayberry dresses eschewed by my old-lady friends and drape sweaters over my swollen middle. I don't think I'm keeping too many secrets anymore, but I imagine that an unspoken rule against pointing to women's stomachs and asking questions is keeping me from having to talk about it.

Leslie says people definitely wait for *you* to bring up your pregnancy, and that I don't. She calls it "the pregnant pause," when, in conversation, people give you the opportunity to mention the other human living inside you. "But you don't seem to follow the same conversational cues that other people do," she says to me in the kitchen. I'm sitting at the table and staring at another plateful of expensive protein I don't feel like eating. "You just look at them and smile," she continues, "which is sort of confusing. You should eat that, by the way."

"Confusing's okay, though, right? I don't feel like eating it."

"If you don't mind hanging out with confused people, I guess." She opens the fridge and stares into it. "Eat it anyway. It's not *for* you, it's for the baby. You don't want to have an ugly baby."

"I just think it's my business, is all," I say, pushing eggs around with a fork. They look cold and slimy. "Food is so boring." I put down my fork and look at her. "I just don't wanna talk about it and I shouldn't have to. Remember that guy at the Rat? I thought he was gonna hit me."

I really did think that guy was gonna hit me. Instead, he yelled, "Haven't you ever heard of birth control?!" I don't even *know* him.

"He was pissed off," Leslie says.

"What the hell does that mean? What was he pissed off about?"

"Well," she explains, "most people think teenage pregnancy's a *bad* thing."

I look at her. "It *is* a bad thing." Leslie takes a bottle of pink juice out of the fridge, then sits in the seat across from me. She nods. "Nineteen is hardly a teenager, though," I say.

"Yeah. But most people think you're *thir*teen."

"What? What do you mean?"

"By 'most people think you're thirteen'? What do you think I mean? You look like a little kid," she says.

I scowl at my eggs. "Well, some people just look like kids; it isn't *my* fault."

"I didn't say it was." She's not paying attention; she's reading the label on her juice bottle. "What's ascorbic acid?"

"Do they really or were you just kidding? Vitamin C."

"I thought that was citric acid." She opens her juice and takes a sip.

"No, ascorbic." I watch her, try to take a bite of an egg, can't do it. "*Who* thinks I'm thirteen?"

She smiles a Leslie smile. "Uh, let me think," she says in a *duh* voice. "Oh yeah, everybody." I slump in my chair. "You're lucky!" she scolds. "You're youthful. And you'll *stay* youthful. Having a baby when you're nineteen means you'll have a nineteen-year-old's body for the rest of your life!"

"It does?"

"Sure!"

"I hadn't heard that," I grumble.

"Well, it's true." She drinks her juice and watches me, a half-smile on her face. "A homeless guy in Santa Cruz told me that."

"Oh, well then, it must be true."

"You're too judgmental. He was a smart homeless guy," she says, leaning forward and shifting into storytelling mode. "Once, I baked him a cake in my tree house 'cause it was his birthday, right? And—"

I squint at her. "What are you talking about?"

"I'm talking about *this*," she says, annoyed. "So, I didn't think it was possible to bake a cake in a tree house, but I was gonna try anyway, you know? 'Cause it was his birthday and nobody but me cared, which was *so* lame."

"That was very nice of you," I say vaguely. I usually enjoy Leslie's stories, but all I can think about is people talking about me behind my back.

"Yeah! So this girl I know brought me a toaster oven and helped me run an extension cord up to—"

Putting my fork back down and groaning, I interrupt her. "Is it my accent?" I ask. "Do they think I'm a hick? I thought I didn't *have* an accent anymore." She looks at me. "I mean, how could I be thirteen? What do they think, I'm, like, a *street urchin*?"

Leslie shrugs, giving up on her story, and looks at my plate. "Eggs. Gross," she says. "You should eat that."

♋ el dorado

these eggs look like eyeballs
and i'm too bored to eat

I'm holding my mother's hand in Atlanta, waiting to cross
the street, when a lady pushes a stroller past us with a
strikingly ugly baby in it. "Mama!" I yell. "That lady's
                got a monkey in her baby carriage!"

Crane is horrified; she pulls me away and hushes me,
hissing, "No, Kristin, it's just a funny-looking baby."

The lady pushes the stroller down the sidewalk. *She's
getting away.* "Mama, please!" I squeal. "I wanna see the
monkey!" I let go of her hand and run to see the monkey.

She catches up with me as I reach the stroller and we
both peer down into it, me excited, my mother panicking.
There is a tiny monkey tucked into a blanket next to the
                       ugly baby.

"Oh my goodness," Crane says breathlessly to the woman in
        her relief. "What a *beautiful* baby!"

Our doormat has a daisy and a postcard on it this afternoon. I pick up the postcard and read it. "On another night, there will be another tree and it will be raining again. I'll be there and you'll be there and then we'll both know." *Geez.* The dripping tree guy from the Rat knows where I live.

Leaving the daisy where it is, I shove the postcard in my pocket and head to baby class. I go to this "baby class" every Tuesday. I don't know what happened to our culture to make it so that we can't even procreate without taking a class about it, but I go anyway, 'cause I know *I* can't procreate without taking a class about it. The other mothers in my baby class are all businesswomen who're married to business*men*. These married professionals are strange, plasticky people.

Maybe strange is the wrong word. *Annoying* plasticky people. I've never met anyone like them before. I wanted them to be smarter than me—I have so much to learn—but they aren't. They're *unkind* and that's the dumbest thing you can be. Not unkind to *me*, just snippy and grabby: negative and selfish. Why be that way?

These couples all say they work in "business." What's "business"? Is it selling something? What do they sell? Shouldn't it matter?

Whatever business is in real life, to them, it's competition. In fact, *everything* is competition to them: get it now, whatever it is, before somebody else does. Husbands and wives compete with each other, couples compete with other couples. It's disconcerting; I thought we were a social species. I guess they're just a dark twist on sociability.

Anyway, both husbands and wives worked in "business" until they made enough money to feel ready to start thinking about discussing the various pros and cons of deciding to engage in the process of planning to clear their schedules long enough to paint the home office a pastel color and put a two-thousand-dollar crib in it, research imported strollers and playpens and wooden toys and baby carriers and changing tables and mobiles and tiny designer outfits, order some videotapes designed to turn their little lump of clay into a future businessperson, sign up for a diaper service and a private nursery school with a waiting list, hire a day nanny and a night nanny and a weekend nanny and a freakin' wet nurse if they still have those, then begin trying to pinpoint ovulation and fertilize that egg in order to have a—*phew*—baby, whatever that is. For years, they've been starting their families. My family got started without me even being consulted.

Which I *know* is my fault and my deal. I try not to judge the yuppies lest I be yuppie-judged. I even want to like them, but they make it hard. They're always snapping at each other and bitching about . . . well, everything: working, not working, working out, not working out, swollen feet, swollen middles (*what'd you think was gonna happen?*), the heat inside, the cold outside, the products they've purchased and the ones they don't yet have, their friends and loved ones. It's angrifying. They have so much and they whine so much.

All that unnecessary stuff and all that unnecessary meanness—I actually feel bad for their future children. I'm afraid they're all getting babies as accessories, 'cause they heard other people had them and they gotta have whatever anybody else has.

At least their kids'll have tons of money.

The yuppies're really gung ho about the whole childbearing thing, which'd be cool if their enthusiasm was focused on growing a baby or raising a child. All they seem to care about is labor and delivery. I don't know any more about having kids than they do, but their attitude seems myopic, like trying to have a wedding without a relationship or a marriage.

They *definitely* take the midwife's assertion that pregnant women are athletes literally, treating the birth day like it's a big race they're in training for—the husbands even calling themselves "coaches." I mean, nobody's keeping score—they gotta know they aren't gonna *win* the birth day race. This doesn't make them any less competitive, though. The women sit on the floor, their husbands holding their feet, and they breathe like champions, first fast, then slow, each coach cheering on his chubby star athlete in preparation for the big day. Except the coaches' definition of cheering is: criticizing.

"No, that's wrong, Trisha. Butterfly breathing—*butterfly*!"

"I'm doing the best I *can*, Jim," Trisha seethes.

"You're gonna have to try a little harder, honey. There won't be time to make mistakes when it really counts. C'mon, we'll do it together." Like he could possibly fool Trisha into thinking they're gonna give birth *together*. Trisha hates Jim by the end of this exercise.

And all any of them want to talk about is pain. They are absolutely terrified of pain.

"How *much* will it hurt? Is it like a migraine or like stomach cramps?"

"Is it an ache? Or a stabbing pain? A burning one?"

It's so boring. And scary. Why are they worried about themselves when they have babies to worry about? I want the midwife to drop her knitting and yell, "Just do it! Just deal!" but I guess she knows that's what the yuppies'll ultimately have to do anyway.

The married professionals and I talk over paper cups of juice during breaks, but we don't *bond*. They seem to be holding back—lots of frozen smiles and uncomfortable silences, as if we have nothing in common except our big stomachs. Now, thanks to Leslie, I know why. It's not 'cause I'm unmarried and unprofessional; it's 'cause they think I'm goddamn thirteen.

When I turn down my street after baby class, I see someone sitting on our front steps. I figure it's one of the Harvard thugs, but I don't have to care. They don't bother me anymore now that I'm pregnant. Fun fact: to a certain kind of man, pregnant women don't exist, don't show up in space. The more visible my gut becomes, the more *in*visible I am to them.

But up close, the guy doesn't look like a Harvard thug. I think I may know him, just can't place his face. He's blocking my way, though, so I gotta talk to him. "Hi." I try to sound friendly.

"Hi," he says, without moving.

"Do I know you?"

"No. Did you get my postcard?" *Oh, the dripping tree guy.*

"Yeah. Thank you." *I knew living somewhere was a bad idea.* "Was the flower from you, too?"

"Yeah." He still isn't moving.

"Well, thank you."

"You're welcome."

What does he want? "I guess I better go inside," I say quietly, but he doesn't budge. ". . . Are you okay?"

For a long time he doesn't say anything. Cars drive down the street, their headlights cutting across his face in the darkness, turning his teeth yellow. *It's so cold out here.* Then he nods. "Yeah, I'm okay."

Slowly, he stands up, then walks down our front steps, crosses the street and disappears into the cold.

Ice on the chain-link fence that surrounds the school
yard glints in the white sun; snow that blew into the
corners of the fence weeks ago is now gray. Construction-
paper Santas on the door of the school blow in the chilly
wind while children in snorkel jackets and ski masks
huddle together to stay warm.

"You should all keep moving," says a fourth grader,
oldest and wisest among us. "If you don't keep moving,
you'll fall asleep and die." Two kindergartners look
terrified. They begin jumping up and down.

A third grader snorts. "Yer mental. We're not gonna fall
asleep; it's too cold." The kindergartners' jumping
slows, then stops.

"That's *why* you fall asleep," says the fourth grader.
"And then you die. I saw it in a movie."

The kindergartners jump around like maniacs, hats
slipping down over their eyes.

The songs have settled on four in the morning as their favorite time of day. They wake up when it isn't day or night—time just *is* at 4 A.M. It's almost always silent, which may have something to do with why I hear music then.

It's sort of a bummer; now that I'm all pregnant-sleepy, the songs're my alarm clock. And I'm everyone else's, 'cause I gotta heave my gut up out of bed when I hear one and grab my guitar. Then I tiptoe down the freezing hallway, the snow outside the kitchen window lit blue by moonlight, and shut myself in the bathroom. I play as quietly as I can, sitting on the edge of the bathtub, but by seven o'clock, the shimmering tile reverb has carried the sound throughout the apartment, waking everybody up.

Luckily, none of my roommates have the stomach for yelling at a pregnant lady—they thank me for helping them get to work on time. God, I hope I'm pregnant forever.

♋ colder

so I feel like **an alarm** clock

My job, as it turns out, is only to shut up and listen.

And it's interesting to watch what songs do unimpeded by me. When I don't struggle against them, they don't have to fight me. What they do then is crawl all around an event and shine different lights on it. They grope for intensity and grab whatever has the most impact, a bewildering free-for-all. *Not safe*. But I don't think we're supposed to be safe.

The songs' fully engaged effort toward life presses on me. By that I mean it leaves an impression. They have fists and heels and tiny lungs, too. They're bad-ass like babies 'cause they have to be—if you're gonna leave inertia behind, you gotta be ready for forward movement.

So I sit on the edge of the tub and marvel at all the fists around me, inside and out, pummeling the universe into a shape that suits them. It's vivid.

Pregnant or not, we *are* going to make a record, in the spring, with Ivo's money. The contracts are signed; we *have* to make a record in the spring with Ivo's money. "Damn straight!" said Dave when we got our copies in the mail.

Tea beamed. "If we can make a baby, we can make anything!"

"I think it's against the *law* to fire a band just because it's pregnant, anyway," added Leslie.

So even if Ivo flies over here and isn't fooled by my little fat kid act, we're gonna make a record called *Throwing Muses*—it'll be an *eponymous debut*. We won't name it 'cause we figure we can't add any more syllables to that: you say "Throwing Muses" and you've already talked enough. Ivo agrees.

I've wrapped my head around it: who quits their job 'cause they're gonna have a baby? Who can afford to? The baby-class yuppies, I guess, but they don't count; they aren't human.

"They're *normal*, Kris," said Dave.

"You didn't meet them," I answered.

♋ juno

now I can be balancing

We're in a freezing loft in a building somewhere across town, which is exactly where we expected to be shooting a video—something we swore we'd never do 'cause videos are so lame. But these filmmakers told us they needed help fighting *their* good fight against all *their* corporate suckiness, so what could we say? And listen to this: the song they chose for the video is "Fish," so they're gonna cut in footage of fish they shot at the aquarium! The aquarium we just *went* to. We're so happy about this.

"We were *at* the aquarium!" we squeal, as if this is an impressive feat. "We looked at fish!" The filmmakers nod, smiling patiently, while we gape at them. "Fish live *inside* the water!"

We aren't lip-synching; we're playing the song live over and over again. One song all day long, with cameras up our butts. This is really, really, really, really hard. I don't mean it's difficult—it's upsetting. "Fish" isn't scary, but it's intense. I try to pretend it's a fake song, but that's like trying to pretend a person is a mannequin.

Fish Jesus floats around the room and Napoleon's apartment moves across its walls, lit by blinking Christmas lights. I see the smoking donut shop women, feel the invisible Animal . . . and "Fish" is mostly green and blue, so everything glows greenish-blue. It's like the world is suddenly dreaming around me. And mothers can't disppear, so I gotta watch every color, see every face, feel every moment. It's too bright, too much.

I talk and laugh with my friends between takes, but during the performances, I have no choice but to be present for the song, to see the dreaming over and over and over again. It's giving me an ulcer. It seems to be taking its toll on the band, too; they're getting edgy.

"Where's that girl with my twig tea?" asks Leslie when we finish playing the song for the hundredth time.

Sitting down in front of Dave's kick drum, I point. "She's in the corner, holding a bunch of coffees."

"Crap," says Leslie.

The guitar on my lap starts to buzz because it's so close to the amp down there on the floor, so I turn down the volume. "Twig tea's schmanky," I say. "It was maybe a little over her head. Or over the diner's head."

"Oh," she says, disappointed. She's about to ask for one of the coffees when a voice yells, "Places!" Leslie's open mouth forms a silent scream.

After this take, one of the directors, a woman named Lisa, takes me aside and asks if it's okay with me if I look pregnant in the video. I look at her, surprised. "I was gonna ask *you* the same thing."

"Well, I think 'Fish' is a sexy, life-affirming song," she says, "not sexy flirtatious, but sexy strong. It'd be great to have such a healthy female image in the video."

"That's a nice thing to say."

"So we can shoot your body?"

"I'm proud of this gut," I answer. "I worked hard to make it wonderful."

"Good for you!" she says, and runs back to the crew to tell them to shoot my body.

♋ fish

stares out of a block of ice
with one melting eye

About a thousand takes later, this day finally ends and we all leave the loft in a van with the crew and our equipment and *their* equipment. This is a lot of people and a lot of stuff; we barely fit. People sit on amps and each others' laps. It's pitch dark out, but I don't think it's nine o'clock yet, so before I get in, I ask the driver to drop me off at the health food store. "If it's still open," I add.

He looks at me, nervous. "Are you sure you're okay to walk home?" he asks. "It's dark and you're . . ."

"Yeah, I can walk. I do it all the time."

When I climb in, he carefully pulls away from the sidewalk. Squirming past bodies and into a small space between some lights and an amplifier, my guitar case blocking my view of the people around me, I listen while they discuss dinner options one word at a time: "Italian?" "Burgers." "Mexican?" "Pancakes." "Pancakes?"

When we pull up outside Bread and Circus, I can't stand up; I'm stuck. "Just a minute!" I call. Two open hands appear next to my guitar case. I grab the hands and heave myself into a crouching position, then scramble over elbows and knees, trying not to hurt too many body parts. "*Sorry! Sorry!*" When I hop out onto the sidewalk, more helpful hands lift the guitar case and push it out the door. Then, as the door is closing, about fifteen more hands wave goodbye. Then the van pulls away in the dark.

God, it's cold out here. It's nice that I can feel cold now, but . . . *god, it's cold out here.* I hurry into the warm store, trying not to bonk my guitar case or my belly on the swinging doors. Luckily, I'm not gonna face anything as difficult as food shopping today; I just need some prenatal vitamins.

On the way to the vitamin section, I see a rack of dingy, purplish-gray lollipops that're probably dyed with beets or spinach or something 'cause they look moldy. I feel a wave of sympathy for the little hippie children who get these in their bag lunches when the other kids at their lunch table are eating Twinkies—*I know your pain*—but I grab a fistful for the band anyway, 'cause they need treats. I know for a fact that none of us will ever, *ever* want to play "Fish" again.

When I'm ready to pay, the hippie chick who tried to sell me leopard steak is at the cash register talking to a heavily pierced guy about natural ointments for piercing-related infections. "You have to leave it on for, like, twenty-four hours and it smells like crap," she says cheerfully. When she sees me, she claps her hands and gasps. "Hi-ee! How're you feeeeling?!"

"Great! How are you?" I put my guitar on the floor and my vitamins and lollipops on the belt.

She rolls her eyes. "Double shift! Would you believe it?" I shake my head. The infected pierced guy watches dully. "Me, neither! It's almost over, though." She picks up a lollipop. "These are *awesome!*"

"Oh, good."

Turning to the guy, she says, "Have you tried these? They're *awesome.*" I try to imagine him eating a lollipop. "Eleven dollars and ninety-five cents." She sticks the sad lollipops in a miniature paper bag with the vitamins while I dig into my coat pocket for some money. "Do you need help carrying these groceries to your car, ma'am?" I look up. Her hands are over her mouth and she's giggling. *Crazy hippie chick.* I laugh mildly as I count out my money. "How'd that protein powder work out for you?" she asks in a baby voice.

I smile at her. "I ate it." She claps her hands again. "You have a good memory," I tell her. "Do you remember what *everyone* buys?"

She nods, looking frightened. "I could work for the government or something!"

"That's true," I say. "You *should* work for the government."

When she hands me my bag, she says to the pierced guy, "Look at this baby ready to have a babeeeee! Isn't she sweet?"

The pierced guy nods at me in acknowledgment and I wave to them both as I walk out. "So this crap smells like *crap . . .* " she's saying when the doors close behind me.

∽ moan

in the deep cold
you can't be brave

The walk home is cold but head-clearing. By the time I turn onto our street, "Fish" is gone, swept away by freezing wind. As soon as I can make out our house in the dark, though, I realize that the dripping tree guy is on our front steps again. *Damn it.* I almost turn around and walk in the other direction, but I have no idea where I'd go—Bread and Circus is probably closed now, and it's too cold to walk anywhere else. *I shouldn't live anywhere,* I think, *I shoulda kept moving.* He watches me approach, but when I get there, he says nothing.

Putting my guitar case down on the sidewalk, I look at him. "How ya doin'?"

"I'm alright." He's hunched in the cold, perfectly still, and I can't get around him.

He's definitely got a creepy vibe. Not a put-on one either. He's dirty. He's really dirty, inside and out. I know how that feels, but I don't wanna get any closer to it right now 'cause I feel like dirty is dangerous. Like it might hurt the baby. I try to gauge how strong he might be in case I have to force my way past him. He looks like he could be pretty strong in a wiry sorta way. The only thing I have going for me is that I'm stronger than I look.

"How're *you*?" he asks.

"I'm pregnant," I say. I have no idea why I say this. I don't know whether I think being pregnant is a defense or a weakness. Probably just losing patience with him.

Suddenly, he stands up and walks down the steps. I take a step backward. *What the hell? I'm afraid? I'm not scared of things. Maybe 'cause the baby's sticking out in front of me.* He holds out a postcard and a chrysanthemum. When I take them from him, he walks away.

I watch him go, then pick up my guitar and walk up the steps. Looking at the postcard in the light, I see that it's a picture of Boston Common. On the back, he wrote, "the next time we sleep."

What?

I decide on the spot to move back to the island for the baby's sake. I earned the rats this year; I wear song tattoos proudly—badges of evil. But evil isn't clean, the air isn't clean, grime is seeping under my skin and creepy is starting to make sense. I'm used to dirty and I don't want to be used to it.

When the time is right, I'll go back to the ocean.

♋ pneuma

pneuma and pollution
don't confuse me any

A girl across the school yard screams. We look at each other, imagining all sorts of wonderful things happening to make the girl scream, then race toward the sound.

It's a foot. Well, a paw. A little black paw, sticking out of the snow in the corner of the school yard. All the kids who own cats start crying.

The wise old fourth grader digs around the paw in the snow and reveals a whole fox. It's incredible, perfect, and frozen stiff.

We all stare. The fourth grader stands back, his hands on his hips, and sighs. "He shoulda kept moving."

Gary's making me dinner because I promised to let him record me playing songs solo acoustic in his apartment if he fed me. "You can sing for your supper!" he said gleefully. Recording alone with Gary looking at me sounds pretty uncomfortable, but I'll do just about anything for calories these days. I'm starting to miss the VIPs and their bottomless expense accounts. I actually dream about items I saw on menus months ago—*so much free protein . . .*

So I ring his bell in the exhaust-infused dark and cold and he lets me into his warmly lit, steamy, lovely apartment. I look around me, stunned. "How did you *do* this?" I ask him, admiring the beautiful furniture, books and paintings. And the fact that the place is so *clean.* "Everybody else here lives in shit." He takes my guitar from me and puts it in his bedroom while I hang up my scarf, hat and coat. *Coat hooks!*

"Shit is a choice," he says as I follow him into the kitchen. He picks up a big wooden spoon and stirs a pot of something with it.

I sit down at his kitchen table to watch him cook. "I guess so."

"No, it's true. People either don't notice the shit or they think it gives them grit cred, but at some point, they make the shit choice."

"Maybe they're poor."

"Some of 'em are poor. Generally not the ones you'd think."

"Really." Gary has a bookshelf in his kitchen. Books are everywhere in this apartment: in neat stacks on coffee tables, on shelves lining the walls. I grab one about architecture and leaf through it.

"Yep. 'Cause the actual poor like to keep up appearances. You don't wanna know how many trust-funders're masquerading as us."

I look up from the book. "They could give their money away and then they'd *be* us."

Gary turns off the stove, then pours pasta out of the pot and into a colander in the sink. "*They* don't resent their money, *we* do." He is enveloped in steam. "Do you want a drink?" he asks through the steam. "Everything I have is alcoholic."

I laugh. "Well, then, no, sir. No, thank you." The light sources in this apartment are all beautiful antique lamps. I tell him I love lamps.

"*Don't* you love lamps?" he says, shaking water out of the colander. "I'd rather sit in the dark than use an overhead light."

"I only have one lamp, so I *do* sit in the dark. Overhead lights're nasty. Light shouldn't shine on *everything*; it should shine on one angle of a few select things."

"You're right." Expertly, he flips the pasta into a wooden bowl. "Let's get you another lamp so you can put it next to something you like and angle it to shine on your favorite part of it."

I laugh. "Okay." Next to the sink is a little rubber monster, its mouth open in a silent roar, its arms raised in the air. "Nice monster."

Drying his hands on a tea towel, Gary looks at it. "Thank you. Roaches pour out of its mouth every morning."

"Oh my goodness. Is that bad or cool?"

"Mostly bad. A *little* cool." Gary stirs the pasta, then spoons some onto a plate. "Not cool enough."

"We have roaches, too," I say. "But they aren't in anybody's mouth." He places two beautiful plates of food on the table and sits down across from me. "Gary, this is so nice of you."

"Are you hungry?"

I put the book I've been looking at on the shelf. "I'm always hungry." Sitting back down, I reach for my fork and realize it's lying on a cloth napkin. "Oh my god."

Gary stops eating. "What's wrong?"

"You have cloth napkins."

"Is that bad?"

I shake my head at him. "You're wild."

"No one's ever called me 'wild' for having cloth napkins before."

"That doesn't make you any less wild." I glance out the window. Snow is falling. It looks very beautiful from in here. "It's snowing."

Gary watches the snow fall for a minute, then looks back at me. "I have to show you a photograph after dinner," he says. "Remind me."

"Okay. Hey, did you know we made a video?" I remember we're supposed to be having dinner and try the pasta. It tastes like something from one of the VIPs' restaurants: very schmanky. "This is great, Gary."

"Thank you. I thought you said videos were lame."

"They are. That's why we made it."

"Hmmm."

"We're helping the filmmakers fight suckiness," I explain.

"If they can't manage it," he says, "you could always take your name off the project."

"Sure. And take my song out of it. And my face and my body. They shot my body, Gary."

"Ow." I nod. He pushes pasta around on his plate. "This isn't al dente. I'm sorry. I was thinking about shit and lamps. Your fault." He looks at me accusingly and puts down his fork. "It seems to me," he says, "that music

has been in film for such a long time, it shouldn't be such a leap to imagine
that film images could also serve music. Without sucking, I mean."

"That's pretty much what they said. And fish're gonna swim by. That
should be cool."

"Really? That sounds . . . silly."

"It does. But fish aren't silly. I bet the fish'll pull it off." We watch the
snow fall out the window.

"Remind me to show you that picture," he says.

"Okay."

The snow is falling slowly, gently rising on wind currents and floating
down past the window. Then the wind picks up. Flakes in chaos create patterns in the air, flying *up*, then coming together—schools of fish—crashing
into the building, tearing down toward the ground.

"And we're gonna make a record," I say slowly, mesmerized by what's
outside.

"I heard."

"Thanks to the Gary tape."

He looks at me. "You made that tape, not me."

I shake my head. "I didn't do anything but hang with rats and eat Froot
Loops."

Gary leans over and turns off the lamp on the table so we can watch the
snow fall in the dark. It's like being in a movie theater.

♋ beestung

snow rides the wind down
and drives past the window

Dude and I are camping outside the hospital where Crane
is in labor because neither of us is allowed in. We
consider this a terrible injustice, so we camp on the
hospital grounds in protest. And 'cause it's fun.

Until it gets dark and starts pouring down rain and I
realize there's no TV. "Jonesin' pretty bad, huh?"
asks Dude.

"Pretty bad," I answer.

"I know something that's better than TV," he says,
pulling the tent flaps aside.

We watch the rain fall into the grass and mud, spattering
across the parking lot. The raindrops are black, blue,
clear and silver.

"This *is* better than TV," I whisper.

SPRING 1986

When we pulled up to this place in the middle of Nowhere, Massachusetts, we were shocked. Our idea of a recording studio is a rat-infested black hole in a part of town where it's always night. That's just all we've ever known about recording studios. We love that they're horrible bunkers in war zones and that so much beauty can be created there.

This place is a mansion at a petting zoo: an enormous house, plus the studio itself and then a barn full of cute animals. Which is nice, I guess; it's just weird. As creepy as dirty can be, I suppose there was something invigorating about our filthy world—we felt indomitable there, safe. 'Cause we were surviving. Places like this are where clean gets a little not okay.

I can do nature's version of clean and beautiful, but rich people's clean, beautiful buildings make me suspicious. 'Cause I figure soon I'll get thrown out, I guess, but also 'cause I imagine they're dishonest—hiding something darker. That they must be dirtier than the dirty places.

Why do people think comfort is comfortable? *And how much is Ivo paying for this?*

As we got out of the van, studio employees grabbed our bags and began showing us around the enormous facility. This place is huge; we were completely disoriented by the end of the tour. There's actually another studio *behind* the studio we'll be working in. The furniture is luxurious and everything is made of polished wood—it even smells good.

I whispered, "What *is* this?" in Tea's ear and she whispered back, "It's *fancy.*"

Then we were separated, marched upstairs and placed in our own private rooms, alone with our bags. Which I guess is also fancy, but it made me lonely.

My room is made entirely of wood, like everything here, and it has cool medieval windows. They put a cradle next to my bed because I'm pregnant and they had a cradle. I don't actually have a baby yet, though, so I filled the cradle with tapes.

I couldn't think of anything to do in my wooden room. I looked out the window for a while, then stuck a tape in the fancy stereo system on my bureau, watching the moon while music played. I don't listen to much music. The more you love music, the less music you love, 'cause you get picky—we take our religion seriously. Bad music is angrifying and good music is so painfully intense. But I needed some company, so I chose a soundtrack for the moon very carefully and let it be my friend for the better part of an hour.

Eventually, though, the tape ended and moonlight was starting to make the room feel creepy, so I wandered downstairs where Tea, Leslie and Dave were sitting around a table near the kitchen in silence, looking tense.

I took an apple from a fruit bowl on my way over to them and Dave shook his head slowly at me. I mouthed "No?" at him and he mouthed "No" back, shaking his head faster. Quickly, I tried to replace the apple, but before I could, a lady in a chef hat and apron grabbed it out of my hand and put it on a plate. Then she handed the plate to me with angry eyes and a forced smile. "I'm the chef," she said. *Oh.*

Balancing my apple on its plate, I walked over to my bandmates. "She's the chef," said Dave quietly. I nodded.

Leslie leaned over and whispered, "She took my ramen noodles."

"She's making *me* a glass of water," said Tea, her hand over her mouth.

"Why?" I whispered.

"Fancy," said Dave.

Tea nodded. "It's fancy," she said.

"We wouldn't understand," Leslie smirked.

"No," I answered, staring at my apple plate. "We wouldn't."

Making a record isn't the release that playing a show or making a demo is; it's a particularly vivid circle of heaven and hell. Like skiing down a mountain and off a cliff. *Wheeeee! Whooooa!*

Without lithium in my system, my hands no longer shake, so I can play anything I want, perfectly, the first time around. I had no idea this could ever be a bad thing. When we first started recording, we were *on* with a capital O, busting our asses to serve the song, re-create the sculpture, give it a body worth its soul. *Here we are, makin' a record that's not gonna suck. This is important—make this one great!*

We were terribly nervous, our muscles never let go (mine didn't, anyway), but we did it: a perfect first take, technically and magically sound.

The song came flying into the room with everything intact—a soul *and* a body, unkempt and breathing, like anything that deserves to live on planet earth. Enthralled, we worked hard to keep it up in the air, growing it limbs and a heart, a beautiful coughed-up liver. And impossibly, it got real: a lovely, hovering freak. We couldn't believe it—we did it. On the first try.

As we listened to the final chord fade, we waited, tense and exhausted, to hear that the tape stopped, that we could breathe, then move on to the next song. But "Try it again!" was all we heard in our headphones.

So far, we've played one song for seven hours. And thanks to Gary calling us athletes and teaching us to "identify our curve," we know we were used up and sucking after exactly four takes. The song left the building a long time ago and shows no signs of returning. We can no longer create a body in the room; we're just playing instruments for no reason, dead notes, getting more anxious and depressed with each take.

Our high-strung Liverpudlian producer Gil just met us—he doesn't know the good takes are over and he missed them. To him, it just sounds like we need more practice, which makes him nervous. "Try it again!" he calls out whenever we get to the end of the song. The repetition is unbearable.

And if we *ever* get a good take of this song, there are a dozen more waiting, just as intense as this one. Ivo didn't choose any of our fun songs for this record—the country-punk ones that are such a relief to play. Probably 'cause he's English. "Country" isn't *his* country. I was cool with that at the time, but now I'm realizing that every song on this record is gonna hurt and hurt bad.

I know how lucky we are to be here. I know how few bands *ever* get to this point. I remember all the work we did to earn this opportunity, how many years of practice and playing out. I know a lot of money is at stake and a lot of people are relying on me; I know our futures depend on the performances we capture *now*; I know, I know. But this is like being trapped on a roller coaster.

'Cause even when a take is dead, *I'm* not—the song grabs me as it races past, like "Fish" did at the video shoot, thrusting shapes and colors and memories in my face. And because of the baby, I can't disappear, can't hide. I have to sit through every single goddamn note. I can only describe the effect as . . . anguish.

If I were a crier, I'd be in tears.

♋ catch

catch a bullet in your teeth

But my bandmates are here and their presence is comforting. It's their record, too. I gotta keep it together for them.

Technically, we're sitting in a circle facing each other, because that's how we said we prefer to work, but we're so far apart, it doesn't matter. I can't watch anybody else's hands 'cause I can't see them. And Dave isn't even here. He's in an isolation booth behind glass. Our amps are in other isolation booths, behind more glass, so there's no actual sound in the room, no pulsing energy—just cold measuring. The record is supposed to sound live, like the demos, but this feels more like an operation than a show: clinical and cruel. Guts as plain old organs.

I don't like science anymore, I think, *I can't like it—we're chaos people. I want my art back.*

The studio and control room are both enormous, full of more shining glass and that clean polished wood that's everywhere here. The carpet is plush and elegant. It's . . . someone else's world. We don't belong here.

We can't even talk to each other 'cause I'm the only one with a mic. I whisper into my bandmates' headphones, "*I don't like fancy*," and they shake their heads mournfully at me.

♋ rat

it occurred to me that someone
might not understand our world

Our poor producer hasn't stopped running around the studio listening for a "*booze*" since we started recording seven hours ago. He's really hyper. Ivo sent Gil to us, having made the match himself. "Gil's a good one," he said. And Gil does seem like a good one; we all feel sorry for him, he's so frustrated. He came all the way here from Liverpool, just to pace and sweat. We blame oursleves.

"I hear a *booze*, I hear a *booze*! Do you hear a *booze*?" he chants, racing around the airless studio, running his hands through his curly brown hair. We hold our instruments, wide-eyed, hands over the strings to keep them quiet, and watch Gil run back and forth.

When he bends over to look behind an amp, his glasses fall off. Swearing, he dives after them, freezes and stares into a corner, then turns to look at us. We stare back blankly. It's like watching a cat chase a mouse, except that I've heard of mice. *Booze* is studio lingo with which I'm unfamiliar. Gil uses a lot of words we don't know. "Is that it?" he asks no one in particular. "Is that the *booze*?"

Finally, Leslie says. "Gil, we don't know what a 'booze' *is*."

"*A booze, a booze*," he cries frantically, testing cords and inputs and tapping microphones.

The assistant engineer, a young American man who came with the studio, follows him through the room, looking sheepish. "I think he's hearing a buzz," he says quietly to Leslie.

Her face lights up. "Oh! I know what *that* is!"

"Gil's speaking *English*," clarifies Dave into his snare mic from behind glass.

Gil is a lovely man, just a little keyed up. "Of course I'm hearing a *booze*, there *is* a *booze*! Don't you hear it?" He flicks a switch on the back of an amp, checking the grounding, and we hear a snapping sound. "Aaah!" Gil yells, jumping backwards and sticking his finger in his mouth. "Another fucking shock!" he yells through his finger. "What the fuck's the matter with this country? It's been shocking me since the bloody plane landed! I wore me jumper and me pumps today, and I'm *still* getting shocked!" Leslie shoots me a look.

Tea looks deeply confused. "But you aren't wearing a dress, Gil," she says carefully. "*Or* high heels . . ."

Gil looks at her, his finger still in his mouth, then he grabs a fistful of his sweater and says angrily, "*This* is a jumper!" Pointing at his sneakers, he growls, "*These* are pumps!"

"Gil's speaking *English*," whispers Dave into our headphones.

By midnight, the buzz is gone, one song is done, and the workday officially ends. I yelled all day long. It felt . . . unkind.

What we did was, we took the song apart, played each piece separately, then stuck the pieces back together. In my opinion, it didn't work. We'd torn the song's limbs off, sewed them back on and then asked it to walk around the room. Of course, there's no song left anymore; we killed it. It's just a corpse—a neat, clean, sterile corpse—and corpses can't walk.

I crawl upstairs to my wooden room and run a bath, trying to wash off this day. Dirty and clean are confusing me. Some clean is seeming dirty and some dirty is clearly clean:

A living song is dirty, a dead one clean.

Art is dirty, science clean.

Cities are dirty, nature is clean.

Crazy is dirty, health is clean.

Us poor people are dirty but pure of heart, and rich people are clean on the outside but so dirty where it counts that they hoard money they don't need. Is that right?

This all seems true, but there's something wrong with it.

My belly dances in the water. Tiny heels and fists push my skin around. *What an adorable monster.* I stay in the tub for hours. The water gets cold.

I don't know if I've let music down or music's let me down. *Whatever.*

I decide this is no place for a baby. With this thought, I choose the baby over music, and water becomes my friend again. Somehow, this bath washes off all my song tattoos.

☺ some catch flies
i am clean

Gil's wife is as pregnant as I am, back in Liverpool, so Gil and I talk baby together at breakfast. While we talk, the chef fusses around us with an angry smile and then leaves to go bang metal things together in the kitchen. "Apparently, babies're very small," says Gil, staring into the distance. "And noisy."

He's afraid his wife'll go into labor while we're making this record. "I'm not usually this nervous," he says, cleaning his glasses with a shaky hand. "Every time the phone rings, I nearly jump out of me skin." He glances at my protruding belly, pressed against the table, and his pale face gets a little paler. "And you aren't making me feel any better."

"Sorry."

"It's not your fault. It's, you know . . . pregnancy's very beautiful," he adds, distracted, sucking down another cup of tea. Then the phone rings and Gil does nearly jump out of his skin, shuddering impressively. When the phone is answered and no one tells him to get on a plane, he exhales and replaces his cup on its saucer with a sigh. "Do I seem nervous to *you*? I mean, exceptionally so?"

"Well, I don't really know you. You do seem a little . . . caffeinated, I guess."

He stares into the distance again. "Yeah," then pours another cup of tea.

The chef races into the room and stands at the table, staring at us. When we look up, she asks us if we'd like another pot of tea. She stresses the word "another" as if we'd already drunk enough for ten people because Gil *has* drunk enough for ten people this morning. "Yes, please!" Gil answers, a little too loudly.

"Maybe if you didn't drink so much tea, you wouldn't feel so tense," I suggest.

"Huh?" He looks into his cup. "Tea calms me down."

"It does?"

Gil thinks. "Maybe that's just in England."

"I hear tea's better there."

He squeezes some pale brown liquid out of a tea bag and frowns. "Yes," he sighs. "Yes, it is."

I walk into the Chattanooga church holding my
grandmother's hand. The building is cavernous, echoing
with loud organ music. The people around us are dressed
up: the women wear pearls and diamond pins and smell like
hair spray, the men wear suits and string ties and smell
like mouthwash.

My hair is always down, my mother makes all my clothes
and I'm usually allowed to go barefoot. This morning,
though, I'm wearing a starched, store-bought dress and
tight, hard, unyielding shoes. My hair is pulled back so
tight my eyebrows are on wrong. I've been pressed and
primped to the point of immobility because I have to go
to church.

I want desperately to leave. Outside is right outside and
I can't get there.

Jesus would hate this place, I think bitterly.

I can't scream anymore. In these headphones, a real lung-ripping scream would sound like an explosion. I mean, if you just stand in front of the microphone not making a sound, you can hear your *clothes*. Singing is like a freight train running through your head, and screaming is just . . . out of the question; it can't happen.

Back in my real life, when evil would kick in, it *wanted* the explosion, wanted my lungs ripped open and I did, too. Screams'd just fly out of my mouth then, but right now, I'm wasting everybody's time, singing as if the words and notes were dead. Expensive hours are going by while I . . . I don't know, my version of humming along. I sound like anybody. I fake scream: a tame yelling that sounds like loud singing—just stupid.

But I don't care, because it's safe. The song can't get me *or* the baby if I fake it. It reaches for me when it races past and I lightly step out of the way, watch the roller coaster from a distance. No heat, no pain, no nothing. I've shaken off the witch's curse *and* the Doghouse.

Last night, after the tattoos went spinning down the drain, there was nothing left underneath but some girl wrapped in a towel.

Standing in front of the mic, useless, I realize I no longer think like a musician. I try to remember what that was like. *What did I used to say?*

That I had a calling, I was on a mission.

That music is beautiful math, that it's owning violence.

Songs are electricity, my religion.

Music is how we respect hurt *and* happiness.

Hmmm . . . nope. I feel like I could just wander off.

℗ firepile

```
count the tires one more time
count the times i let the air out
```


So we move from take to take, erasing every vocal I put down. It's Gil's job to coax an authentic performance out of me and instead, we're just taking a lot of walks. Gil's going quietly crazy. "Take five," he says cheerfully, through gritted teeth. "Come outside with me, Kris. Let's take a walk."

I swore I wouldn't waddle like the married professionals when my middle got this big, so I use these walks to practice my Not Waddling. One foot in front of the other. We always take the same route down a rural lane, past farm houses, orchards and lime green hills, then along a dirt road that ends in the petting zoo barn full of lambs and calves and bales of hay. It really is pretty here.

I know I should be more frustrated than this, but I'm feeling vague, enjoying the view. I never wanted that horrible voice to happen in the first place—it's hard to be upset about it not happening. And I don't want yesterday to repeat itself; I really don't think I have it in me. Giving up feels so much better. *So I lost music. Big deal. It was never very nice to me anyway.*

Gil, however, is not feeling vague, is not enjoying the view. He looks pained. "You don't sound like *you* when you sing. What is it, Kris?" Putting an arm around my shoulders, he asks sweetly, "Are you not angry enough? You want me to say something insulting?" He pushes his glasses up his nose and squints into the bright blue New England sky as we trudge down the road yet again.

I grin. "You could try. I'm not easily insulted. I'd probably just agree with you."

"What *would* make you angry?" he asks.

"I don't know. You just made me sing the same song all day; I should be pretty pissed off right now. I don't think that's it, though. The songs aren't *angry*; they're intense. A song doesn't have to be dopey to be happy."

He stops and looks at me. "You think your songs are *happy?*"

"Well, maybe not 'happy.' Celebratory.*"

"So why don't you sound like yourself?" He squints into the sky. "What'd make you sound *celebratory?*"

"I do sound like myself. That's the problem. This is *my* voice. The songs' voice is the one you're looking for and I honestly don't know where it is."

Gil's eyes widen. "The songs' voice?"

"Yeah."

"The song isn't Kristin?"

"Oh god, no." *Geez, that'd be awful.* "It's best if I'm not feeling anything. Otherwise, I crawl into the song and start messing it up. Like I just did." He stares at me for a second, then starts walking again.

I catch up as best I can without waddling. *One foot in front of the other.*
"You can still say something insulting, if you want, Gil. I deserve it."

He can only come up with a half smile. "Would you like to talk to Ivo?
We could call him when we get back to the studio."

"You mean for a pep talk?"

"Input," he answers.

"Sure," I say, "but I don't know if it'll help."

"Are you *sure* the song isn't you, Kris?" asks Gil.

"Well, if it is, then it's evil me."

He looks very sad. I don't know if he's feeling sorry for me, for Ivo or
for himself. Maybe he's feeling sorry for our doomed record. "So why isn't
she here?" he asked.

"Evil me? I'm kind of relieved she isn't here. I don't like her very much.
She's not a good babysitter."

He stops walking and brightens. "You're worried about the baby?"

"Yeah. *Duh-uh.* Evil Kristin screams pretty loud."

"Right." He rubs his hands together, looking busy again. "Evil Kristin
is *supposed* to scream loud. I could take your vocal out of the cans; then you
wouldn't be so loud in your own head. You could really let go. I reckon you
know the feel of the notes by now, so your tuning'll be okay." He looks
excited.

Staring at the ground, I think, *The baby'll still hear it.* But when I look
up to respond, I see two Doberman pinschers tearing down the hill behind
Gil in total silence. They're in full attack mode, heading straight for him,
and they aren't making a sound.

Gil looks back at me with mild concern. "What, you don't want me to
take your voice out of the—"

"Gil, run!" I scream, pulling him down the road.

"Christ!" he yells when he catches sight of the Dobermans, then races
alongside me as they leap into the air, mouths open, a few feet away from
the back of his neck. I hear an awful *clang!* as they're jerked backwards on
chains. We stop running and turn to look. Both dogs have fallen to the
ground and are now lying in the grass in a tangle of chains and spit, looking
pathetic.

Gil leans forward, hands on his knees, like he's gonna puke. "Are you
okay?" I ask him.

"Oh god," he says. "My heart."

I stare at the strangled dogs on the ground—they look worse than Gil.
"Are *they* okay?"

Gil looks up. "They don't look so good, do they? It's their own fault. They almost gave me a heart attack. Fucking American dogs."

"I think Dobermans are German." The dogs're lying on their sides, drooling, and they aren't moving. I feel bad for them. "They were just doing their job, Gil."

Gil shakes his head and stands upright, takes my arm and begins to walk slowly down the road. "How 'bout we go do *our* jobs, Kris?"

Poor Gil. "Sure thing, boss." We walk in silence. "Why didn't they bark?" I ask him.

"That'd just give us time to get away," he sighs.

The song "Vicky's Box" pours into my head. Gil's blasting me with the track, but he's turned my mic way down so evil Kristin can work without any censorship from me. He sits in the control room, looking tense and pale. I yell pretty loud, I think. Probably out of tune. I don't know; I can't hear it. Sorta don't care. The vocal is Gil's problem; the baby is mine.

"Better," says Gil's voice in my headphones after the first take. "But not quite evil. Pretend a Doberman's after you." He turns to say something to the assistant engineer and then hits the talkback button again. "What's this song about?"

"About? Hell, I don't know."

"I heard the word 'blow jobs.'"

"That's two words."

He stares. "Is that what it's about?"

I know he's baiting me, but I have no good answer. "Yeah, Gil, it's about *blow jobs.*"

He smiles. "I just want you to put yourself in the song. What do you *think* it's about?"

"My roommate, Vicky, painted some cool stuff on a box when she was moving and some of it turned up in a song."

He looks stunned. "Really? 'Vicky's Box' is a song about *Vicky's box*? A box owned by someone named Vicky?"

"Mostly," I say, embarrassed. "That's why it's *called* that."

"Huh." He seems disappointed. *Why do people want you to make shit up?* He opens his mouth to say something and then closes it again.

"What?"

"Nothing."

Gil turns off the talkback mic and says something to the assistant engineer. The engineer has a long answer with a lot of pointing and gesturing in it. Then Gil says something else and points at me. They talk for a long time while I stand there watching them, wishing I could read lips. *He's probably speaking English again, anyway.* Finally, he hits the talkback button, and I can hear what's going on in the control room. "Kris?" he says.

"Yeah?"

"Is Vicky a gay man?"

Oh, for god's sake. *That's* what they're talking about? "Gil . . ."

"Yeah, Kris?"

"Please stop listening to the lyrics."

"Okay." He rolls tape. "It isn't *just* about a box, though, is it?" I don't say anything. "Right. This is the one, Kris."

But it's not the one and neither is the next take. I don't know what to do: call back that terrible voice I never asked for in the first place? Bring heat and electricity to the body I now share with an innocent baby? I can't *make* myself sing right; it either happens or it doesn't. The Monster Body simply doesn't wanna be a mouthpiece for the Brain That Wouldn't Die anymore.

This was all a stupid idea in the first place—why can't anyone see that?
So I run away.

I'm trying to teach Zoë to bark. She sits in front of me and I say "woof" over and over again while she watches. She turns her head so far to the side, it looks like it'll twist off, but she doesn't bark.

Eventually, I get bored and sit down. "Look," I say. "If a bad guy comes to our house, you gotta let us know, okay? Whine or something." She looks at me. "It's important."

Zoë sighs, then lies down with her chin on my lap.

♋ red eyes

two fists of rose hips
red eyes

in springtime you come home

I stand on the edge of a cliff, staring at the ocean, the school behind me. This was our view from the library bathroom. Looking up at the window next to Betty's toilet seat, I wonder if she still hangs out in there without me.

Spring is happening again. *Again! What a great deal we have here on earth.* Sunlight on the water is literally dazzling—I squint painfully but can't look away—and in the air is *rosa rugosa*: rosehips, beach roses.

I try to button my sweater 'cause it's flapping around in the breeze, but my stomach sticks out too far.

Standing at the pay phone in the student lounge where I used to buy Betty candy to fuel her show-biz spiels, I wait for her to answer the phone. It rings and rings. Finally, she picks up. "Surprise!" I yell. "It's me! I'm here, Betty—at school! And I signed us up for a seminar; an easy coupla credits before summer classes. C'mon."

I can't wait to pick up where we left off. I can finish my degree and she can give me advice that I ignore. She's gonna be so happy. "Aren't you supposed to be in the studio?" Betty asks suspiciously. "Making a record?"

"I *am* in the studio making a record. Technically."

"Huh?" She doesn't sound happy that I'm back. "What do you mean, Krissy?"

"It was awful. And dumb. So I ran away. I don't believe in making records anymore; you can't measure music," I explain. "It doesn't matter; just drive over and take a class with me. It'll be great. It's a beautiful morning. I can see the fairy tree from here."

"Don't believe in it?" she asks.

"No. Turns out it's ripping the arms and legs off a song and then sewing them back on. The song can't walk and nobody notices." I wipe some dust off the leaves of a potted plant. "Plus, I'm just plain bad at it. They make us play the same song so many times, I don't even know what I'm doing anymore."

Silence. "So you just ran away?"

Grrrr. Hang up and drive over here. "I didn't *just* run away . . . I ran away for a reason. I don't belong there. I missed the ocean. I missed *you*." She says nothing. *Why isn't she happy?* I try this: "I wanna go back to school 'cause I'm thinking, you know, that if I don't plan for my future, I won't have one."

It doesn't work. Betty just sighs. "Are you taking care of yourself?"

People ask me this all the time. Like I might forget I'm pregnant and chug a six-pack or something. "Absolutely," I say. "Eating, sleeping, breathing—the whole deal."

A couple of girls with clipboards post themselves in front of me and begin stopping people on their way to class to discuss some issue. I turn away from them. Betty switches to her I–don't-have-time-for-you voice. "You *sure* you're feeling well?"

"Everything's fine. I finally have my head on straight." She says nothing. "Could you please go to school with me? We go to school at the beach, remember? The *beach*, Betty."

"I know where we go to school, sweetie, but I can't take any more of your classes. Do you know they're making us dissect cats?"

I loved dissecting cats. "They're *dead* cats. Cat cadavers." I look up at the bulletin board next to me, read a roommate-wanted ad, one asking for a ride to New York and one that just says, "Help, I need help," with a phone number attached. *Help, I need help?*

"I'm planning a headache for that day." *Poor Betty. It takes weeks to dissect a cat.* She says something muffled to a person in the room with her. I watch a spider walk up the stem of the dusty plant while I wait for Betty to talk to me again. The spider catches me watching it and freezes.

I can't believe she doesn't even care that I'm here. She was supposed to be happy. I'll just explain to her that there aren't any dead cats in this class. "Hey, Betty, the seminar is Art Therapy. Get it? Isn't that funny? 'Cause art is the opposite of therapy! It *makes* you crazy!"

Betty sighs again. "You don't talk that way around other people, right?" She sounds like I'm making her tired. "I have to go, honey, but tell me—do you really think your record's going badly?"

Shit, I think she's blowing me off. "I don't know. Probably. The English people took out all the fun songs."

"You don't have any fun songs," she says distractedly. I roll my eyes. I guess it was presumptuous, thinking she'd have nothing to do on a Saturday morning. She's probably got a date with a priest. "I talked to a Holly-wood friend about you and he says you need a *single*."

"Do you know what a single is, Betty?" I ask, annoyed. "It's a dumb song, a bad song. Bad enough to get played on the radio. That's just public humiliation—what's the point? I'd rather be good in private than bad in public."

"Well, maybe just some up-tempo numbers, then."

"We're plenty 'up-tempo,' we're just not in the right—" I can tell she isn't listening. "Never mind."

In a singsongy way she asks, "Do you like living in the recording stu-dio? I *loved* recording studios."

"Well, this one's a rich-people farm. They cook for us and stuff; we don't get it. It's too sterile. Hey, wanna go to school? School is important, remember?"

She drops the singsongy thing. "I *do* go to school, Krissy. I didn't quit." *Ow.* "You know what I think? I think you're under a lot of pressure, with the baby coming and making your first record. Maybe it makes you want to go back to a time before you had these stresses in your life."

She is blowing me off. "So you're a psychology major after all."

She doesn't laugh. "I'm going to give you some advice now." *No shit.* "Don't ever run away from your commitments. You'll have more options open to you if you *don't* run away. Does that make sense?"

I say nothing. *I shouldn't have said that I ran away. I should have put it differently. 'I've come to a decision' or something dramatic like that. Then she'd be on my side, welcoming me back, not lecturing me.*

"We all have a snake," Betty continues, "and right now you need to—"

"What?" It's like she slapped me.

"I said we all have a *snake* and yours is—"

"We all have a *what*?" My head's pounding along with my heart.

"I don't mean it literally. I'm just trying to say that if you don't face—"

"Did you say we all have *snakes*? Why did you say that?"

She sighs. "Krissy, if you'd let me finish, I could tell you." I sit, stunned. *I never told her about the snake.* "I have a snake and you have a snake. We all have to face our demons some day, sweetheart, and that day'll be the scar-iest you ever lived. Then you'll wake up the next morning and realize your snake is still there, that you have to face your demons again. But it won't be so scary this time. Once you see your shadow, you'll realize that the rest of your life will be spent staring it down, but you know what?"

"What?"

"You can do it."

"Yeah. Thanks, Betty." *Christ.*

"Krissy, you have a calling, so make this record. If you hate it, you never have to make another record again."

She doesn't understand. I slide to the floor. The issue girls turn around to stare at me, their clipboards at their sides. "Promise?" I ask.

"I promise," says Betty. "If this record's as bad as you think it is," she says cheerfully, "you won't be *allowed* to make another one!"

I laugh uncertainly. "Not 'bad' exactly, just hard."

She's talking to somebody else again. *I'm losing her.* "Go back to work, sweetie." *Now she's gonna go dancing off with some priest and leave me here alone.*

"I gotta take this seminar anyway, Betty. I mean, it's a 'commitment' and all. Why don't you just sit in?" I'm getting desperate. "Please?" *Help, I need help.* The lounge begins to fill with students talking and buying styrofoam cups of coffee between classes. They look happy. *I miss my life.*

"You're gonna be great, sweetheart," says Betty. "It's a new chapter! I love you. You're super. Fall in love!" and she hangs up. *Bummer.* I lean against the dusty plant where the spider is still frozen in terror.

"Miss you, Betty," I say to the dial tone.

My aunts—Lily White, Frank, Sister, Tony and Weeza—are
sitting around a table, slicing strawberries and shelling
pecans for pie. They talk and laugh, their hands moving
expertly. Frank looks out the window. "It's getting
dark," she says.

Lily White, the youngest, knows what this means to
children. She smiles at me, her fingers pink with
strawberry juice. "When the stars come out, they're
telling you it's their turn to play," she says.
"They help us say goodbye to one day so we can see a new
one tomorrow."

I wanna go back to the ocean or sit under the fairy tree. The buzzing fluo-
rescents are gross and the other students don't look promising.

The first thing the teacher asks us to do is lie on the floor. What is it
with college professors and lying on the floor? This time, though, I have
the opposite experience from my deep relaxation freak-out in Dude's
class. I could no more jog around the room than . . . I don't know, *stay
awake*.

So while the teacher drones on about swaying trees and gentle breezes,
I don't stay awake; I just pass out. 'Cause I'm not me anymore, I'm
pregnant.

I wake up as the other students are shuffling around, grabbing art supplies
and moving desks into groups. *Crap. I slept through the assignment.* Following a woman with blond ponytails and glasses over to the art supply cabinet,
I copy everything she does, taking a gigantic piece of paper, some colored
pencils, charcoal and a drawing pen from the cabinet, and scooting a desk
over to her group. Surreptitiously peeking over some shoulders to see what
"art" we're supposed to do, I notice the other students are all drawing
animals. *Okay . . . I can draw an animal.*

The paper is enormous and difficult to manage. I try spreading it out
on the desk, but it spills over the side, so I put it down on the carpeted floor.
Then the pen I'm using tears a hole in it. *Goddamn it.* I grab a small book
off a nearby shelf, place it underneath the paper and, stretching my arms
out past my enormous stomach, draw a tiny blowfish in the exact center of
the paper.

While I'm coloring it blue, the instructor calls for everyone's attention
and asks that we begin discussing our imaginary animals with the other
people in our group. *Imaginary?* Quickly, I draw a horn on my blowfish's
forehead, then sit down at a desk, leaving my drawing on the floor.

A painfully nerdy guy sitting across from me stands up, offering to go
first. "I drew myself as the Golden Eagle of Fantasy," he says nervously,
holding up an incredible picture of a shining eagle on top of a mountain,
surrounded by vivid blue sky. It looks like a frame from a government-issue
comic book. *How did he have time to do that? He must have brought it from
home.* Every inch of the magnificent eagle is colored in varying shades of
gold, with silver cross-hatching. It glares at us from the paper, wings out-
stretched.

"That's *you*?" I ask, without thinking.

"Why 'fantasy'?" asks a middle-aged woman pointedly. *Do you have to ask?*

The nerdy guy clears his throat. "I feel at home in the realm of fantasy and I'd like to bring a more dreamlike quality to my everyday life." He has memorized this short speech.

The woman smiles knowingly. "I feel like you have a lot to offer this world, but you keep it locked away inside you." She has stiff, puffy, jet-black hair and dark red lipstick and she wears many, many silver bracelets. Her black pantsuit makes a crinkling sound every time she moves. Like when she says "locked away inside you" and folds herself up as if she's locking away inside her all that she has to offer this world.

Golden Eagle nods noncommittally and sits down. Then the woman reveals her picture. It looks like a pony with butterfly wings. Her paper is completely filled with color, like Golden Eagle's, but she can't draw as well as he can. The butterfly pony is crooked and distorted. It could be a butterfly . . . camel? Whatever it is, it stands in a meadow, eating a square-ish apple, its horizon and ears masked by an enormous rainbow.

She stands. "I am Metamorphosis," she says. "Ever changing, I am in flux, yet constant like a river."

Huh. We all look again at the pony. It doesn't look constant like a river. It looks lumpy.

"Where'd it get the apple?" asks a heavyset man in a Budweiser T-shirt. "I don't see an apple tree."

Metamorphosis turns her drawing to face her and looks at it. "There's an orchard nearby," she answers quickly.

"Oh." He seems unconvinced.

The blond woman I'd followed over here points at the pony's butterfly wings. "When you fly," she asks, "where do you go?" *Oh for christ sake.*

Metamorphosis smiles. "I'm a healer. I break through the illusionary walls of space/time to bring clients into balance on a quantum level." *God, Betty, what you're missing.*

The ponytails lady smiles back. "I, too, am a quantum field dweller," she says, standing and holding up her picture. It looks like puke—a big pile of puke. Her picture fills the paper, too, but with what? "I am Amoeba," she says proudly.

A quantum-field-dwelling pony and a quantum-field-dwelling amoeba. Do they think the quantum field is an apartment complex? Metamorphosis presses her face up against Amoeba's drawing, squinting. Slowly, she sits back down in her chair, the wind knocked out of her quantum sails.

"That's *nice*," offers Golden Eagle. Amoeba pushes her glasses up her nose and looks at the group expectantly for questions and comments, but we're all busy grimacing at her puke picture. Eventually, she sits back down.

Then the Budweiser guy stands up, placing his picture in the center of the desks. He has drawn Batman. No one says anything. "I'm Batman," he says.

Golden Eagle looks terrified. Metamorphosis stares at the guy's drawing, then at his face. "What did you say your name was?"

"Batman."

"No, your real name."

"Oh. Bob."

"Bob, I believe the assignment was to identify our personalities with a mythical creature—"

"Batman's not real," he says defensively. "He's mythical."

"—of our own invention," finishes Metamorphosis, inventor of the butterfly pony.

Amoeba cuts in, looking sorrowful, her glasses glinting, ponytails swishing. "So it can't be human."

Bob thinks for a second. "Oh yeah. Batman's human. He just wears a bat *suit*, huh?"

"Yes," says Amoeba sadly.

"I see what you're saying," says Bob, folding up his drawing.

Metamorphosis stops him with a bangled, manicured hand. "No, Bob," she says. "Tell us *why* you're Batman. If it's important to you, then it's important to us." Amoeba nods vigorously, not to be outdone.

"Well," says Bob. "I'm a rebel." He looks at us all. "Of *society*," he articulates. He looks around again, with growing desperation, then points at his drawing impatiently. "And so's Batman!" Golden Eagle and I nod with tight, gruesome smiles on our faces.

"Stay focused on the assignment, Bob. Tell us where you live," says Metamorphosis gently. "What are your immediate goals?"

"In the Bat Cave, see?" Bob, exasperated, points at a penciled semi-circle over Batman's head. His picture looks like it was drawn by a six-year-old. "I guess my immediate goals," he adds miserably, "would be to . . . fight crimes."

Golden Eagle says, "That's important." *This can't possibly be educational—I can't wait to get back to the studio. Boy, Betty, when you're right, you're right.*

"I may have misunderstood the assignment," Bob mutters, looking at the clock. *Four more hours to go, Bob.*

Metamorphosis won't let him off the hook, though. "Tell me," she presses. "How did you become interested in art therapy?"

Bob looks like he's under attack. He starts talking fast. "I'm-a-maintenance-professional-employed-by-the-University," he says. "Completing-my-degree-nights-and-weekends."

"I see," says Metamorphosis, looking smug. "And what is your degree in?"

Bob's crumpling. Golden Eagle looks like he's gonna die. "I'm . . . undecided," says Bob quietly.

Golden Eagle comes to his aid. "Sometimes a *double* major is the only option for those of us with varied interests," he says hopefully.

Bob looks over at him, grateful. "Yeah, pro'bly." Art therapy creates strange bedfellows.

There is a tense silence; then they all look at me. *Shit.* I'd hoped we'd run out of time before we did me. Batman was making it look possible. I look up at the clock in spite of myself. *Four more hours to go, Kris.* Then I pick my drawing up off the floor and spread it out on the desks. It's difficult to see the tiny blowfish in such a huge expanse of white. Golden Eagle, Metamorphosis, Amoeba and Bob all stare at my dumb little fish. *Help, I need help.*

"Who *are* you?" Amoeba asks me.

"I guess I'm a . . . blowfish," I say, looking down at the pathetic blue dot. "With a horn."

Metamorphosis cocks her head to the side, trying to understand. "Where do you live?" she asks. "What are your immediate goals?"

I think for a second. "I live underwater." I can't think of any pressing mission I might take on in the form of a blowfish with a horn on its head.

They all look from the drawing to me. Bob says to Golden Eagle, "Aren't those things poisonous?"

Golden Eagle nods. "I think so. If you eat them."

"Do they bite?" asks Bob. "Do they got that kinda poison?"

"No, I don't think they're aggressive."

"Not like a piranha."

"No."

"Those things're nasty," says Bob.

"Yeah," agrees Golden Eagle.

I wonder if I can sit down yet. I begin lowering myself into my seat when Metamorphosis sticks out a hand and pokes at the blowfish violently and repeatedly. I stand back up. Her shiny red nails strike angrily at the little fish. "It! Makes! Me! Sad!" she says shrilly, punctuating each syllable with a jangly blow to the paper, "that you live in a sea of nothingness, with no immediate goals, no friends and nothing to *eat!*"

"Do I?" I ask, looking again at my drawing. *Maybe there's an orchard nearby.*

Amoeba heartily agrees. "I feel sad, too," she says, shaking her ponytails from side to side.

Bob and Golden Eagle look sympathetic. Golden Eagle says, "Some people are natural loners."

Bob nods. "Poison's like a superpower . . ."

♋ bright yellow gun

i think i need a little poison

Headlights race past in a spring drizzle. The nausea's coming back. Nobody told me about third-trimester morning sickness. I don't even know where I am right now. I can't make out highway signs through the mist and rain; they're just green and white blurs. Watching them whiz by makes the nausea worse.

The bus driver and I are the only people on the bus who aren't asleep. No old ladies to sit with, no goth knitters, but pregnant women are never alone. I'm gonna miss my dancing belly when it's gone.

The bus driver catches my eye in the rearview mirror. "Where you headed, ma'am?" he asks. I'm *ma'am* now 'cause of the gut; everybody calls me that. I'm in the grown-up club. "You going home?"

"Nope, leaving home."

"Going to visit relatives maybe?"

Wow. Do people still "visit relatives"? This guy lives in an old movie, just like Betty. I wish I was an anachronism. I bet it's nice. "I'm working, actually."

"So am I!" He laughs. "Would you care for a pretzel, ma'am? I got a whole bag of 'em." He holds the bag out to me and the bus swerves into the other lane.

I grab the seat in front of me. *Ugh, this isn't helping.* "No thank you, sir. I'm not feeling well."

"Pukey?" he asks, interested.

I laugh. "Don't worry. I won't throw up on your bus."

"It ain't *my* bus!"

"Well, just the same. I'd rather not throw up at all."

"I know a guy," he says, looking at me in the rearview mirror for emphasis, "I know a guy who never once puked in his whole life."

"Wow . . . *cool.*"

"It's cool as long as he don't eat poison or nothing," he says seriously.

"Yeah, I guess he can't eat poison."

"Naw, but my *wife*," he catches my eye again, "all you gotta do to make my wife throw up is say *fruitbread* to her."

"Fruitbread?" *What the hell is fruitbread?*

"You could say, for instance, 'banana bread' to her and she would vomit."

Oh. "Wow."

"You could also," he continues, grabbing a pretzel out of the bag and eating it, "you could also say, for example, 'banana' and 'bread' to her in the same sentence and she would then vomit."

"Gee . . . I guess you gotta be careful. She could throw up at the grocery store."

"That's right." He nods. "It happens with all the various fruits," he says. "And breads."

The windshield wipers wheeze rhythmically; rain spatters the glass.

Dave and Gil are sitting at the dining room table with crumb-covered plates in front of them when I get in. They both look spent. I take off my damp sweater and put it on the back of a chair, then sit down with them. My wet hair drips onto the table.

Gil smiles kindly. "Had to do some thinking?" I nod. "It's okay. We laid down some drum tracks. Dave got three songs done . . . sounds really good."

I look at Dave, stunned. "You can play without me?"

"Yes," he says for Gil's benefit, shaking his head at me. *Whoops. Poor Dave.*

"Is there anything to eat?" I ask, looking over their shoulders into the kitchen to see if the scary chef is there.

"She went home; we can finally eat," says Gil. "We were starving." Dave looks too tired to move. He manages a wan smile. "Look, Kris. I'll fix you something to eat, but we have to call Ivo. He wanted to know as soon as you got in."

Shit. I suck and now Ivo knows it. Gil walks over to the phone and takes a piece of paper out of his pocket. He dials two numbers, then checks the paper, then dials two more numbers. It takes forever, giving me plenty of time to get nervous. *I run away too much and now I'm in trouble. It's Ivo's money I'm wasting. I wonder what the queen sounds like when she's mad.*

Finally, Gil finishes dialing and waits. I can hear the phone ringing— two short rings, silence, then two short rings again. Sounds like Pink Floyd. *I bet everything's just a little different in England,* I think. *They have phones, but they ring funny; they have tea, but it tastes better.* "Hey," says Gil suddenly into the receiver. "Kris's right here." He holds the phone out to me.

I take it and push it under my wet hair. "Hi."

"Guess what I saw in the park today," Ivo says through the familiar long-distance static.

"What?"

"This old man, a very old man with a cauliflower ear, was sitting on a park bench, feeding a bunch of pigeons, right? And his cauliflower ear was fucking enormous, never seen bigger. So while I'm walking by, I see one of the pigeons hop up on his knee, yeah? And then a few more hop on his lap; some fly up onto his arms. He's got like a dozen pigeons on him. And these are filthy London pigeons, mind you."

"Ew."

"And he doesn't notice or he doesn't care. He just sits there with pigeons all over him."

"Hmmm."

"Right. Then they start hopping up on his shoulders and his head like they're gonna *eat* him."

"Aw, crap."

"Yeah, they're *crapping* on him."

I giggle. "Geez."

"—and then they start nibbling at his bloody cauliflower ear! And he's letting 'em! They just keep chewing on his filthy old ear and he keeps throwing bread on the ground, like he doesn't know they're there!" *God, I love Ivo.* "Eventually. The birds. Engulfed. His entire. *Body*."

Laughing, I settle into a big, squishy chair next to the phone. "Know what *I* saw today?"

"What?"

I tell him the story of Golden Eagle, Metamorphosis, Amoeba and Bob. I leave out the Betty heartache and make it sound like my day was hilarious. As he laughs, I start to believe that my day really was hilarious. Then I realize that it was. Ivo *is* an angel. Possibly misguided, but still. "Do you have the blowfish?" he asks, chuckling.

"It's in the pocket of my sweater. It's probably wet."

"I'd like you to send it to me, please."

"I don't see that happening."

"Do your best," he says briskly. "Good luck tomorrow. Goodnight, Kris."

"Bye, Ivo." As I hang up the phone, I notice that Dave's gone. Or else he slid under the table; he looked like he was about to. Gil has put a plate of scrambled eggs and toast at my seat. "Oh, Gil, thank you! You didn't have to do that."

"I can only make breakfast, sorry. And I can't find any butter."

I sit down with him. "I can't believe you did this."

"Not a problem, Kris."

I start eating, then stop. "Gil."

"Yeah?"

"What time is it in England?"

He checks his watch. "About 4 A.M."

Wow. "Ivo's great."

"Yeah," he agrees. "Ivo's great."

Music's screaming in my ears to keep me from hearing my own voice. The headphones are at top volume and my vocals aren't in the mix at all. It's a strange effect. Like a hurricane sucking words out of your mouth.

Gil's glasses are reflecting the glass of the control room window; he's staring at me with empty Little Orphan Annie eyes, framed by the curly brown hair that's looking more unkempt by the day. I want to do this right for Ivo, for Gil, for Gary, for Betty, for my bandmates, but, honestly, I don't know how—I'm just going through the motions. What I'm doing isn't art or science or inspiration or craft or *anything*, really, except self-parody. I'm simply fulfilling a commitment. *I probably shouldn't have taken that bath.*

"I know going through the motions when I hear it, Kris," Gil says kindly into my headphones.

"Yeah, me too."

In Roxbury, I used to kill. Just shake apart every time I put down vocals— shake apart willingly—the rats running around me. Not enough rats here. Not that I care. Hey, maybe that's it: I don't care anymore. Should I care about not caring?

"Is there anything else I can get you to make you more comfortable?" Gil asks with his spooky Little Orphan Annie stare.

"Rats."

"What's wrong?"

"Not enough rats here," I answer.

"Not enough *what*?"

"*Rats.* They used to crawl around my feet."

Gil pauses to think, but it doesn't work. "What the bloody hell are you talking about?"

"This studio is too nice; it makes yucky people like us feel out of our element." *There, I said it.*

"Right. Do you want me to fuck it up a little?"

"Would you? That'd be so nice. Just fuck up the place, Gil."

"After this take, dear," he says. "Rolling." As the song begins, I hear him say, "This is the one, Kris."

Of course it isn't the one, 'cause it's never the one. Afterwards, Gil actually leaves the control room to come and talk to me. *I'm in trouble again.*

He stands in front of me with an empty Coke can and smushes it in his fist, drops it on the floor. "Better?" he asks.

I laugh. "Better."

"Right. I'm going back up to the control room and you're gonna blow the roof off this filthy place."

"Okay." When I see his Little Orphan Annie face back at the desk, I thank him. "I know fucking up the place isn't in your job description."

"You write my job description," he answers. "I'll do whatever you tell me to."

"Right back at ya, sister."

"Okay, then," he says. "Blow the roof off this filthy place."

"Yes, sir."

Gil rolls tape. "This is the one, Kris."

I don't blow the roof off. Tattoos don't glow. No heat, no electricity, no roller coaster, no beautiful coughed-up livers. I feel fine.

And guilty. *What're the odds a witch'd be driving by right now? I could run out into the street . . .*

"Do I have to take you for another walk?" Gil scolds gently, sounding tired. "How did you *used* to get the songs' voice to kick in?"

"It just did whenever I picked up my guitar," I say quietly. It's sorta hard to root for Gil when he's rooting for *evil*.

"AH-HA!" he screams into my brain. Quickly, I grab my headphones and rip them off.

"Ow." I wince at him through the glass and he motions for me to put the phones back on.

"Sorry, Kris, I forgot how loud your cans were," he whispers. "I'm bringing you your guitar and you're gonna play it while you do this vocal, got it?"

"Isn't it gonna bleed onto the track?"

He laughs. "Not if I can get you screaming again." He's excited again. *That's nice. It won't last long, but it's still nice.*

Gil appears in the room, holding my guitar. I take off the headphones and reach for it, but I'm moving too slowly for him; he's really excited about this new idea. Deftly, he places the strap over my shoulder and swings the guitar away from my big belly. He even moves my hair out of the way and shoves the headphones back on my head. Then he races to the control room, saying something I can't hear to the assistant engineer, motioning and gesturing. Gil can't *wait* to try this new experiment. Poor Gil. It'll be a relief when he finally gives up.

Maybe I should start planning my life. All art therapy aside, education is important. I can't be fucking around, not with the baby coming. I wonder if McGill University would still let me in. After the baby's born, we could both go be Canadian.

"One minute, Kris," Gil whispers in my head. He's still pointing and talking in the control room; the assistant engineer's listening and nodding. *They're probably tearing apart my goddamn lyrics again. Glad I can't hear it.*

I'll fulfill this commitment, then move to Montreal. I could teach the baby French instead of English. That'd be funny. None of my friends would understand it when it talked.

Gil hits the talkback, whispering, "You ready?"

I stick a thumb up at him. *What are we trying now?* I look down. *Oh yeah, my guitar.*

"*Rolling!*" he whispers as the track begins.

Bass and drums start this song. I listen and then begin playing along with the guitar that's already there 'cause Gil is watching so intently. I feel silly.

"*This is the one, Kris,*" whispers Gil. And I smile up at him, thinking, *No, it's not.*

I sing on cue. Can't hear it, of course, but I feel it in my rib cage, not my throat. *Weird.* Like the baby, it's in my middle, alive and swelling and needing to come out.

Then the roller coaster races by and grabs me by the hair. Heat builds, my skin fizzes with electricity, colors appear, blotting out the studio around me, "now" becomes memories, vital sounds fill my chest—all this in an instant. The last thing I think is, *this is one beautiful coughed-up liver.*

☞ long painting

static played through my middle
seared my gut

When the song ends, I look down at my guitar, impressed. Quickly, before its spell fades, I try to understand. *Evil Kristin makes me care,* I think, *about everyone and everything.*

Or maybe she's just what it sounds like when you care so much that you flip the fuck out.

I hear nothing from Gil in my headphones. Then I look up at the control room window and see him jumping around, waving his fists in the air and dancing in silence. Gil dances in as I'm taking off the headphones and guitar. "You done it, Kris, you done it!" he cheers and pulls me into the control room to listen back.

My bandmates are sitting on the floor, smiling. *Were they there the whole time?* Gil laughs delightedly. As the song plays back, I put my hands on my stomach. The baby isn't moving.

☞ white trash moon

out of the chaos
my us
and your little fontanel

I'm lying in bed, listening to a tape, and the baby's dancing, thank god. Little fists and feet going a mile a minute. Babies just don't dance to Throwing Muses, I guess—nobody does. I remind myself that babies sleep a lot in utero, that all mothers freak out when their bellies are still, that evil isn't necessarily *evil* . . .

Gil and I decided that our only rule for recording vocals is: no singing. Works for me. Singing's stupid, at least when I do it, but evil . . . maybe I shouldn't call it "evil" anymore because there's something okay about the mess, the chaos, the noise. It does seem to be an intelligence. I ask myself Dr. Syllables' question, "Are you peaceful?" and think, *Well, yeah, I am peaceful.* Peace just isn't necessarily quiet.

I have to remember what I learned playing guitar on the edge of the bathtub all those cold mornings in Boston: fully engaged efforts toward life pummel the universe into a shape that suits them—they *are* the universe, after all. So it's in a song's nature to leave an impression. I shouldn't expect anything less.

Now I have to be as bad-ass as a song or a baby. If I'm gonna leave inertia behind, that is. I silently promise this baby that I'll be ready for forward movement when the time comes.

And I will be. Because vital means you can do both dirty *and* clean. Science measures art: this studio helped us harness our chaos. The ability to navigate a pristine or polluted terrain is inherent in our changeable natures: strong people can breathe anything and they can live anywhere, like snakes. Light and dark are two different moods a mind shines on the subject matter at hand. All humans embody this dichotomy and music's just what that sounds like.

None of this is special; it's merely extraordinary. It's falling in love—with this moment, with all moments.

♋ status quo

peace isn't quiet

So I don't write songs to describe what it's like in here; it's just like this in here so that I can write songs. And I absolutely did not invent them.

Sitting in a tree, I look out over my swing set, over
other trees and into the fields behind our house.

A cloud of birds erupts from one of the trees: a hundred
dark birds, scattering up into the sky.

We've reached a détente with the chef: we're allowed to boil water. This way, Gil can have his buckets of tea and Leslie can have her ramen noodles. Anything else, the chef gets to put on a plate. She's calmed down a little, seems to have figured out that we aren't assholes, though we all still avoid eating when she's around.

This morning I told her I just wanted an apple, so she put one on a plate, then insisted on "making the baby breakfast." It was very sweet of her, especially since she's not a very sweet person. I'm just not hungry and she makes me so nervous, I don't think I could eat the baby breakfast even if I *was* hungry. Maybe I can smuggle it out in a napkin to the little animals in the barn. I've been looking for a way to get them to like me.

The record is really flying along now, though we're still amazed that we can play a transcendent take and then a crap one. We "identified our curve," alright: it's a disintegration that is both instantaneous and remarkable. Crap takes vary in their crappiness, but there's rarely anything actually wrong with them except "feel"—they simply don't have it.

After five years of playing shows, we thought we were in love with music and music loved us back. But music's been waltzing into the room, sparks flying, giving us big, fat kisses and then waltzing right back out again, leaving us very much alone. None of us can put our finger on the mechanism behind the spark. It's either there or it isn't and everyone can hear the difference; a dead body may have all its parts intact, but no soul animates it and we all know what that looks like. Luckily, we only need each song to waltz into the room once.

And every time we get a keeper take, Gil lets us take a break so we can wander out to the barn to see the animals. None of us would ever go, say, read a book or make a phone call because the petting zoo babies are so painfully wonderful. Their facial expressions alone are enchanting—like the fish in the aquarium plus goofiness. I can't believe anybody ever finishes a record with all this dangerous cuteness around. Baby animals'll keep you from getting *anything* done.

In the barn, Leslie always climbs a ladder into the hayloft. An actual freakin' hayloft. She loves it up there. And Tea and Dave position themselves on the fence at the calves' pen. Perfect, tiny cows, the calves have mouths full of hay and big old purple tongues that stick out when they chew. They're really beautiful.

But the lambs are my favorites; they run around like they don't have knees. The lambs're so much like the toddlers in my midwife's waiting room, it's uncanny. This is how vegetarians are born, I guess. I sit on the floor, holding a lamb on what's left of my lap because *they like to be held*. The lamb snuggles up against my big belly and bleats at the other lamb as it runs by, kneeless. "We're never gonna finish this record," I say. "It's too cute here."

"Murder," says Dave vaguely, his chin on his arms.

"Just 'murder,' that's it?" asks Tea.

Leslie calls down from the hayloft, "Don't you wanna kill anybody specific?"

"When I kill them, it'll be specific," says Dave. "For now, I just wanna book a murder."

I squint at the back of Dave's head. "What're you guys talking about?"

He turns around. "Future crimes," he says, bending down to scratch my lamb under the chin.

"I'm gonna free lab animals," says Tea.

"Well, god, Tea, you could do that *now*. It can't be that hard . . ." The lamb looks over at me and bleats, sticking out his little, pink, potato chip tongue. I laugh. "He likes me 'cause I gave him bacon."

"Oh no!" says Tea, looking stricken. "You gave him bacon? Sheep don't eat bacon."

"Well, neither do I. He didn't eat it, though; he just sorta played with it. Then Tripod ate it." Tripod is a three-legged cat here who has run of the place. He hangs out in the control room and listens while we work. "Now Tripod likes the lamb."

Leslie looks at me from her hay bale. "That's not cool. Bacon's bad news."

"Tripod thought it was pretty good news." The lamb hops off my lap to play with the other lamb in the straw.

"Freeing lab animals is harder than you'd think," says Tea. "I've looked into it."

"We could free some farm animals," I suggest. Tea looks thoughtfully at the calves. "Can I book a crime?" She nods. "I wanna pull off something . . . complicated . . . that would hurt mean people and help nice ones. Or Robin Hood money from somewhere bad to somewhere good." I think. "And it'd take place in the Everglades."

Dave looks at me. "I want in."

"No dice, you already got your murder." The lamb comes ambling back, so I pick it up and put it on my lap.

"I think my murder could play a role in your grander scheme," he says.

"Oh, you wanna be under my auspices? Okay. What're your qualifications? You were an owl keeper, right? That could come in handy."

One summer, Dave and I worked at the bird sanctuary on the island. My job was great: I took little kid campers on hikes and taught them how to make herbal mosquito repellant, I fed orphaned baby foxes, raccoons and sparrow hawks. *Dave's* job was killing mice and feeding them to the owl. The mice were cute and frightened and the owl was huge and very scary: blind in one eye and really pissed-off. It lived in a smelly pen far away from all the other animals. Dave hated his job, though he can now do excellent impressions of a sweet mouse about to die and an angry owl about to eat it. "Tea, Dave could help you free *owls* before he killed his person—"

"Is freeing owls all you can do, Dave?" interrupts Leslie.

"He can kill mice, too," I say. "I've seen him."

"Don't make me kill mice," Dave says quietly.

"You can borrow my hair spray," says Leslie.

"Well, no, he wouldn't wanna use up his murder . . ." I reply. "*Free* the mice!"

"Yes!" yells Tea. Dave looks relieved.

Leslie's voice echoes from the top of the barn, "Counterfeiting! The perfect, victimless crime!"

"I think we could work that in," says Dave. "If you're talking Robin Hooding in the Everglades—"

"I'm confused," I interrupt. "Who're you murdering?" Dave starts to answer when Gil comes in to get me for the next vocal. "Gil, if you could commit any crime—" I begin, then notice that he looks upset. "What's wrong?"

"Deep Purple's kicking us out!" he yells.

"Deep what's *what*?"

"Deep fucking Purple is kicking us out of the bloody studio right in the middle of the fucking session!"

Leslie sits up and swings her legs over the loft. We look at each other. "What's 'deep purple'?" I ask.

She looks grim. "It's an old-fart band."

"An old-fart band with wads of cash," says Gil bitterly. "Collect your bags and move into the control room. They don't want to have to see you lot, so you have to vacate any room they might feel like walking into."

My stomach drops. Dave's eyes are huge. "*What?*" he says.

"We can't finish the record?" I ask.

"I'm fighting to keep those fuckers out of the studio itself as long as they'll stay out, but you have to leave your rooms and you aren't allowed anywhere else in the building. No food, no telephone." He shakes his head. "I don't believe this."

We don't move, just sit in silence. "Look," continues Gil. "We'll do everything we can today, but we'll never be able to finish. We'll just have to save the rest of the recording for the mix in London next month."

Dave and I look at each other. We both know I can't go to London next month; that's when the baby's due. I push the lamb off my lap and stand up.

Gil looks defeated. "When you leave your rooms, spit on the floor."

We file out of the barn. Dave and I walk together. "I'll go to London," he says. "I'll make sure it's good. Just do whatever you can today."

I look at him. "What're we, cursed?"

He smiles. "Let's plan our crime."

My mother tells me that she was "sad" before I was born.
I ask her what she was sad about, but she won't say.

"It doesn't matter, because after I had you, I was happy
again. Because you were perfect. Because all babies are
perfect. Do you know what I mean?"

I don't. I think of the ugly baby with the monkey friend.

"I could hold you and say, 'This is my baby,' and then
everything was okay."

In the hospital, they put me in the shower room, alone. It looks like a shower room in a correctional facility: gray on gray. Just shower heads on the walls and a big drain in the middle of the floor.

This pain is sending me out of myself, is not limited to my systemic reality. It's more like a shift in the room. I pass out between contractions and then wake up as the next one begins, the sound of the shower spray getting louder and louder as I come to.

Like slow flashing lights: one bright minute is silvery water pouring into the drain, then darkness. The next bright minute opens to a world of cold metal. Not the way cold metal looks, but the way it'd feel to be made of it. Then it's dark again.

Water pours over me. I'm curled up in fetal position.

☺ hysterical bending

a girl body's solid
how do I melt

without dying?

A little universe. With eyelids, shoulders and tiny lungs, yeah, but also with fingers, toenails and knees. Babies *are* perfect.

Another hell to another heaven—and this has been going on for millennia. *Crazy.*

Now I know I'll never be numb again. A mother is condemned to feel everything forever. And I'm finally afraid, condemned to *fear* everything forever. But that makes sense: feel someone else's pain, feel someone else's everything.

And he's my baby, so everything's okay.

I absolutely did not invent this.

♋ cartoons

i wasn't staring
i was just looking far away

dazzled by something i forgot

ABOUT THE AUTHOR

Kristin Hersh recorded with 4AD records until 2007, when she helped found the nonprofit Coalition of Artists and Stake Holders (http://cash-music.org), recording and releasing music without the aid of a record company. She is entirely listener-funded and makes her music available, free of charge and free to be shared, via Creative Commons BY-NC-SA licenses (http://creativecommons.org).

For more information or to get involved with CASH Music, please visit http://kristinhersh.cashmusic.org.

Kristin's personal Web site and the online home of Throwing Muses and her newest musical project, 50FootWave, is http://kristinhersh.com. There you'll find a mailing list and regularly updated content, including a forum, a shop, essays, new music, tour dates and more.

Throughout the first year of this book's publication, Kristin is making available a series of four intimate session recordings in which Throwing Muses performs songs from the book *Paradoxical Undressing*. These collections will be available for download via her Web site and will be released in four special-edition compact discs entitled *The Season Sessions—Fall, Winter, Spring* and *Summer*.

Readers can access these free, high-quality digital downloads on the first day of each season, beginning September 21, 2010, by visiting http://kristinhersh.com/seasonsessions and entering the first word found on page 10 of this edition.

E-mail Kristin: kristinhersh@cashmusic.org.